Bone Wars

BONE WARS

The Excavation
and Celebrity
of Andrew Carnegie's
Dinosaur

TOM REA

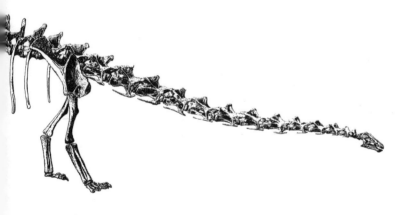

UNIVERSITY OF PITTSBURGH PRESS

for Adam

Published by the University of Pittsburgh Press, Pittsburgh, Pa., 15261

Copyright © 2001, University of Pittsburgh Press

Manufactured in the United States of America

Printed on acid-free paper

10 9 8 7 6 5 4 3 2 1

The art on the title page spread is redrawn from John Bell Hatcher's 1901 monograph, *"Diplodocus* Marsh, Its Osteology, Taxonomy and Probable Habits."

Library of Congress Cataloging-in-Publication Data
Rea, Tom, 1950-
  Bone wars : the excavation and celebrity of Andrew Carnegie's dinosaur / Tom Rea.
      p.   cm.
Includes bibliographical references and index.
  ISBN 0-8229-4173-2 (cloth : alk. paper)
  1. Paleontology--United States--History--20th century. 2. Diplodocus. 3. Carnegie,
Andrew, 1835-1919.   I. Title.
  QE705.U6 R43 2001
  560'.973'09034--dc21

                                                        2001003336

CONTENTS

ACKNOWLEDGMENTS

This book began one windswept day in January 1990, when Brent Breithaupt, curator of the University of Wyoming Geological Museum, and I rode with two other friends in a Subaru out north of Como Bluff to look for the spot where *Diplodocus carnegii* was dug out of the ground in 1899. We didn't find it, that time. But Brent's enthusiasm for the bone diggers—especially for one of them, Bill Reed—was infectious, and from Brent I caught the bone bug. An editor at my newspaper agreed to let me write a feature on Reed, the dinosaur, and related subjects for a supplement marking the hundredth anniversary of Wyoming statehood. In succeeding years, I wrote about other dinosaur finds—and sometimes crimes—around Wyoming, often quoting Brent on their meaning and significance. His good-natured support has been part of this project from the start.

Later I visited Pittsburgh, where I had grown up admiring the dinosaurs at the Carnegie Museum of Natural History. There in the archives of the Big Bone Room in the museum basement, under the careful stewardship of Elizabeth Hill, I found a rich mine of correspondence surrounding the discovery and subsequent celebrity of *Diplodocus carnegii*. The correspondents' personalities were vivid in their letters. Combining the archival material from the bone room with other material then housed in the museum annex, the museum library, the Carnegie Library of Pittsburgh, and the Historical Society of Western Pennsylvania, I found I had a story before me, one that in the past had been told only sketchily, and told wrong in many of its most important details. Equally important, I found in Betty Hill a person who knew the archival material top to bottom and to whom the actors in these events—Reed, Wortman, Hatcher, Holland, and Carnegie—were very much alive. Throughout the writing of this book, I've checked my assumptions and conclusions with Betty. We disagree, I think, on only one of them.

At the Carnegie, I am also grateful to Deborah Harding, who oversees the anthropology collections—including Holland's letters—at the museum annex, to Bernadette Callery and her staff at the museum library for access to so many of Holland's letters there, to *Carnegie Magazine* editor Bob Gangewere for his thoughts on Andrew Carnegie's personality, to Curator of Vertebrate Paleontology Mary Dawson, who quietly encouraged her staff to help me out, and to curator Chris Beard, who read a draft of this book and steered me to some interesting contemporary science on sauropods.

In Wyoming I need especially to thank Beth Southwell, a paleontologist and volunteer at the UW Geological Museum, whose generosity and expertise on dinosaurs, their early collectors, and especially on the Fossil Fields Expedition of 1899 saved me mountains of time. It was in Beth's Toyota that she, Brent, and I finally did find the *Diplodocus carnegii* quarry, one hot day in August 2000. Paleontologist Bob Bakker and geologist Melissa Connely, then both connected with Casper College's Tate Museum, kindly let my son Max and me accompany them and their crews of dino-digging vacationers for two days' work on sauropod and *Allosaurus* bones at Como Bluff in the summer of 1999, providing me more insights than they may have known.

UW History Professor Phil Roberts helped me thread the labyrinths of nineteenth-century land and mineral-claims law in the West, and UW History Professor Emeritus Roger Williams, author of a biography of the great botanist Aven Nelson, helped me better understand Wyoming university politics at the turn of the last century. At the university's American Heritage Center, archivists Ginny Kylander, Matt Sprinkle, and Leslie Shores helped me find photos and documents. Rebekah Johnston at the Historical Society of Western Pennsylvania helped me locate photos, as did the staff at the Wyoming State Archives in Cheyenne. At the Casper College library, my old friend and former bookstore colleague Kevin Anderson cheerfully gave me many hours of his time scanning photos and documents into electronic sendability. But I couldn't have researched the book at all without Laurie Lye and her assistant Kirsten Olson, whose good-humored skill at the interlibrary loan desk transformed the Casper College library into one as big as any in the world.

Among scholars I owe a profound intellectual debt to Ronald Rainger, of Texas Tech University, whose book on Osborn and especially whose 1990 article in *Earth Sciences History* on Wortman, Hatcher, Osborn, and Holland helped me see the class tensions behind these men's professional relationships. I also need to thank Jack McIntosh, now emeritus at Wesleyan University, the world's leading authority on sauropods, who seems to know off the top of his head the condition, whereabouts, catalog number, quarry site, and collector of every sauropod ever dug, and who assured me Hatcher's designation of *Diplodocus carnegii* as a separate species was sound.

I'm also grateful to Don Baird, retired curator of the geology museum at Princeton, who told me his father's story about Holland's medals, and to Michael Woodburne of the University of California, Riverside, for his expertise on recent fossil discoveries in Antarctica. Hugh Torrens, historian of geology at Keele University, in Staffordshire, U.K., helped me take Prof. Lankester at his word when he said *Diplodocus carnegii* had been erected in the Natural History Museum's Gallery of Reptiles only because the Hall of Paleontology was already full. Closer to home, Jerry Nelson of Casper College helped me with Como Bluff and Rocky Mountain geology, and Will Robinson of Casper College and Scott Seville of the University of Wyoming/Casper College Center helped me think more clearly about evolution.

My Wyoming friend and now transplanted New Yorker, Mike Fleming, scouted the archives of the Osborn Collection at the American Museum of Natural History, and found for me some revealing letters on the competition between the American and Carnegie museums. Michael Kohl, of the University of South Carolina, co-editor with McIntosh of Arthur Lakes's journals from Colorado and Como Bluff, kindly provided me with a biographical sketch of Reed written by his son-in-law in the 1950s, a document I had been unable to find anywhere else. Similarly, David Rains Wallace, author of a recent book on the Cope-Marsh feud, provided the clue I needed to locate at last the correct source for the "Most Colossal Animal Ever On Earth" newspaper story.

Natrona County High School language teachers Scott Underbrink and Kay Freire in Casper, and my daughter, Hannah, helped me translate some Hatcher and Holland correspondence from French and Spanish. A couple of friends, Paul Hannan and Cherie Winner, read early chunks of the book and did their best to liven my approach; my friend George Gibson did the same and, crucially, helped me narrow it; and my newspaper comrade, the gentlemanly Dan Whipple, first gave me rein years ago to write enough on this subject to become absorbed by it in the first place.

I need to thank copy editor Cynthia Wells for her close attention to my prose. I need to thank as well the cheerful staff at the University of Pittsburgh Press for their support, and especially Cynthia Miller, the director, for her straightforward encouragement and patience.

I'd finally like to thank two geologist relatives, my uncle Bart Rea and my brother Dave Rea, for years of answering questions from an amateur. My wife, Barbara, who's impatient with bluster and loves the truth, was my best reader and ally of all.

Bone Wars

Chapter 1

DIPLODOCUS CARNEGII

The standing skeleton of a dinosaur gives off an unearthly grandeur—grand because of the size, unearthly because the bones leave its living bulk to the imagination. The skeleton is an idea, an armature of what really lived. Like all ideas, it stands for itself but allows room for speculation to meander among its parts. The legs may recall tree trunks, the ribs hint at shipwrecks, but the long arch of vertebrae—tail to spine, to neck, to head— displays a mesmerizing logic. At any natural history museum one may find a person gazing up at a dinosaur for a full half hour. A good museum needs high ceilings. Meaning gathers up there in the darkness, above the skulls.

At one o'clock in the afternoon on Friday, May 12, 1905, Andrew Carnegie presented the trustees of the British Museum with a plaster-of-paris replica of a dinosaur that bore his name, *Diplodocus carnegii*. More than two hundred people had packed into the Gallery of Reptiles in the natural history museum in South Kensington, in London, for speechmaking and ceremony. The dinosaur, 84 feet long over its curves, nearly 15 feet high at the hips, was mounted on a platform down the long axis of the room. The skeleton was made of exact copies of bones found six years earlier on the plains of southeast Wyoming, not far from the tracks of the transcontinental line of the Union Pacific Railroad.

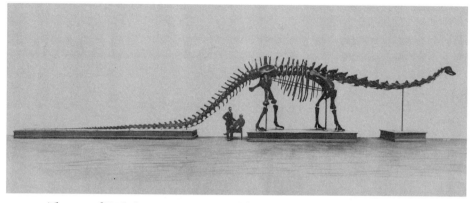

The cast of *Diplodocus carnegii* prepared for Kaiser Wilhelm II of Germany, with Arthur Coggeshall, *left*, and William Holland on hand for scale. Casts eventually went to nine national museums in Europe and the Americas; the dinosaur was the first that millions of people ever saw. Courtesy of Carnegie Museum of Natural History, Pittsburgh, Pennsylvania, originally published ca. 1908 as Carnegie Museum, Paleontological Illustrations, no. 1.

The guests sat on chairs on either side, and the speakers stood a few feet off the right front leg of the skeleton. Daylight flooded down from clerestory windows. Late arrivers stood in the aisles between the chairs or against glass museum cases along the walls. On hand were scientists, the press, generals, admirals, painters, writers, a few lords, many knights, members of Parliament, and a liberal sprinkling of married and unmarried women. The men wore morning coats and high collars, the women wore dresses and hats.

Professor E. Ray Lankester, director of the museum, rose to speak after the crowd had settled. He linked the size of the dinosaur with the size of Carnegie's generosity. The professor was courteous, yet in the spaces between his words lay discomfort with the *direction* of Carnegie's gift—eastward across the Atlantic. Politely, obliquely, Professor Lankester let it be known that this museum in the capital of the world's greatest empire had no real need of such generosity. The Hall of Paleontology was already full, he noted, making it necessary that the new specimen be erected instead in the Gallery of Reptiles.

He went on to attribute to Carnegie the insight that all Ameri-

can progress—including its forms of government and its great mechanical inventions—had been founded on British ideas. Even the
centerpiece of the day, the *Diplodocus*, the professor joked, "is an
improved and enlarged form of an English creature, for we have recently discovered in the Oxford clays a specimen of a dinosaur not
quite as large as *Diplodocus*, but in a measure a rival. (Laughter.) You
will find the remains of this creature in the Hall of Paleontology."
Then the professor read out a brief letter expressing the thanks of
King Edward VII to Carnegie.

Carnegie's turn to speak came next. Short, white-bearded,
round-faced, sharp-eyed, Carnegie was a vigorous sixty-nine years
old, his health buoyed by the sport he called "Dr. Golf" and by a vast,
unreflective self-confidence. In 1901 he had cashed in his steel holdings, nearly all of them based in Pittsburgh, and had converted them
into the largest liquid fortune in the world. Now he was four years
into the full-time job of giving the fortune away, and he enjoyed giving some of its fruits to a king, even if the king hadn't shown up to
accept them.

"You will have seen from the published accounts how it comes
about that this gigantic monster makes his appearance and takes up
his abode among you," Carnegie began. "You owe this to one of
your former Trustees who, although no longer of your Board, I am
sure retains his interest in your work unimpaired. I refer to His Majesty, who, even in his recreations, seems to keep his eyes and mind
ever open for opportunities to advance the interests of his country
in every department of national life, from the peace of nations to the
acquisitions of his Museum."

World peace was a subject close to Carnegie's heart. By 1905 he
believed that his own personal wealth and influence could bring it
about. Personal contacts among the powerful, Carnegie thought,
would end war, just as his own personal contact with the king had
brought about this gift of a dinosaur.

"His majesty when at Skibo expressed the hope that the Diplodocus before us might some day be seen here," Carnegie continued. In the autumn of 1902 the king had visited Skibo, Carnegie's
castle in Scotland, where the tycoon spent every summer and fall.
Over lunch, the king had inquired about a drawing of a dinosaur

skeleton on the wall. Carnegie explained to his guest how a Wyoming dinosaur had won a Scottish-American plutocrat's name because of some stories in the New York newspapers. It was a remarkable tale. The guests in the Hall of Reptiles would have been familiar with its main outlines if they had been reading the London newspapers during the previous month.

Late in 1898, Carnegie had come across news items trumpeting the discovery in Wyoming of an animal of unimaginably huge proportions—120,000 pounds in weight and 130 feet long. Carnegie asked William Holland, director of the new Carnegie Museum in Pittsburgh, to go get it. The newspaper reports turned out to be less than accurate, but Holland did manage inside of a year to get the first bones of one of the largest dinosaurs then known from Wyoming back to the fossil labs in Pittsburgh, where they could be prepared for display. To do the work, Holland hired William H. Reed, a former buffalo hunter and railroad man, and two seasoned paleontologists from the American Museum of Natural History in New York. He handled the politics himself, bluffing and flattering his way through the corridors of Wyoming power and western land law, making three trips to Wyoming in the space of five months. The first *Diplodocus* bones were shipped by rail to Pittsburgh in the fall of 1899.

Holland was also lucky enough in the following year to hire the brilliant paleontologist John Bell Hatcher to supervise the scientific investigation of the fossil, and to oversee its preparation for study and display. Hatcher wrote the monograph on the dinosaur, and it was an illustration from that monograph which the king saw on Carnegie's wall in 1902.

Over coffee, perhaps, or cigars, the king inquired if he, too, could get a *Diplodocus*. Carnegie must have been pleased. Granting the king's wish would place his own power on equal footing with that of the world's greatest empire. The request went out to Holland: Can we get the king another dinosaur? Not likely, Holland replied. But we could, perhaps, make molds and construct a plaster copy.

Carnegie paid for everything. The work took the full-time labor of up to four men for a year and a half. Hatcher was in charge of the operation, with young Arthur Coggeshall, formerly of the American Museum of Natural History, in charge of the details of mold making, plaster casting, and display. The plaster bones were crated in Pittsburgh and shipped to London early in 1905. Holland and Coggeshall followed in March to supervise the assembly and erection of the skeleton.

"It is doubly pleasing," Carnegie continued that May afternoon, "that this should come from the youngest of our museums on the other side to yours, the parent institution of all, for certainly all those in America may be justly considered in one sense your offspring; we have followed you, inspired by your example." Carnegie had long been eager to show Europe that American science, like its new industrial capacity, was world class. He was determined to appear magnanimous. He praised Holland for having "conducted the first party to the Far West and organized victory" and went on to note that some of the crates which had crossed the Atlantic full of plaster bones would return filled with fossils of which the British Museum had duplicates. "An alliance for peace seems to have been affected . . . Thus you, Trustees of the old museum, and we, Trustees of the new, are jointly weaving a tie, another link binding in closer embrace the mother and child lands, which never should have been estranged, and which, as I see with the eye of faith which knows no doubt, are some day—some day—again to be reunited. (Applause.)"

The Scottish-born Carnegie had left his homeland with his family when he was a boy. Poverty forced them to emigrate. They went to Pittsburgh, where he made his first fortune. During the second half of his life, however, he spent as much time in Britain as in the United States, and his dream of a reunion between the two nations, plus Canada, was an open secret.

Lord Avebury, a bald man with white muttonchops, spoke next, on behalf of the trustees. Though he protested that the "size of the animal does not indeed necessarily add much to the interest," he seems to have been as stimulated by the skeleton's magnitude as was everyone else that day. He noted, slightly incorrectly on both counts,

On May 12, 1905, fashionable Londoners gathered for an afternoon of speechmaking to celebrate Carnegie's gift of a dinosaur to the king. Lord Avebury is speaking; William Holland is visible just behind Avebury's left arm. Photo first published in *Annals of the Carnegie Museum*, vol. 3 (1905): plate xvii.

that the *Diplodocus* was "the most colossal quadruped which has yet been discovered; and it is not likely that any much larger ever existed." He further noted the surprisingly small head, given the size of the body.

It then fell to Holland to acquaint the audience with some of the animal's natural history as it was then understood. The fossil stump of a palm tree had been found near the dinosaur bones, leading to the conclusion that *Diplodocus* lived in a tropical climate, and ate "the soft succulent vegetation of the shores and marshes which it haunted." The animal was primarily an eating machine, Holland said, "simply intended to convert vegetable fiber into flesh, upon which the carnivorous dinosaurs of the time fed." He was right that the climate of the time was tropical, if probably wrong about the dinosaur's habits and surroundings.

Diplodocus was in fact the longest, though not the most massive, dinosaur known at the time. That honor went to the genus *Apatosaurus*, then and now more popularly known as "Brontosaurus." Both *Apatosaurus* and *Diplodocus* were sauropods—the long-necked, long-tailed, elephant-legged, small-headed dinosaurs whose shape is now so familiar. *Apatosaurus*, though shorter than *Diplodocus*, was so stocky that it may have weighed three times as much—thirty-five tons compared to eleven, according to some estimates. Both flourished during the Jurassic period, around 140 million years ago. Even larger genera of sauropods have since been found; *Brachiosaurus*, for example.

The size of the sauropods led early paleontologists to conclude that the animals must have lived in swamps, believing that immersion in water would have been necessary to buoy all that bulk. Many paleontologists now, however, understand sauropods to have been dry-land tree browsers, inhabitants of an ecological niche similar to the ones occupied today by giraffes or elephants on the Serengeti Plains of East Africa. Like the Serengeti, Wyoming in the Jurassic swung between distinct wet and dry seasons, and supported large herds of plant eaters whose populations were controlled in part by far smaller numbers of carnivores.

Holland modestly passed to O. C. Marsh, the great paleontologist from Yale, the credit for having first named the *Diplodocus* genus and to Carnegie the true credit for discovery of the specimen being celebrated that day. "To Mr. Carnegie's intelligent appreciation of paleontological science and his generosity, far more than to my humble efforts," he said, "are to be attributed the discovery, not only of this great animal, but of a multitude of other strange creatures, the remains of which we have secured for the Museum of which I have the honor to be the Director."

Holland's modesty hides the love of command which had driven him to carry out Carnegie's wishes. His ambition had led him through stints as a clergyman and university president and now to his position as a museum director with substantial real estate holdings in Pittsburgh, a love for butterflies, and a knowledge of six or eight modern languages. In paleontology, however, he was self-taught, a state of affairs that caused some friction over the years with the more professional men he hired. His eyes were on the next big task of his career: expanding his museum.

The Carnegie Institute in Pittsburgh first opened in 1895 and included a library, music hall, art gallery, and natural history museum, all paid for by Carnegie. Holland came on as director of

the museum in 1898. By the spring of 1899 the impending acquisi-
tion of a dinosaur spurred Carnegie to come up with more money,
and plans began for a major expansion. Construction was underway in 1905, transforming an elegantly Italianate public building
into one far more massive in bulk and French in style. "In the Hall
of Dinosaurs in the Museum of the Carnegie Institute in Pittsburgh," Holland told his audience, "it is our wish to assemble and
display a series of skeletons representing the more striking forms of
dinosaurian life. The present specimen may be regarded as a sort
of first fruits of our undertaking. Such an enterprise involves the ex-
penditure of no little labor and of much money. Fortunately, the
kindness of our Maecenas, the distinguished founder and benefac-
tor of the Institute, has never failed to provide the sinews for our
scientific war."

A genuine competition was under way at the time among
American natural history museums, for splendor as much as for
specimens. America's most memorable dinosaur halls—at the
American Museum of Natural History in New York, the Carnegie
Museum in Pittsburgh, the Smithsonian Institution in Washington,
D.C., the Peabody Museum at Yale—all were built and filled in the
first quarter of the twentieth century. Our notion of natural history
museums as temples to science, with the dinosaur exhibit their central shrine, dates to that time. Smaller institutions around the country—the little University of Wyoming, for example—followed suit as
best they could. As a result, vertebrate paleontology remained a
museum-based science, as had much of natural history throughout
the nineteenth century. Darwin, for example, had strong ties to the
British Museum, where fossils he sent back from the Beagle voyage
were examined and described by other scientists. Natural sciences
that depended on collections depended on museums to house their
resource materials. But, by 1905, that was changing.

The information amassed during the nineteenth century's in-
creasingly organized labors in descriptive science bred more and
more hypotheses. Scientists needed to test them—to run experiments—and experiments were more likely to occur in university
laboratories. Experimental biology—genetics in particular—was already regarded by most life scientists as the true frontier of the pro-

fession, not the erection and display of extinct fossil vertebrates. By contrast, leaders of natural history museums at the turn of the century began just then to articulate the triple mission they had haphazardly been undertaking for years: collecting specimens, maintaining them in an orderly fashion for study, and educating the public by means of displays. Museum administrators discovered that people loved dinosaurs and would flock to grand halls to admire them. Far into the twentieth century, that gave vertebrate paleontology, and particularly dinosaur paleontology, a financial and political power base that greatly outweighed its intellectual prestige.

Meanwhile, there was no room for *Diplodocus carnegii* at the Carnegie Museum in Pittsburgh when the fossil was cleaned and prepared, so the cast intended for Carnegie's gift to the king was first mounted in an exposition hall miles away. The original was finally erected in 1907, when the doors opened to the expanded institute with its newly created Dinosaur Hall. By mid-century, ten complete dinosaur skeletons would fill the hall, along with a number of other marine and flying reptiles from dinosaur times. They all still may be seen there today.

Before concluding his remarks, Holland praised a colleague whose absence he may have felt with some pain. "I should be false to the promptings of my heart," he said, "did I not allude tenderly and in terms of highest appreciation to the labors of Professor J. B. Hatcher, my learned colleague, who for fully eighteen months devoted himself to superintending the restoration of the object before us, but who unfortunately was stricken down in the midst of his activities by the hand of death, a premature victim to the hardships and exposures of those expeditions, which Mr. Carnegie, who always sees things from an interesting angle, has designated as 'annual holidays.' Mr. Hatcher was one of the most successful students of paleontology whom America has produced."

Hatcher's reputation, like the reputations of so many people who die young, will always be bound up with the question of how much more he would have accomplished had he lived longer. While still in his thirties, before he came to work for the Carnegie Museum, he had suffered severe attacks of rheumatism on Princeton-sponsored expeditions to Patagonia. He was then beginning to develop a hypothesis of global proportions. By the time he came to Pittsburgh in 1900, he had formulated the notion that the land masses of South America, Antarctica, and Australia once had been joined, and he began pressuring Holland for help in getting to Antarctica to test his ideas. But he never got there, and it would be sixty years before geologists would work out comprehensive, theoretically consistent answers to all the questions Hatcher had begun to ask.

Lord Avebury introduced the final speaker, Sir Archibald Geike, geologist and fellow of the Royal Society, and asked him to say a few words on behalf of the geologists of England:

"It is a great pleasure to possess this gigantic creature in the flesh (Laughter), or at least in the bone (Laughter), and to be able to study the animal in its entirety, and thus to interpret other forms, the separate and fragmentary bones of which hitherto were all that we knew, but the significance of the scattered remains of which now becomes plain to us," Geike said. Here, at last, was a scientist speaking. He was talking about the logic of the full form of the animal, how the parts each have so much more meaning when the whole can be seen. The reason to collect fossils is to compare them with one another, so that the forms of life may be better understood. It seemed appropriate, Geike went on, that "such a monster as this" would come from a continent so vast in resources. American scientists were to be envied for having these resources available to them. And, not failing to render his praise to the emperor of the day, he concluded, "Supported by the beneficence of such a far seeing man as Mr. Carnegie, we may expect that the student of paleontology in America will achieve discoveries even surpassing in interest those which have already been made, and that, bit by bit, the wonderful story of the evolution of existing forms of life, through forms, many of them long since extinct, will be deciphered. (Applause.)"

Then the meeting broke up, the guests got a chance to shake hands with Mr. Carnegie, "and the assembled company leisurely examined the skeleton, which appeared to create much interest in the minds of all."

As it turned out, the international journeys of *Diplodocus carnegii* were just beginning. The crowned heads of Europe, as they were then called, were eager for a gift like King Edward's, and Carnegie proved equally eager to continue demonstrating his imperial generosity. In the next decade, he had more *Diplodocus* casts made in Pittsburgh and shipped to museums in Berlin, Paris, Vienna, Bologna, St. Petersburg, La Plata in Argentina, and Madrid. Holland and Coggeshall accompanied the casts and supervised their assembly at each location. *Diplodocus carnegii* gained international fame. It was the first dinosaur millions of people ever saw.

How that came about may be traced back twenty-eight years to Wyoming Territory at a time when there was a brisk trade in buffalo bones on the plains, but few had noticed fossils.

Chapter 2

THE FREEHEARTED
FRONTIER HUNTER

O ne afternoon in March 1877, gun in hand and the fresh hams
of an antelope slung over his shoulder, Bill Reed found dinosaur bones weathering out of a bluff in southeast Wyoming, just a
mile and a half from the Union Pacific Railroad tracks. Long experience as a hunter told him that these were not the bones of any kind
of living animal. Remarkably, he also knew who might know more
about them—America's most famous scientist, who already had a
reputation in the West for paying money for ancient bones.

Just then Reed was working for the railroad in a spot as lonely
as any of a thousand other stretches of the West—except that the
tracks, and their train traffic, ran right by. He was twenty-eight years
old, in the full competence of his youth and always with an eye out
for better prospects. He'd been born in Connecticut in 1848 and had
moved gradually west with his family, serving in the Civil War as a
teenager. After the war, railroads were expanding in all directions.
Reed joined the laborers extending the Union Pacific across the continent. He worked first as a snow shoveler, then as a hunter, providing game to feed the construction crews. Buffalo herds were still vast
when tracks came across southern Wyoming in 1868 and 1869, and
they were the laborers' main source of food.

Reed returned to Michigan to marry and farm, but his wife died
after their first child was born. Probably leaving the child with relatives, he roamed west again. By 1874 he was back in Wyoming with

William Harlow Reed, fossil
collector, who first came to
Wyoming as a laborer and hunter
for the Union Pacific Railroad.
Courtesy of the Yale Peabody Museum,
Yale University, New Haven,
Connecticut.

the railroad. He and a partner, William Carlin, held jobs at tiny
Como Station on the tracks about sixty miles northwest of Laramie.
In March the high plains there are bleak and windy. Among Reed's
tasks would have been to keep them both in meat.

Carlin was station agent; he handled ticketing, shipping, and
bookkeeping. Reed was section foreman, boss of a small crew of laborers who kept ten miles of track in good repair. As such, they were
part of a new bureaucracy, America's first really big business. The
railroads depended for revenues on the nickel-and-dime accounting
of men like Carlin, and for safety on the vigilance of men like Reed.
And in bringing more and more white people to the West, the railroads brought a new industrial economy. By 1877 Laramie had
evolved from a violent, end-of-the-tracks tent camp into a town with
a steel mill where worn railroad rails were melted down and rolled
into new ones.

At Como, however, the vast plains with their older economy
pressed in all around. The two men would have had plenty of time
to talk. They didn't know what kind of bones they had, exactly, but
fossils were already winning some notoriety in the West. For several

years, reports of big-bone finds had been coming from places as far apart as the Dakota and New Mexico territories. Closer to home, the two men probably knew of the discovery in Colorado that spring of bones of huge, ancient beasts. Now they'd found huge bones, too. While the wind blew around their shack, they decided what to do.

The discoverers of bones at one Colorado site—near Morrison, west of Denver—soon would sell them to the phlegmatic paleontologist Othniel Charles Marsh, who ruled the Peabody Museum at Yale College. Fossils discovered one hundred miles south of Denver, at Cañon City, that year would end up in the hands of the mercurial Edward Drinker Cope, the Quaker naturalist from Philadelphia. Both men were already famous for their brilliant science and deep pockets.

The logistics of Western scientific exploration were well established by the late 1870s. Army expeditions locating railroad routes had mapped extensively before the Civil War. After the war, an expansive Congress financed four government surveys, supplied from Army posts, whose members explored primarily for mineral riches. But they also took thousands of photographs and carefully described flora, fauna—and fossils. The government also financed lavish publication of the surveys' findings. Cope worked as vertebrate paleontologist with two of the surveys. One published his study on the Tertiary—that is, post-dinosaur—fossils of the West, a massive book that came to be known as "Cope's Bible." Marsh, meanwhile, managed to wangle Army escorts for fossil-hunting expeditions of Yale students, which he led from 1870 through 1874. But after the four government surveys were consolidated into a single U.S. Geological Survey in 1879, it was Marsh who came out on top, winning the post of vertebrate paleontologist for the entire agency—and the staff, budget, and publication support that went with it.

Marsh learned to spend government money instead of his own; Cope eventually went broke trying to increase his personal resources by investing in New Mexico silver mines. Their generation-long rivalry—often it's been called a feud—destroyed them both. But before they died—Cope in 1896 and Marsh in 1899—the two of them together scientifically described about 1,600 species of previously unknown extinct vertebrate animals.

Reed and Carlin decided to approach Marsh in disguise and so signed the first letter they wrote him "Harlow and Edwards"—their middle names. Perhaps they wanted to shroud their news from any passing Cope informants. Perhaps they'd been prospecting on company time and didn't want their supervisors to know. In any case, Marsh received their letter from Laramie in July 1877 announcing the discovery, "not far from this place, of a large number of fossils, supposed to be those of a *Megatherium*, although there is no one here sufficient of a geologist to state for a certainty." A *Megatherium* is an extinct giant ground sloth from the Pleistocene epoch, many tens of millions of years more recent than dinosaur times. Still, it's a paleontological term, and shows that one of the two, probably Reed, had some knowledge of fossils already. A few bones had already been dug up, the letter writers said, and they claimed to know the location of many more:

We are desirous of disposing of what fossils we have, and also, the secret of the others. We are working men and not able to present them as a gift, and if we can sell the secret of the fossil bed, and procure work in excavating others we would like to do so.

We have said nothing to anyone as yet . . .

One shoulder blade was four feet, eight inches long. A single vertebra was two and a half feet around and ten inches thick.

As proof of our sincerity and truth, we will send you a few fossils, at what they cost us in time and money in unearthing.

We would be pleased to hear from you, as you are well-known as an enthusiastic geologist, and a man of means, both of which we are desirous of finding—more especially the latter.

By January 1878, Marsh knew that Cope had gotten wind of the Como discovery, and at that point he agreed to pay "Harlow and Edwards" each $90 per month to excavate what would turn out to be one of the greatest troves of dinosaur bones ever found. It was better than railroad pay. The first great dinosaur rush was on.

Flesh decays, but bones may last. Especially if a flood comes to bury an animal soon after its death, the bones have a chance of lasting

eons. During the Jurassic period, 140 million years ago, the climate in what is now Wyoming alternated annually between dry and wet seasons. Rivers wound eastward across a mostly flat landscape. They flowed past conifers and gingko trees near their banks, alongside tree ferns and shrub-sized cycads.

Dinosaurs reached their greatest number and diversity during the Jurassic, the middle of the three dinosaur periods—Triassic, Jurassic, and Cretaceous—which together make up the Mesozoic Era, the middle time of life on earth, dominated by the great reptiles. The Jurassic dinosaurs are perhaps the most familiar: the thirty-five-ton *Apatosaurus*; its shorter, box-headed cousin *Camarasaurus*; the lighter, longer *Diplodocus*; *Stegosaurus*, with its high, humped back, back plates, and tail spikes. All of them browsed their favorite plants at what is now Como, keeping an eye on members of their own herds while watching out for speedy *Allosaurus*, the big-headed two-legged predator.

Meanwhile, the rivers shrank in the dry seasons and swelled over their banks in the rainy seasons, leaving new layers of mud, silt, or sand—depending on their speed, volume, patterns of outflow, and what kind of country they were draining in the first place. If a dinosaur died, it would most likely rot quickly. Scavengers would scatter its bones and insects would clean them before they, too, finally decayed into something else. But if a dinosaur happened to die by a riverbank in the rainy season, and the river flooded the carcass before much of it was dragged off or eaten on the spot, then the flesh would still rot, but the bones, encased in mud now, might mineralize. And the resulting mineral would keep the animal's shape—right down to predators' teeth marks on the bone, or the grooves left by blood vessels, or the wear marks of tendons where they stretched from bone to big-bellied muscle.

The rivers went on flooding and shrinking, flooding and shrinking, now and then preserving bones, until, fairly suddenly, after fifty million years of unchallenged hegemony, the big Jurassic dinosaurs disappeared. The life forms of the Jurassic gave way to the life forms of the Cretaceous, the last of the dinosaur ages. Diversity among dinosaurs decreased. *Allosaurus* was replaced in the big-predator niche by *Tyrannosaurus*, which was twice as large. Flowering plants appeared.

During the Cretaceous, a shallow sea bifurcated the North American continent, sometimes stretching all the way from the Arctic Ocean to the Gulf of Mexico. The western shore moved west or east across what is now Wyoming as the water level rose or fell. The continents themselves, meanwhile, had broken apart after an earlier union and by the Jurassic and Cretaceous eras were moving gradually away from one another. Then, as now, these great landmasses were floating on the hot mantle below them. North America was moving slowly to the northwest. And then, as now, the sea-floor plate under the Pacific was diving into the mantle under the North American plate as it moved.

That diving under and moving over of plates along the western edge of North America brought pressure to bear on the interior, knotting the rocks into complex associations; when the pressure released a little, the rocks bobbed upward, starting the Rocky Mountains. The uplift continued past the end of the Cretaceous and into the beginning of the Tertiary Period—the Paleocene and early Eocene epochs—when, with dinosaurs gone, mammals expanded rapidly in numbers, kinds, and size, though they would never come near the size of the larger dinosaurs.

Meanwhile, the sideways pressures had folded the older, river-deposited layers of the Jurassic rocks and the limy, sea-deposited layers of Cretaceous rocks into new shapes, just as a handkerchief will fold if you lay it flat on a table, then move its opposite sides toward each other. Four parallel upfolds, or anticlines, ran roughly northeast-southwest between mountains to the south and north of what is now the Como area. Those folded layers rose again, together, as the Rockies rose. But even before the Rockies reached their maximum height—much higher than they are today—the weather was wearing them down. Frost, rain, and relentless wind scoured enough debris off the mountain tops to nearly fill all the basins between mountains in Wyoming with sand and dirt. Wind-blown ash from volcanoes erupting far to the west filled the basins the rest of the way, right up to the tops of the mountains.

Wind kept blowing and water flowing, carrying the sediments away from the basins again. Eventually the tops of the four upfolds were again exposed. Then the tops, too, were scooped away, leaving the outermost sides of the old folds as long, low ridges, like Como Bluff. Finally, the edges of the river-deposited layers where the Jurassic dinosaurs had died were re-exposed on the steeper, inside slopes of the eroded anticlines. And that was where Reed found his bones.

Como Bluff stretches in a narrow, mostly treeless ridge about seven miles from its western to its eastern end. Steep, crumbly slopes line the north face. The south face slopes more gently, covered with grass and some sagebrush. The entire bluff rises four or five hundred feet above the plains around it.

On the north face the mostly gray, sometimes greenish and ochre, layers of the Morrison formation—soft sandstones, shales, and clays of the Late Jurassic—are clearly visible to a geologist or anyone else with an eye for rocks, though to others they appear unremarkable. At wetter times of year, spring-fed rivulets flow down the north face of the bluff to little Lake Como near its western end. Years ago, Como station lay on the tracks nearby. From the top of the bluff you can see horizons in all directions. Elk Mountain, a large right triangle lying on its hypotenuse, dominates the west. In the middle distance lies the little town of Medicine Bow, still clinging to the tracks as it did 120 years ago. To the south, the Snowy Range shoulders up from Colorado. Laramie Peak shows the apex of its blue cone far to the northeast. Until 1900, the railroad wound north of the bluff, more or less along the meanders of Rock Creek. Trains would have been frequent from the earliest days, as would have been the handcar traffic of the maintenance crews.

By the spring of 1879, Carlin had defected to the Cope teams also digging in the area, and Reed was working alone. The rewards were enormous; limb bones appear to have been strewn about like logs. They were stacked in a wheelbarrow, wheeled to the nearby tracks, loaded on a handcar, and trundled to Como station. There the men built packing boxes for the bones and shipped them off by rail. Reed's discoveries ranged from the huge *Apatosaurus excelsus* still at Yale to the teeth and jaws of the tiny *Dryolestes*. The discovery of

Como Bluff, Wyoming, with Elk Mountain in the background. Dinosaur bones were plentiful when Reed first found them here in 1877, within wheelbarrow distance of the tracks of the transcontinental Union Pacific Railroad. Courtesy of *Casper Star-Tribune* Collection, Casper College Library. Photo by Zbigniew Bzdak.

this animal, the first Jurassic mammal found in North America, proved that mouse-sized furbearers were scurrying, and surviving, under the giant reptiles' feet.

Competition between the Cope crews and the Marsh crews at Como intensified throughout 1878 and into 1879, as both scientists pressed their collectors for bones. In desperation Reed once smashed bones at a quarry he was finished with, so there would be nothing left for the Cope men—no small crime by modern scientific standards. Another time, he shoveled dirt and rocks from the steep bank above a Cope quarry down onto the rival diggings.

In May 1879 Marsh sent Arthur Lakes, an English-born naturalist and schoolteacher, up from the Colorado dinosaur quarries to reinforce Reed. The daily journal Lakes kept, and the sketches and watercolors he made during his ten months at Como give an unmatched picture of the place—its geology, fauna, flora, economy, and human society. When he arrived, Lakes found a dozen men around the stove at the station house, smoking and playing cards. But only one was the center of attention:

Amongst them was a tall swarthy complexioned man with a handsome face dressed in a full suit of buckskin ornamented with fringes after the frontier fashion.

The broad brimmed white felt hat on his head had the front rim thrown up like a vizor and perforated by a gun-wad punch. He was standing with his back against the stove, the most striking and commanding figure of the group looking the ideal of the frank, freehearted frontier hunter.

I asked, "Is Mr. Reed here?" and he answered, "that is my name" and gave me a very hearty welcome. He had been expecting me for some days . . . "

They quickly became friends. Lakes, the Oxford-educated naturalist, was smitten by Reed's skills, yarns, and curiosity. After a week Lakes was describing Reed as

a splendid shot, a keen sportsman, a lover of nature, natural history and scenery, [with] a wonderful power of close observation which with his occasional intercourse with stray naturalists and scientists had made a very fair naturalist of him. He had become too a fair practical geologist and had increased his knowledge of that science by the study of books lent him. A man of much force of will and character qualifying him as a leader, freehearted and generous to a fault and honest and honorable. We get along first rate together, sleep in the same bunk, eat and drink and share all things in common except the prevailing western habit of profanity . . .

He has an endless fund of stories of the wildest character of his experiences in the parks and mountains amongst Indians, bears, desperadoes; stories which bear the character of truth. He is quite our leading spirit around here.

Como consisted of a red station house, a red bunk- and boardinghouse for the maintenance workers, and, for the locomotives, a red water tank "like a huge coffeepot," Lakes wrote. None of these buildings remains.

Lakes bunked first with Reed in a tent at a spring up on the bluff. After a few days "the navvies," as Lakes called the laboring hands, persuaded the two men to move down to the station—perhaps in an attempt to ease tensions between Reed and the three Cope men who were also camped there. Reed and Lakes pitched their tent at the station, then spruced it up with a gunnysack carpet and a pantry of wooden boxes.

For Lakes, the place was Eden. The station lay a few hundred yards from the shore of Lake Como, named by hopeful railroad surveyors a decade earlier for the beautiful Italian original. A mile long and half as wide, it is shallow and has no outlet; its waters are alkaline and undrinkable. Such white-rimmed ponds are common in that country; they expand and contract as the year cycles from damp to dry. In springtime, in Lakes's description, Lake Como teemed with life—millions of mosquitoes, thousands of tiger salamanders; also cowbirds, blackbirds, mallards, coots, grebes, avocets, phalaropes, terns, gulls, and muskrats. Cheerfully, the men plundered all that plenty. One day in July, Reed returned from the lake "with twelve dozen eggs they had collected from the grebes nests in the rushes in about an hour. In former years as many as seventy five dozen have been collected in a day," Lakes wrote. Besides hunting antelope and an occasional deer or elk for food, killing went on for sport, or something more like pure exuberance. Both men were happy to shoot at eagles, shrikes, a sage grouse, gulls, beavers—creatures they had no intention of eating. Of course, they killed coyotes whenever possible. "R feels particular delight in slaughtering these," Lakes wrote, "in revenge for their nocturnal howls which have so often kept him awake at night."

Guns were for celebrating, too. First thing on the Fourth of July, "Reed sat up in bed and shot a hole through the tent with his revolver." Later that morning all hands grabbed their pistols and went after rabbits in the sagebrush, then adjourned to a beer keg by the water tank, then to a dinner cooked by Mrs. Chase, wife of the new station agent, then back to the beer keg. That evening, presumably after cleaning up the big meal she'd cooked earlier in the day, Mrs. Chase "was unwell." A midwife arrived from Medicine Bow in a fast carriage. At 9:05 p.m. "Mrs. C presented Como with a Fourth of July baby daughter. We had rabbit stew for supper and so ended the glorious 4th and the moon came up a red ball over the bluff."

Also that summer, Marsh and Cope paid separate visits to their quarries, the closest they ever came to meeting at Como. Marsh arrived in early June. The professor enjoyed breakfast with all hands, followed by a ride along the tracks in the "rubber car," drawn behind the hand car and named for its rubbernecking passengers. At the quarry Marsh separated the bones he wanted from the ones he didn't and "devolved" the ones he didn't want "to destruction," Lakes wrote—apparently a second reference to smashing bones. The next day they visited a quarry near the west end of the bluff, not far from the station, where, under Marsh's ebullient leadership, they found a new dinosaur. Cope showed up in early August. Lakes confided to his journal, perhaps with twinges of disloyalty, that he found Marsh's rival likable, and the two talked about England. For everyone's pleasure, the great naturalist sang a song that ended with coyote yips and howls.

But, as the summer progressed, indications of a rising tension between Reed and Lakes began creeping into Lakes's journal. Digging bones is hard, dull labor. Both men worked hard, but Reed worked harder, and by August he was disgusted with his educated colleague and ready to quit. Lakes, for his part, was following Marsh's instructions by often spending more time sketching than digging. His watercolors show long views of the bluff and scenes of the men working. In one, titled "The 'Pleasures' of Science," Lakes sketched himself and another man quarrying bones in driving snow. More important to subsequent science, Lakes measured the rock layers and left detailed, labeled drawings, which have enabled modern paleontologists to relocate nearly two dozen quarries the Marsh crews dug in those years. Reed was not a record keeper: he was after bones, bones, bones.

By fall they were working on opposite ends of the bluff and seeing little of each other. Relations thawed somewhat on New Year's Day, which was warm and sunny. All hands celebrated with a test of marksmanship. "Reed made the best shot & I next," Lakes wrote. Then the days turned bitter cold, but work went on. When Lakes widened a big trench, in his enthusiasm for *Stegosaurus* bones, he barely escaped a cave-in. The men reported frozen ears; when Reed froze a foot they had to "make a fire to thaw him."

Still, Reed found game in the worst weather. On the coldest days, they stayed inside and Reed told stories. Regardless of the feelings between the two men, Lakes could not keep from recording the tales. Once, after a heavy snow, "on passing near a snowdrift they found bushels of birds alive in it. They caught fifty of them." There are other stories:

Reed told us about seeing a puma spring on a elk. The latter tried hard to throw him off. Reed waited till the puma had killed the elk and was sucking the blood from the throat. Then he whistled, the puma looked up and Reed fired and killed him....

Reed told of a big pyramidal crystal of quartz eight feet long he found in a cave near North Park.

Reed's West was an Aladdin's cave of wonders.

The Cope threat dwindled considerably after 1879, leaving as the primary sources of stress at the diggings Marsh's failure to pay anyone on time or to make clear who was in charge. Still, Reed stayed loyal. His brother, who had come west to join him in the work, was killed in the summer of 1881 after he dove into Rock Creek one hot Sunday morning and hit his head on a rock. Reed worked harder than ever after that, and his letters became less and less enthusiastic.

In 1883 Reed went into the sheep business and failed spectacularly, losing 1,100 head, nearly half his herd, to bad weather. Badly in need of money, he fell back on the work he knew best. But Marsh would only pay him by the piece now, though for years they squabbled over what kind of payment they had agreed on. After 1886 the letters stop altogether. Marsh, meanwhile, was reaching the peak of his fame and power. In 1890 Reed contacted Marsh again, saying he had been making a living with his team of horses where he could, most recently by cutting hay. Shortly afterward he returned to railroad work but wrote to ask Marsh if there might be a job collecting fossils in Alaska, where Reed had heard the government survey might be starting some projects.

The request came to nothing. Marsh's ten years as paleontologist for the U.S. Geological Survey ended in 1892 and with his appointment went most of his perks and influence. Congress had grown reluctant to pay for science in a contracting economy. Marsh's luxurious monograph on *Odontornithes*, a genus of toothed birds from the Cretaceous chalkbeds of western Kansas, attracted derision in the House of Representatives. "Birds with teeth" became a rallying cry in a war on government waste. Behind it all were Cope and his allies, who had been maneuvering in Washington against Marsh for years.

In the mid-1890s Reed finally got steadier work, and in 1896 he was hired full time at the University of Wyoming as assistant geologist and curator of the university's so-called museum, a hodgepodge of fossils and other miscellany crammed into corners and a few available rooms of the two main buildings. The collection totaled eighty tons. The fossils, primarily Jurassic vertebrates, were so numerous that, at least for a time, the collection rivaled Marsh's Jurassic collection in size.

Despite having a new employer, Reed kept his old customer. Near the end of 1896, Marsh paid $65 for parts of four skeletons of *Baptanodon*—a seagoing Jurassic reptile. In the same correspondence Reed mentions that he has a few bones from a huge dinosaur. But Marsh, for the moment, was interested primarily in the low-growing, palmlike Jurassic conifers called cycads. It appeared that Reed would have to save the dinosaur for another buyer. Still hoping for a sale, Reed wrote Marsh in June 1898, saying that he had found some cycads in rocks just above the layer that had yielded *Baptanodon* a few years earlier. But mentioning the *Baptanodon* sent him off on a tangent:

By the way that makes me think of another matter that I want to call your attention to I have two letters where you promise to give me credit in your monographs for my work and all of my Discoveries who found the first baptanodon and where is the credit you have described 17 new mammals I found the first Jurassic mammal found in america and all of the 17 came from a quarry that I found and where is the credit all the credit I have ever seen is for Brontosaurus of course I thank you for that but give the devil

W. H. Reed, shown here with a sauropod femur, began collecting fossils for the University of Wyoming in 1896. In 1899 he went to work for the Carnegie Museum. Courtesy of S. H. Knight Collection, American Heritage Center, University of Wyoming.

his due but if I remember correctly there are several more dinosaurs that
should be credited to me.

It was true. Reed's finds provided early and solid evidence for
Darwin's theory of evolution by natural selection, then still quite
young. And they had boosted Marsh's prestige in his long battle with
Cope. But not until the end of the letter does Reed get to the real
source of his resentment. He has learned that Marsh can't remember his name:

Now here comes another matter that I don't like last week I met Dr
Wortman he said he met you several times last winter and once spoke of
me but you could only remember me as <u>Moss</u> <u>Agate</u> <u>Bill</u> now that is a new
name to me and I never heard it before and I don't want to hear it again if
that is the only way you rem[em]ber me after all the years of hard work
and poor pay and shaby treatment. why I believe I am as near being a
gentleman as some that fill higher walks in life. . .

For years he had suppressed this resentment of the poor man toward the rich, the Westerner toward the Easterner, the scrambling
toward the powerful, the autodidact toward the professor cloaked in
honors and degrees. That he could write such words and send them
off shows that personal feelings were closer to the surface then, in an
innocent way that now seems odd. Or perhaps he was simply tact-
less—the blunt end of the quality Lakes was describing when he
called him "frank" and "freehearted" so many years before.

The pressures Reed felt also flowed from the way science was
done at the time. Biology and the earth sciences were still primarily
descriptive: Plants and animal specimens had to be gathered and
classified. Rock formations had to be mapped, their chronology
figured out and their nomenclature standardized. The work, though
often tedious, was a great intellectual and logistical adventure. But
hired collectors of flora, fauna, and fossils were not well paid; one
of the few rewards for their work and hardships was a chance to rise
out of anonymity when their names were attached in scientific publications to some newfound thing.

Change was coming, however. A new kind of field scientist began appearing at the turn of the century, more professional than the

collectors who had served the professors of earlier generations. The new professionals' collecting led them to make hypotheses of their own, which in turn demanded yet more specimens against which to test the ideas. Marsh would not live to see the change. But others of his class—big-city museum directors, administrators, patrons of science—would be sometimes baffled by the intellectual ambitions of their employees and often resentful. At the same time, the newer scientists would demand greater care in the collecting. Veteran collectors—men like Reed—would have to relearn their craft from younger men if they wanted to keep their jobs.

Reed was probably writing Marsh from the cabin he had built in a spot sheltered from the wind in the Freezeout Mountains northwest of Como, and had named "Happy Holow." Those hills and swales are treeless, the wind more or less constant. The Dr. Wortman he mentions was Jacob Wortman, a paleontologist from the American Museum of Natural History in New York, whose crews were also prospecting southeast Wyoming then. A moss agate is a pretty rock that an amateur might admire. Reed, who knew the rocks and fossils of Wyoming as well as anyone, was stung. His handwriting is large in the letter, and gets larger as his feeling increases:

Dr Wortman speaks very highly of you but says he considers it very singular that you have not given me credit for my work if I have done all I claim now as W.H. Reed I should be glad to make you a present of 2 or 3 of these cycads but as moss agate Bill I cant do it so you wil have to wate til fall and get them from the curator of ower museum.

yours in camp
W. H. Reed
Medicine Bow, Wyo

Marsh answered immediately. Eager to soothe, he said he'd pay "full value" for the cycads and would be sure to credit Reed in upcoming monographs. The great naturalist was at risk of losing one of his greatest collectors:

I wish to be a friend to you in any way I can, and I want you to be the same to me. Various people have tried to make trouble between us, and we may have misunderstood each other on some points, but I have always spoken in the highest terms of you as a collector and as a man, and remember with much pleasure the days I have spent with you in fossil hunting, and only wish I could be with you again, as we can both be of service to each other in many ways.

Marsh doesn't deny having used the nickname. He simply figured its use would never get back to its owner:

I am very sorry to have used the name you referred to. I do not remember to have used it to anyone who knew you, and had I supposed that you would be offended, I should never have done so.

Finally, Marsh tries to bridge the gulfs between himself and Reed—income, class, background, geography—by mentioning a celebrity acquaintance:

I heard the expression, once only, years ago, just as I heard my friend Cody called "Buffalo Bill," and this, I believe, he has never objected to.

Oddly, it worked. Who knows? Perhaps Reed, like Cody, a former railroad buffalo hunter, was flattered. Buffalo Bill was America's Western star, enjoying with his Wild West circus a new kind of nostalgia-based fame, made possible by mass advertising and fast railroad travel. A mollified Reed wrote back on July 8, 1898, to say, "I believe you intend to do about right" and to recommend that Marsh send whatever he thought the cycads were worth directly to the university.

His own career prospects were more on Reed's mind than anything else. When he wrote Marsh two months later, Reed was guessing that his university's troubles were likely to continue:

Ower university is so poor that I am thinking of leaving it and trying to work independent and sell my fossils in europe or to some other american museum and If I do I shal want some recommends from you.

The Westerner in him, if that's what it was, was restless again. He may or may not have known it, but his job search was about to land him in a full-page story in one of the largest newspapers in the world.

Chapter 3

THE MOST COLOSSAL
ANIMAL

*A*ndrew Carnegie returned to New York in the fall of 1898 after
a year and a half in Europe. He was on the edge of great
changes in his life, beginning to realize as he approached his sixty-
third birthday that he wished to sell off his steel interests and give
all his time to philanthropy. After a summer at Skibo, a winter at
Cannes, and another summer and fall at Skibo with his wife and their
only child—Louise Carnegie was forty-two, and Margaret already
two and a half—he may have welcomed the return to the bustle of
New York life. But he had a family of his own now. Business, a world
to which he had brought huge changes, may not have held for him
the attraction it once had.

In December, Carnegie saw reports in the New York papers
about a remarkable dinosaur found in Wyoming the previous summer. While one article was headlined simply "The Dinosaur of
Wyoming," another, which ran in a special Christmas edition of
William Randolph Hearst's *New York Journal and Advertiser*, pulled
out all the stops: "Most Colossal Animal Ever On Earth Just Found
Out West," ran the headline across the top of the page. A drawing of a long-necked, elephant-legged dinosaur, slightly bulbous
but generally sauropod-shaped, dominated the center of the page.
It reared back on its tail in a tripod position and peered into an
eleventh-floor window of the New York Life Building, one of Manhattan's fashionable new skyscrapers. A trolley car was passing be-

Andrew Carnegie was sixty-three in 1898, nearing the time when he would cash in his steel interests and turn to full-time philanthropy. Library and Archives Division, Historical Society of Western Pennsylvania, Pittsburgh, Pennsylvania.

tween the creature's back legs and its tail, which lay switching in the street.

Headlines in smaller type declared: "When It Walked The Earth Trembled Under Its Weight of 120,000 Pounds"; "When It Ate It Filled a Stomach Large Enough To Hold Three Elephants"; "When It Was Angry Its Terrible Roar Could Be Heard Ten Miles."

A photograph in the upper-left-hand corner of the page showed a thickly mustached man in shirtsleeves, long cuff-protectors, and a lab apron standing next to a massive leg bone slightly taller than himself. The *Journal and Advertiser* story identified him as "Bill Reeder" of Wyoming, discoverer of the beast the paper was calling *Brontosaurus Giganteus*. Carnegie must have felt good reading the news. He'd already taken steps to get that very dinosaur for himself.

Carnegie had plenty of money, partners who managed the day-to-day operations of his steel interests in Pittsburgh, a castle in Scotland, and a brownstone in New York at 51st Street and Fifth Avenue. Construction had recently begun on his new mansion, a sixty-four-

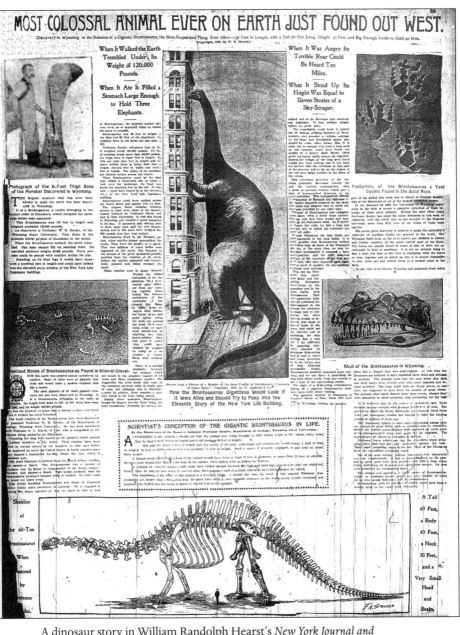

A dinosaur story in William Randolph Hearst's *New York Journal and Advertiser*, December 11, 1898, caught Carnegie's attention. Image electronically combined from McGinnis, *Carnegie's Dinosaurs*, 13, and Library of Congress microfilm.

room house forty blocks uptown. The great majority of his wealth, however, was still tied up in his steel mills, coal mines, coke ovens, limestone quarries, iron mines, ore boats, and railroads. For a generation he had spearheaded American steelmaking by constantly reinvesting profits in technical improvements, thereby steadily driving down the price of steel. Gradually he bought more deeply into the raw-materials and shipping ends of the business, until he had a vertically integrated system that would become a model for twentieth-century commerce. His first priority had always been to make steel, not money; the great wealth he had amassed was a by-product. As a result, Carnegie was largely responsible for transforming American business. It's unlikely that the United States would have become the world's leading manufacturing power by 1900 if Carnegie's competitors had not been scrambling for decades just to keep up with him.

Carnegie was a small man—only five feet, three inches tall, with small hands and feet and a high voice. He was one of the very few tycoons of the so-called Gilded Age who came from genuinely humble beginnings, in fact, real poverty. His interest in dinosaurs was only a small part of his life, but it may be read as part of a general fascination with size, with bigness. That fascination seems logical in light of his slight stature and his lifelong memory of the moment when the Industrial Revolution drove him and his family out of Scotland, the lowest ebb of their fortunes.

Andrew was twelve in 1848 when he, with his mother, father, and brother Tom left the village of Dunfermline at the head of the Firth of Forth for Glasgow, there to board a ship to the New World. His father, a skilled cottage weaver and the son and grandson of weavers, had lost his livelihood to the steam-powered textile mills. The family borrowed money to emigrate and chose Pittsburgh as their destination because they had relatives there. Carnegie's mother mended shoes and took in washing to make ends meet; his father never found steady work again. The young Andrew started work almost immediately, first as bobbin boy in a textile factory, then as a deliverer of telegrams. He made the most of this job, becoming a cheerful, familiar presence to Pittsburgh's most prominent businessmen and learning telegraphy himself. One of the businessmen hired him to run a private telegraph operation for the Pennsylvania Railroad. Seven years later, a few weeks after Andrew turned twenty-four, he was superintendent of all the railroad's operations in western Pennsylvania.

Carnegie made his first fortune by investing some of his salary in the newly discovered oil fields of northwestern Pennnsylvania. After the Civil War, he quit his job with the railroad and added to his fortune by investing in railroad bridges, sleeping cars, and telegraphy, and by selling bonds for American companies to European investors. Only then, in his mid-thirties, did Carnegie narrow his field of investments and go full bore into manufacturing. One of his favorite mottoes was "Put all your eggs in one basket—and watch the basket."

From his first years in Pittsburgh, he maintained close connections with relatives back in Dunfermline. Carnegie had inherited a Scotch shrewdness from his mother that motored him quickly upward in the business world. From his uncles, grandfathers, and father he learned by heart great stretches of the poetry of Robert Burns, and a political idealism which motivated him all through his life. The Scotsmen he had lived among called their politics Radical, which meant democratic. Like most of the other weavers and artisans in Dunfermline, his relatives subscribed to Chartist ideals. Economic justice, they believed, would only come to Britain when it adopted such democratic forms as salaries and annual elections for its members of Parliament, a secret ballot, equally proportioned electoral districts, elimination of property requirements to hold a parliamentary seat, voting rights for all men, and the abolition of the monarchy. Enact those measures, the thinking ran, and adopt the forms of a modern democratic republic, and nothing would stand in the way of peace and prosperity for all. Throughout his life, Carnegie always would believe that changing the political forms would change men's hearts. He saw his life as a simple demonstration of that truth. In Scotland, where democratic forms were lacking, economic advancement was blocked. In America, where the forms were in place, he had found nothing but wide roads open to success.

In 1867 Carnegie and his mother left his younger brother Tom, by now a business partner, behind in Pittsburgh, and moved to New

York, then, as now, the national center of business and finance. Carnegie was thrilled to be invited into the city's intellectual salons. His New York and British connections eventually led to friendships and correspondence with Mark Twain, the poet Matthew Arnold, the British Liberal statesman John Morley, and, most significant, Herbert Spencer, the British philosopher and inventor of Social Darwinism.

As Carnegie's fortune grew, he allowed himself more time for public affairs on both sides of the Atlantic. By the mid 1880s he was spending half of every year in England and Scotland, first in rented castles and later at Skibo. Eventually he would write eight books, sixty-three articles in high-profile national magazines, thousands of personal letters, hundreds of letters to the editor, and many speeches, ten of which were widely distributed as pamphlets. All of his writing was bursting with social, political, and economic optimism. For a time in Britain he owned seven daily newspapers and ten weeklies, aimed in the short term at advocating for the passage of the Reform Act of 1884, which embodied Chartist ideals. He also became self-appointed kibitzer and confidant to William Gladstone, the Liberal British Prime Minister, and to six American presidents, from Grover Cleveland to Woodrow Wilson. He was untroubled by any inconsistencies between his Radical politics in Britain and his steady backing of Republican politicians in the United States. The Republicans propped up high tariff barriers, which protected his steel from British and other foreign competition. Business was business, after all.

It was a busy life. By the 1890s Carnegie was rotund, with a trim white beard and a beaming countenance. In cartoons he often looks like a short Santa in a tweed suit or, if his Scottish connections are pertinent, in a kilt and Highland bonnet. His biographer, Joseph Wall, describes him making a speech in Scotland for democratic causes. He would step from behind the lectern to get closer to the crowd: "Frequently rising to his toes and pumping his short arms vigorously, to his critics in the audience he looked like a bantam rooster ready to crow. But to his Radical supporters he was the tough little man ready to take on all comers in the ring."

"All is well, because all grows better," Carnegie repeated, again and again. The motto fused his native optimism with a misunder-standing of evolution. By way of Herbert Spencer, evolution became mixed up in his mind with progress, biological change with moral improvement. Evolution, we now know, only means that living or-ganisms either adapt to changing conditions or go extinct. It is not the "ability" to adapt that allows a species to survive. It is something more like luck—a happy correlation between the changes a species undergoes and the changes that occur around it. Evolution does not imply that species that survive and prosper are "better" than species that do not. But, like others who find themselves at the top of the heap, Carnegie secretly suspected that his virtue had something to do with his success—and, therefore, that success and virtue went naturally hand in hand.

In fact, his belief that "all grows better" allowed him to become skilled at ignoring things that were not going well. When his busi-ness practices collided with his Liberal political ideals, business won out. The pressure he imposed on his companies to drive down the costs of steelmaking encouraged constant reinvestment and techni-cal innovation but also meant that his managers jumped at any chance to keep wages down. In a widely read essay in 1886, Carnegie proclaimed trade unionism a good idea for managers and workers, as it solved disputes in ways that allowed both to prosper. "There is an unwritten law among the best workmen: 'Thou shalt not take thy neighbor's job,'" he wrote. But by 1892 workmen's wages were growing faster than Carnegie liked. Production was growing and prices were falling, as industrial methods became more efficient. At the Homestead mill, on the Monongahela River near Pittsburgh, a three-year union contract was due to expire in the summer of 1892. The leaders of the six local lodges of the Amalgamated Association of Iron and Steel Workers expected to renegotiate something at least slightly better. But Carnegie had other ideas. When, in April, he left the country for his summer-long retreat to Scotland, he and his top manager, Henry Clay Frick, agreed that the union would have to be broken.

Frick was a brilliant capitalist whose methods were unclouded by liberal ideals. That spring he ran the mills full out to stockpile steel. He also ordered a high stockade of boards, complete with rifle ports, built around the Homestead mill and down to the riverside piers, to protect the mill and any shipments that might land there. And he contacted the Pinkerton Detective Agency. In June he made the workers an offer he knew they couldn't accept. When the union men, an elite of eight hundred skilled workers, were barred from their jobs, the other three thousand workers at the mill struck in sympathy. The mill was closed by lockout and strike. A week later the Pinkertons—three hundred strong, armed with pistols and Winchester rifles and wearing blue coats with bright brass buttons— were loaded into two covered barges and towed upstream during the night.

Early on the morning of July 6, the barges floated down to the mill, ostensibly to secure it for the company. The workers had been warned, however, and turned out to meet the Pinkertons on the river bank, armed with guns, shovels, and sticks. A day-long battle fought with guns, dynamite, and fire ended in a standoff. Ten strikers and one Pinkerton had been killed. The agents, still on their barges, surrendered out of exhaustion and thirst. The workers agreed to give them safe passage through the town. But, walking and crawling away from the river through a long gauntlet of laborers and their wives, three more Pinkertons were killed before the rest reached the safety of the jail. The governor called out the National Guard. Eight thousand troops came to Pittsburgh to restore order, and stayed through the fall.

Meanwhile, the company reopened the mill with strikebreakers, Frick survived a murder attempt by the Lithuanian-born Nihilist Alexander Berkman, and by winter the strike disintegrated. Most of the union leaders never worked in the trade again. Frick hired back— at the new, lower wages—only the men who forswore the union forever. Pay scales fell or flattened as production continued to rise. Unions faded from American steel mills over the next ten years until they were gone entirely, not to return to the industry until the 1930s. Carnegie had no more labor troubles.

Later, he often said that the whole affair was due to his own seclusion and unavailability in Scotland and to Frick's ruthless provocation of the workers. If only he had been in Pittsburgh, all would have worked out differently, and better, Carnegie maintained for the rest of his life. None of that was true, and much of the world was unimpressed by his rationalizations. "Say what you will of Frick," the St. Louis *Post-Dispatch* editorialized, "he is an honest man. Say what you will of Carnegie, he is a coward. And gods and men hate cowards." Carnegie's reputation was so low after the Homestead strike that organizations from the Glasgow Free Trades Council to the Cleveland Chamber of Commerce banned him from membership. Top Republicans blamed Benjamin Harrison's loss to Grover Cleveland in the presidential race that fall directly on Carnegie. In their minds it was clear that the strike had roused national sympathy for working people and had swept Cleveland, the Democrat, into office. Closer to home, thousands of Pittsburgh workers in all kinds of light and heavy trades showed their disgust by protesting the city's acceptance of Carnegie's gift of a public library—and a museum.

The protests and the slights were no match for the optimism of a man who never knew failure. The Carnegie Institute, composed of a public library, an art gallery, a music hall, and a natural history museum, opened in 1895. It was the first of Carnegie's institutional charities, and he was confident it would better the lives of the masses in Pittsburgh whose toil had brought him such huge profits. His optimism continued to balloon into the idea of a "Race Alliance," a confederation of the English-speaking peoples of Britain, Canada, and the United States, which he began to write and speak about in those years. "The Reunion," as he also called it, was the world's best hope for peace and prosperity.

By the summer of 1898, as the Spanish-American War headed to a quick conclusion, his passion for international affairs spread to criticism of the proposed treaty between the United States and Spain. He was convinced that American leaders had made a terrible blunder, and he promptly set out to change public opinion about the war. American victories in Cuba and the Philippines the previous summer had led to Spain's swift defeat. At first, when it looked like a fight for Cuban independence and a chance to kick one more European power out of the American hemisphere, the war had seemed just and necessary to Carnegie. However, with the fall of Manila to Commodore Dewey's white battleships, plated with steel from Carnegie's mills, the war became a grab for empire. Carnegie's liberal con-

science convinced him that empire would bring only pride and cor-
ruption—and more war.

U.S. negotiations with Spain started in July. Carnegie began
sending big checks to the New England Anti-Imperialist League. In
the August issue of the *North American Review* he let off his first salvo
against the new American imperialism. He distinguished between
colonies, such as Canada and Australia, where white people had
been able to "establish and reproduce our own race" and dependen-
cies, of which India was the prime example, a "grievous burden" to
Britain because it "cannot reproduce its own race there." The Philippines would become a dependency to the United States, as would
any territories outside the northern half of the Western Hemisphere. And trying to govern and educate a people so different and
so far away, he argued, would make hypocrites of the governors:
"With what face shall we hang in the school houses of the Philippines our own Declaration of Independence, and yet deny independence to them?" And he could see no logic in guaranteeing the independence of two million Cubans while denying it to seven and a
half million Filipinos. His political instincts, for once, turned out to
be sound. The United States lost just one sailor in fighting the Spanish in Manila Bay, but four thousand American soldiers and forty
thousand Filipinos would die over the next four years in an ugly
guerrilla war, as U.S. troops fought the same insurgents who had
been fighting against the Spanish when the Americans first arrived.

Carnegie's article had no effect. Soon after it ran, he wrote from
Skibo to the *Times* of London to suggest that the United States and
Britain swap island possessions. Britain could have the Philippines;
the United States, in exchange, would get Bermuda, plus all British
possessions in the Caribbean. The British government, not surpris-
ingly, remained silent. Under proposed treaty terms, the United
States would pay Spain $20 million for the Philippines. Carnegie pro-
posed to pay $20 million of his own funds to the U.S. Treasury if the
Philippines were given independence, but his offer was turned down.
His wilder schemes having failed, Carnegie could think of only one
other alternative, far more mundane: block the treaty in the Senate.
Nothing could be done there until after the New Year.

It may be that the reports of the dinosaur's discovery that December of 1898 gave Carnegie an idea for a project that, while still large, had more straightforward chances of success. Certainly it would prove less complicated than questions of U.S. foreign policy, or, for that matter, than the question of what to do about his own profits.

These profits were now increasing geometrically. Carnegie knew that if he was going to make a coherent project of giving away his fortune, as he had long claimed was a rich man's duty—"The man who dies thus rich, dies disgraced"—he would have to start very soon. Giving it away would be a big job, perhaps even a bigger job than making it had been. Profits from the Carnegie Steel Company were $3 million in 1897, $10 million in 1898. His top managers were estimating that they might reach $25 million in 1899. If the company was to maintain its long tradition of stability and success, most of that money would have to be reinvested—not distributed among the partners, as they would like. For years, Carnegie's constant insistence on reinvestment had meant few or low dividends for himself and his partners. They chafed but had to submit; they owned only small slices, while Carnegie owned 58 percent.

Now, however, profits were so enormous that simple plant improvements would not absorb them. It was time to go into entirely new businesses. Only in the last few years had Carnegie and his partners expanded into iron ore, buying mines in the fast developing Mesabi Range of Minnesota, and Great Lakes ore boats and a railroad to ship the ore to Pittsburgh. Together with their long-held investments in coke and limestone much nearer Pittsburgh, they now controlled all the raw materials they needed, as well as the blast furnaces and rolling and plate mills to turn the raw materials into steel. If they were to keep reinvesting, the logical move was into finished products: wire, nails, springs, axles, pipe—even steel railroad cars. It meant moving from big business to empire.

It would be one of the biggest choices of Carnegie's life: whether to plunge yet again into new ventures, or finally to wrap his arms around the vast wealth he could call his own, take it, and leave the fray. Leaving would mean finding a way to turn his holdings into assets both liquid and secure. Most likely that would mean dissolving the outdated partnership structure and becoming a modern corporation, with publicly traded shares of stock. All the company's holdings would have to be assigned their true value, not the artificially low ones he had imposed for years. Partners who wanted to could then cash in their gains, bypassing the old agreement under which remaining partners had the right to buy out any exiting partners at the artificially low values. It must have seemed a murky prospect; outcomes in matters like this were much harder to predict than the next two quarters' prices or profits. Soon he would direct Frick, still his partner and top manager, to draw up some cashout options. Conflict with the partners was beginning to appear inevitable.

The museum of the new Carnegie Institute acquired some big skeletons in the first few years after it opened in 1895, including an Irish elk with a six-foot antler spread and a mammoth. From the start, however, Carnegie had something bigger in mind. As director of the museum, he had landed a man he'd had his eye on for a decade, William Jacob Holland—a linguist, lepidopterist, Presbyterian minister, and now chancellor of the booming Western University of Pennsylvania, which before many more years would become the University of Pittsburgh.

When the institute was dedicated in 1895, Carnegie invited his friend O. C. Marsh of Yale out to Pittsburgh for the ceremonies. From the speaker's dais—and probably without telling Marsh beforehand—Carnegie announced his hope that Yale and the nation's greatest paleontologist might be able to spare a few dinosaurs for Pittsburgh. But by 1898 nothing had come of the hope, and Marsh would die before anything did come of it.

And now, in the papers were reports of an unexpected treasure—a dinosaur that was apparently complete, and so huge it appeared no one would ever find anything bigger. A man might or might not be able to buy the Philippines, Carnegie must have thought, and the time to swap all his steel holdings for something as uninteresting as cash might or might not have arrived. But certainly a person of means could acquire a dinosaur. Holland had plenty of experience as a university chancellor—Carnegie often addressed him in letters as "My Lord Chancellor" or just "My Lord." But Holland was now a museum director, too, and in that capacity hadn't been tested. It would be interesting to see what the man could do. "My Lord—cant you <u>buy</u> this for Pittsburgh—try," Carnegie scrawled along the margin of the modest New York *Post* story. "Wyoming State University isnt rich—<u>get an offer</u>—hurry AC."

Chapter 4

CULTURE IN
THE IRON CITY

H olland sprang into action as soon as he received Carnegie's request. On December 4, 1898, he sent Reed a telegram and followed it with a quick, handwritten note. He got right to the point:

My attention has been brought to an account of the recent discovery by yourself of a fine dinosaurian. I have wired you as to the matter I supplement by these lines. I should like to know about how perfect you find the skeleton to be and if there is any chance of our being allowed to acquire it by purchase if we should choose to do so. If there is any chance of our becoming the possessors of these remains I might undertake to come out to Laramie to talk the matter over with you. Please let me hear from you.

Holland probably regretted in the months to come that he had shown himself, so early in the game, to be so eager.

He next wrote to Carnegie for advice: If Reed wanted to sell, would it make sense to go out to Wyoming to make a deal? How much did Carnegie want to spend? Dinosaurs, Holland noted, "are scarce, you know." Yet, more than scarcity, the logistics involved would be likely to make the cost of getting a dinosaur for the museum high. He added several other cautions: that in order to acquire the dinosaur they probably would have to hire Reed, temporarily at least; that the museum expansion already under discussion would need to include a big new hall "for the display of such a monster"; and that mounting the specimen "will be the most colossal undertaking of its kind in the history of the world." Holland was eager to show he was up to the challenge: "I can do it, but it will cost some time, labor, and money."

Carnegie didn't bother with a separate sheet for his reply. On the bottom of Holland's letter, he scrawled his response: "See what you can do. I should like to do the Colossal for the Colossal by the Colossal Lord Chancellor. AC"

Holland's job as chancellor of the Western University of Pennsylvania was his second career; museum director was his third. He had been born in 1848, the same year as Reed, but in Jamaica, where his parents had been temporarily posted as missionaries in the Moravian Church. While still an infant, he came with them first to Ohio, then to North Carolina, and finally to Bethlehem in eastern Pennsylvania, the latter two places centers of the two branches of the Moravian denomination in America. In his youth Holland appears to have acquired a deep love for the natural world, especially insects. But his education aimed him for the ministry. He attended the Moravian College in Bethlehem, then Amherst College in Massachusetts, where he received bachelor's and master's degrees.

After teaching high school for two years, in 1871 he entered Princeton Theological Seminary, a stronghold of Presbyterianism. In 1872 he was ordained in the Moravian Church, but the Princeton influence seems to have moved him toward the much larger and more mainstream Presbyterian denomination. On graduating from Princeton in 1874, he took a job in Pittsburgh as pastor of the Bellefield Presbyterian Church in the Oakland area, then a countrified locale just becoming fashionable. Pittsburgh, then as now, was one of the main centers of Presbyterianism in North America. As late as 1890, with immigrants flocking in from southern and eastern Europe, 40 percent of the city's congregations were still Presbyterian.

In 1879 Holland married Carrie Moorhead, the youngest daughter of John Moorhead, an iron manufacturer who later went into banking. By the mid-1870s the Moorheads had been prosperous enough to buy an Oakland mansion—a Victorian hybrid with a cupola, a Greek-revival portico, and four Ionic columns. Holland's marriage, and the connections available through his congregation,

Carnegie directed William Jacob Holland—clergyman, linguist, lepidopterist, and director of the new Carnegie Museum in Pittsburgh—to get the dinosaur. Library and Archives Division, Historical Society of Western Pennsylvania, Pittsburgh, Pennsylvania.

brought him into Pittsburgh's most elite social circles by the mid-1880s. The Hollands often fled Pittsburgh's hot summers for Cresson, a town in the Allegheny mountains fifty miles to the east. Carnegie and his mother for many years kept a summer house nearby, even after moving to New York. Sometimes the Hollands found themselves dining in the inn at a table adjoining Carnegie's.

The two men became friends, although one was an ambitious young clergyman and the other, thirteen years his senior, already was a multimillionaire industrialist. They took walks in the woods, Holland teaching the older man the names of plants and birds. But it was back in Oakland that their friendship would bear its fullest fruit, for it was there they built the first of many institutional charities to bear Carnegie's name.

Oakland lies about four hilly miles east of "the Point," in downtown Pittsburgh, where the Monongahela River, flowing up from the south, joins the Allegheny, coming down from the north, to form the westward-flowing Ohio. Gravity faced the city westward from the start, as it grew from trading post to fort to the bustling little river port Meriwether Lewis found when he had his keelboat built there in 1803 before heading down the Ohio and up the Missouri to the Rocky Mountains. Add coal, limestone, iron ore, and half a million people, and by 1898 Pittsburgh was the fifth or sixth largest city in the nation and the greatest center of manufacturing in the world. Steel, of course, was king, but glass, aluminum, canned food, turbines and generators, and river and railroad traffic all crowded close around.

Along with the products came by-products. The rivers were fouled with factory, human, and slaughterhouse wastes; the air was so thick with smoke that there were days each winter when the streetlights were still on at noon. Coal dust sifted into curtains and onto window sills. Workmen's baths were black at the end of the day. Worse still was the wreckage of human lives. Long working hours were common in all walks of life, but after the Homestead Strike in 1892, the steel mills settled into a steady pattern of twelve-hour shifts seven days a week, with only alternate Sundays off for the shift workers. Those Sundays came at the expense of a "long turn," when a man changed shifts from day to night or night to day, and put in a full twenty-four hours at the blast furnace or rolling mill. The work was hot, loud, and horribly dangerous. Men of working age died from accidents at four and five times the rate of the rest of the population, and many more were maimed than killed. Children suffered the most from the bad air and bad water. At the turn of the century, a third of all deaths in Pittsburgh were of children under five. Week after week, year after year, decade, finally, after decade, it went on, with exhausted fathers strangers in their own households and mothers' lives narrowed to a long domestic battle against dirt, ill health, and short funds. It was often a losing fight.

This was the sea on which Holland's fortunes floated; all that production also meant great wealth, for a few. For decades many owners and managers worked hours equally long, if not as dangerous, as their workers did. By the 1890s some began to want more ways to enjoy their accumulating capital. There were few amusements, other than brothels and churches, for anyone of any class. Pittsburgh had theaters and opera houses, but no museums, no lyceums, few libraries, no concert halls. The city prided itself on not being a cultured Boston, New York, or Philadelphia—on being a place where work got done, and that was that. Near the end of the century, a few of the wealthiest citizens decided it was time to spend some money and add some urban grace.

Henry Phipps, a steel partner of Carnegie's since the 1860s, gave the elegant Phipps Conservatory—a spacious, rambling greenhouse filled with botanical exotica—to the city in 1893. Political boss Christopher Magee and his partners in trolley companies and municipal graft built the city a zoo in Highland Park in 1898, and stocked it with animals.

Oakland, lying up away from the rivers where slums crowded around the steel mills and glass factories, was less smoky. Manufacturers in the 1870s began to leave downtown, where they had lived near their offices, and to build mansions in outlying areas. Oakland became one of several East End neighborhoods with leafy names that shut the mills out of mind: Shadyside, Squirrel Hill, Woodland Road, Point Breeze. Newly electrified trolley cars made it easy to commute downtown. Some of the capitalists began giving lavish parties. Some of their wives started settlement houses with the goal of "improving" the poor.

Carnegie no longer lived in Pittsburgh after 1867, but he never forgot that the city was the source of his wealth and power. By 1890 he had financed two libraries near Pittsburgh—one in Braddock, a riverbank town where he owned mills, and one in the city of Allegheny, where he had spent his adolescence, north across the Allegheny River from the heart of the city.

Pittsburgh proper still had no public libraries, but not for lack of attempts by Carnegie. As early as 1881, he had offered to donate $250,000 for a library if the city would maintain it. The city councils, with no legal way under Pennsylvania law to tax themselves for library maintenance, turned him down. By 1890 state law had changed. Carnegie offered more this time: $1 million for a building that would include a library, art galleries, a natural history museum, a meeting room and lecture hall for Pittsburgh's struggling learned societies, and a splendid music hall. The councils accepted, and a library board of directors was formed. By 1892 the building's foundation was finished. Construction continued despite angry and widespread opposition from the workers of the city against accepting any gift from the man who owned the Homestead mill.

The new building lay on nineteen acres of land Carnegie had bought from Mrs. Mary Schenley, a rich widow who still owned thousands of acres of undeveloped land in the East End. The structure, of light gray sandstone with a red tiled roof, had an Italian feeling. Two tall, bell-less Italianate bell towers—*campanile*—flanked the curved front of the music hall on the north end of the building, facing Forbes Avenue. In a panoramic photo of Oakland from 1900, the institute looks from a distance like a mosque and the towers like squared minarets. Phipps's glass conservatory is dimly discernible in the background, and on the right, further west along Forbes rises the swank new Schenley Hotel. Grassy stretches separate the buildings; in the further background, Mrs. Schenley's fields quilt the hills. Quite suddenly, Oakland had become a campus of culture in an iron world. The steel king's new institute was its palace.

Holland left the ministry in 1891 to become chancellor of the Western University of Pennsylvania. During seventeen years as a clergyman he had gained considerable skill and local reputation as an orator. But the pulpit appears not to have been able to contain him, perhaps because of his ambition, or perhaps because of his curiosity about the world. More than one of the colleagues and scholars who wrote about Holland after his death used the term "Renaissance man" to describe the breadth of his skills and interests.

He learned Latin and Greek as an adolescent, then at Amherst traded a fellow student Greek lessons for Japanese. By the time he entered seminary at Princeton, he had enough Hebrew to win the institution's top prize for that language; by the time he left, he'd learned Chaldean and Arabic, too. Somewhere, he acquired French, Spanish, and German—enough German to correspond with German scientists and collectors once he became director of the museum and enough of all three to make speeches years later to scientific societies in Paris, Berlin, Vienna, Madrid, and La Plata, Argentina.

Butterflies, however, were what he really loved. By the mid-1890s Holland, collecting on his own and buying the services of other collectors, had assembled one of the world's largest collections of Lepidoptera. He donated it to the Carnegie Museum once he began working there. In 1899 Doubleday, McLure & Co. published Holland's *Butterfly Book*. This volume and his *Moth Book*, published in 1903, became standard reference works in their field.

He was also by this time a dedicated amateur oil painter, trustee of a number of colleges and universities, and a businessman with interests in banking and real estate. And he was rich. Requests for loans are fairly frequent in his correspondence, some of them substantial: $5,000 here, $8,500 there. He underwrote the color printing for the plates in *The Butterfly Book*. Some of his debtors were rich themselves. They included Henry Oliver, a partner of Carnegie's who led the business into Minnesota iron mining. Others were more humble, like the man who wrote in March 1899 to thank Holland for his patience regarding a mortgage payment due the previous November.

After Holland became director of the Carnegie Museum, he added publications on paleontology to his list of accomplishments. Though he had studied medicine for a short time at Amherst, he had no formal training in any of the earth sciences. His early correspondence with Reed, for example, shows how little he knew. Some of the men who worked for him noted that his work in paleontology was just adequate; one went so far as to call him a fraud.

His social connections and administrative skills seem to have been the real sources of Holland's mark on the world. In his book *To the River Plate and Back* (1913), about a voyage he took to Argentina, he makes himself out a mild naturalist with time to admire the passing world. But his correspondence—and photos of him—show an aggressive and impetuous man who wants results.

In 1891, when Holland was named chancellor of the Western University of Pennsylvania, that institution included an undergraduate college, graduate programs in civil and mechanical engineering, and the university-run Allegheny Observatory. At the time the university was still located in Allegheny City, just across the Allegheny River from downtown Pittsburgh; not until the following decade would it move to Oakland and become the University of Pittsburgh. Still, it was growing fast. During the 1890s, graduate programs in electrical and mining engineering, medicine, law, dentistry, and pharmacy were added, and the number of students increased eightfold.

Midway through the decade, in 1896, Pittsburgh's politicians were no longer able to ignore the skyrocketing number of typhoid fever cases in their city. They appointed a commission to see what could be done to clean up the city's water supply. Holland served on its key committees and traveled to Europe at his own expense to inspect filtration plants there. He wrote the commission's final report in 1899, recommending the construction of slow-sand filtration plants to clean Pittsburgh's water, which at the time was pumped directly from foul rivers to hilltop reservoirs, then fed by gravity to houses, tenements, and mills. Bitter battles ensued over who would get the construction contracts, with their opportunities for graft and patronage. The struggles penetrated the highest levels of Pennsylvania politics, and construction was delayed, then delayed further. The first plant was not finished until 1907; not until 1913 did Pittsburgh's level of typhoid cases descend to that of other northern cities. Late in his life, Holland would say he was as proud of his work bringing clean water to Pittsburgh as of anything he'd done.

The new library and institute opened late in 1895: this was the ceremony at which Carnegie announced his confident hope that O. C. Marsh would make some Yale dinosaurs available to Pittsburgh. Holland began serving on boards connected with the institute's fledgling art galleries and natural history museum. After the first museum director resigned, Holland took over the job in March 1898 but also retained his university chancellorship for a few more years. Carnegie was a trustee of the university as well, which may have enabled Holland to hold the two jobs simultaneously.

From the start, the director was eager to please his powerful friend. They may not have known exactly what they wanted the museum to be, but they wanted to bring people in. In 1896 Carnegie wrote William Frew, president of the institute's board, that "unless the institution be kept in touch with the masses, and therefore popular, it cannot be widely useful." Museum acquisitions in the early years included the forty-foot-long soul boat of the Pharaoh Seostris II, which Carnegie had purchased in Egypt. It was so big it had to be

stored until the building could be enlarged. The museum also acquired skeletons of a mammoth and an Irish elk, huge mammals
from the last Ice Age, and a dramatic, life-sized diorama of two lions
attacking a desert Arab on a camel.

But still no dinosaurs. By late 1898, this lack would have begun
to rankle. Paleontology embraced an even smaller circle of devotees
then than it does now. Holland knew of the Wyoming discoveries in
the previous two summers by crews from the American Museum of
Natural History in New York. North of Como Bluff they'd found
rich bone deposits, the most famous and productive of which was
the Bone Cabin Quarry, named for a nearby sheepherder's cabin
built sometime before on a dinosaur-bone foundation.

Holland had been director of the Carnegie Museum for only
eight months when Carnegie sent him news of Reed's discovery.
Here was a chance to please the great Scot, outdo the New York museum, and bring his fledgling institution national fame, all at once.
His eager note to Reed was the result. Reed answered Holland's
query the next day in a telegram that dashed Holland's hopes: "Dinosaur not for sale. Have written. W. H. Reed."

The letter Reed sent restored Holland's hopes again. The specimen was "for sale to the highest bidder," Reed wrote, adding "when
I get it out." He included other provisos. For the moment it was still
in the ground, and it might or might not turn out to resemble the
newspaper dinosaur: "the reporter in his article made the usual mis-
takes of a man not up in science." The specimen was still Reed's
property, unlike some of the bones that the reporter had seen, and
it was unrecoverable before spring. Almost as an afterthought, Reed
mentioned that he had found about thirty other dinosaur skeletons
the previous summer. Three were large, one extremely large, and
the rest middle-sized, between thirty and sixty feet long.

Holland wrote Carnegie first. His excitement is palpable: "The
big beast, then, is in the market though yet in the quarry." Then he
checks himself and warns, "The operation, however, is a little like
purchasing a mine, the output of which is problematical." Next day,
writing Reed, he continued the same metaphor: "You are in the position of a miner who has located a 'pay-streak', but how wide and
how long it may be is impossible for you to tell until you have com-

pleted the work of excavation." Then his impatience got the better of him again, and he began pressing Reed for details: How perfect is the skeleton? As perfect as the skeleton of Marsh's Brontosaur? And how much money would Reed want for it? The museum needed something big, Holland wrote, "preferably the biggest specimen that has ever been discovered."

Three different times between December and March, Holland asked Reed for his pay requirements. But Reed was shrewd enough not to answer too fast. He doled out information slowly, never quite pegging a price on the dinosaur or on his own services. He sent along descriptions of the bones he had found, including "the head of a femur fully one-fourth larger than any I had ever taken up." He invited Holland to come out in March and stay at his cabin in the Freezeout Mountains while he looked over the diggings. He boasted of his experience: "For a general knowledge of the geology and fauna of the country west of the Mississippi, from the British possessions to Mexico, there is no man living who is better posted than I am." He detailed the costs of materials and the labor of three assistants that probably would be needed to get the dinosaur out of the ground in four or five months. He said the university had given him a small raise after learning he was corresponding with the museum in Pittsburgh. Finally, in March, Reed played his new trump card. The Wyoming Legislature had appropriated money for a new museum and science hall at the university—$22,000—and the trustees had offered him a better job, "at a fair salary," with the museum. He hadn't accepted yet, but had promised them an answer by April 15. Then he added, "of course, I expect more salary there [the Carnegie Museum] than here."

But not once did he say how much—neither how much he was making nor how much more he expected from Holland. Still, the discovery was now no secret, in Wyoming or anywhere else. Not just the university but the entire legislature seemed to have designs on the dinosaur. That could only raise the price and destabilize any title to ownership. Money would be needed, along with the personal attention of someone who knew exactly what he wanted. On March 19, 1899, Holland boarded a train for Wyoming.

Chapter 5

A LIZARD IN
WYOMING POLITICS

*T*rain service was fast and reliable at the turn of the century. Holland would have made the 1,600-mile trip from Pittsburgh to Laramie in about two days. He arrived at noon on Tuesday, March 21, and found Laramie full of snow. Reed met him at the train, and they spent the afternoon together, meeting the faculty and inspecting the tiny university's huge fossil collection, then crammed into offices, closets, and classrooms in both of the university's buildings. Finally they adjourned to Reed's house. Over tea served by Mrs. Reed, they reached the bargain Holland had found elusive all winter. Reed would work for the new Carnegie Museum for $1,800 per year—a full $600 more than he was making at the university at the moment and $300 more than the trustees had just promised him he would begin drawing July 1. The Carnegie Museum guaranteed him three years' work; in return, he agreed to relinquish his claim to the dinosaur for no extra fee.

His job would be field collector, his first duty to excavate the big dinosaur. The museum would pay for his living expenses in the field, plus tools, a team and wagon, burlap and plaster for wrapping the bones for shipment, and lumber with which to build the bone-shipping boxes. The museum would also pay for two or three "assistants" for the summer work. The term is important, as it shows that both men assumed Reed would be in charge. Reed estimated the "exhumation," as Holland called it, would take four to five months.

Afterward, Reed would travel to Pittsburgh for the winter to help prepare the fossils, then continue spending summers in the field and winters in Pittsburgh for the term of the contract.

Holland hoped Reed's dozens of other quarries—he had mentioned a cached camel skeleton and the skull of a saber-toothed tiger—would quickly catch the Carnegie Museum up with other museums in the East. The American Museum of Natural History in New York, the Field Columbian Museum in Chicago, the U.S. National Museum at the Smithsonian—as well as the University of Wyoming—were all rapidly expanding their fossil collections at that time. None had yet erected any complete fossils of freestanding dinosaurs, though all appear to have concluded that dinosaur displays would increase a museum's scientific prestige and popular appeal. Given his vast field experience, ready fossil supply, and prestigious past connections with Marsh, Reed, in Holland's mind, was clearly the ideal man for the job.

Reed had noted in an earlier letter that it was the snowiest winter he'd known in twenty-nine years in the Rockies—too snowy to hunt bones in the Freezeouts. Any trip for Holland to the bone quarries would have to be postponed. That left only one small courtesy for him to attend to before heading back to Pittsburgh.

"It occurred to me on mature reflection," Holland wrote Carnegie later, "that as I had proposed to take [Reed] from the employment of the Regents of the University of Wyoming it would be no more than civil for me to intimate to the President of the institution what my errand was and what I had done." By the time Holland called on university president Elmer Smiley Tuesday evening or Wednesday morning, the Pittsburgher's presence in town would already have been well known. It would have been considered only polite for the chief executive of one university to call on the president of another.

"I immediately encountered a storm," Holland wrote. More like a tornado, or a typhoon. Reed had told Holland he'd filed a "grub stake claim" to the land where the dinosaur lay—a term that implied he'd filed it on behalf of another backer, probably the university. Smiley's argument was that, regardless of how he had filed the claim, Reed had discovered the dinosaur while employed by the university as a fossil collector and assistant geologist. Anything Reed found was not his, but the university's, and Reed had "no right to sell or transfer." Very well, Holland replied; he was then "prepared to deal in a very generous and pleasant way with them."

Holland managed to calm Smiley down and to persuade him to convene the executive committee of the board of trustees. They were not an impressive group. The president of the board, Otto Gramm, and its secretary, Grace Raymond Hebard, wielded the real power at the university. Gramm was a local businessman who had started out with a drugstore and eventually acquired interests in banking, retail coal sales, and ranching. He appears to have routinely used his political connections to commercial advantage; twice during his long career he was publicly accused of graft, though no charges were brought. Hebard was university librarian, paid secretary to the board, and also a voting board member. For a decade and a half in those capacities she ran the university's day-to-day operations—paying its bills, writing its payroll checks, recruiting faculty and students. The trustees were happy to let her attend to the details, but faculty and administrators resented her influence and control. Hebard would almost certainly have been at the meeting with Holland. The fact that he calls the board members "the gentlemen" probably indicates that it never occurred to him that a woman taking notes could be anything more than clerical staff. Gramm and President Smiley would have been there as well; also probably board members Henry Stevens of Laramie and Timothy Burke from Cheyenne, just fifty miles away by train.

Years later, in a magazine article Holland recalled he was "allowed for two or three hours to sit in the village drug-store and wait, while the mighty body was engaged in consultation." Finally, he knocked, they let him in, and the bargaining began. "I found," Holland wrote Carnegie a few days later, "that they were to a man opposed altogether to allowing the remains to go out of the state of Wyoming."

So Holland upped his offer—generously, he thought. Would they take $2,000 for their land claim, $1,000 for the use of Reed's services for six months, and an agreement to cover all other expenses of digging out the dinosaur?

Not tempting, Smiley said. Impossible, Gramm said—and finally the real reason came out. Not only would the trustees' pride suffer if the dinosaur left the state but, more important, they would lose a political bargaining chip worth tens of thousands of dollars. In the session of the state legislature just concluded, they told Holland, they had used the news of Reed's discovery to convince the lawmakers to approve a $22,000 bond issue for a new science hall, which would include a museum for the dinosaur and all the other fossils now crowding Old Main. It was a substantial political victory, one of the legislature's first moves toward largesse after years of skin-and-bones economizing during the depression of the mid-1890s.

Holland went on to quote Gramm directly. "'If now . . . we should turn around and sell these fossils to the Carnegie Museum in Pittsburgh, a howl would go up over the whole State of Wyoming and it would be as much as our positions are worth to part with these relics. We cannot afford to do it, and we will fight you in any attempt that you may make to get possession of these remains through all the courts of the State. We do not care to entertain any proposition, and we refuse to listen to anything.'"

Another trustee, unnamed by Holland, noted that if "this lizard" was worth $22,000 to the university while still in the ground, then the board should think about what it was worth once excavated and put on display: "'It is the biggest thing on earth,' the man said, 'and we think it is worth a hundred thousand dollars to us.'"

"The lizard," Holland cabled Carnegie when he got back to Pittsburgh, "has gotten into Wyoming politics."

From his Laramie hotel room the night after the meeting, Holland wrote Gramm a letter recapitulating their discussion. Holland felt that his offer had been liberal, conceived in a generous spirit," and he wasn't happy to see it "designated by one of the members of your board as ridiculous." He regretted, he wrote, having to take the news back to Carnegie that the board members refused to make any counter proposal.

Carnegie's name must by itself have been inflating, in the trustees' minds, the price the dinosaur could command. The steel king's wealth was well known, and he wasn't just a rich man; he was a celebrity. As recently as a month before, a front-page article had run in one of the Cheyenne papers about Carnegie's recent purchase of lots far uptown in Manhattan—at Fifth Avenue and 91st Streets, where he planned to build a mansion. Holland, for his part, was the more irritated by the trustees' stonewalling because he knew Marsh had never had to pay for the privilege of digging out an unproven site. He had paid only collectors' wages or flat fees for fossils.

Holland later wrote that the idea for a way to avoid conflict with the trustees and still get the dinosaur came to him from "an old entomological acquaintance and correspondent," who knocked on the door of his Laramie hotel room. It's hard to say who this might have been; neither of the two scientists on the university faculty was an entomologist. It may have been a dreamy way for Holland to refer to himself. The mystery acquaintance suggested, logically enough, that since the dinosaur lay on "Uncle Sam's land," all Holland had to do was go stake his own claim. The letters Holland wrote at the time mention no friendly entomologist, remarking only that he spent a restless night trying to think of a way to "circumvent the belligerent regents."

The next morning he went to find a lawyer and was referred to Stephen Downey. Holland probably couldn't have found a better ally in the state. Besides doing a brisk business in land claims, both for himself and on behalf of his clients, Downey was intimately connected with state and university politics. He had been elected to one term as territorial representative to Congress in 1878. Later he was elected to the Territorial Legislature, and in 1890, as statehood approached, he served in the convention that wrote Wyoming's constitution. He is credited as well with being a founder of the university, going all the way back to 1881 when he wrote to the Union Pacific's chief officers asking for support. More practically, Downey was directly involved in the Territorial Legislature's 1886 logrolling scheme to please its two main urban populations by financing a university in Laramie and a capitol in Cheyenne.

Downey then served as president of the university board of trustees from 1891 to 1897. Any loyalties that service may have stirred in him, however, did not prevent his accepting Holland as a client. For whatever reason—personal distaste for Gramm is not

Laramie lawyer
Stephen W. Downey,
a founder of the
University of
Wyoming, former
Territorial representa-
tive to the U.S.
Congress, and former
president of the
university's board of
trustees, steered his
client William Holland
of the Carnegie
Museum through the
corridors of Wyoming
politics. Courtesy of
American Heritage
Center, University of
Wyoming.

hard to imagine—Downey was willing to work quite competently against the university's interests in the spring of 1899.

Holland paid Downey a retainer and asked if there were any way to get clear title to the land that Reed had "grub staked." There were two ways, Downey replied. One would be to go to the nearest federal land office, in Cheyenne, and there file a mineral claim on the tract. A filer had to advertise his intention for sixty days; if no counterclaim was made, he could then buy the land for $2.50 per acre.

If Holland was willing to pay more—$4.50 to $5.00 per acre, Downey continued, there was another way, little known but legal: Downey could buy enough land scrip to cover the acreage Holland wanted. Such scrip existed in the form of coupons entitling the bearer to a certain acreage of unspecified, unclaimed government land. It had been issued to U.S. soldiers exiting service in the decades before the Civil War; most of it had been used up long before on desirable land in the Midwest. Some, however, was still around at the end of the century, for a price. No advertisement was necessary, and the deal could be completed in a few days or weeks at most—a quiet way around Gramm and his cronies.

Holland was back in Pittsburgh by the following Monday, March 27. He sent Carnegie a long cable, and a much longer letter. At first, he advocated using the land scrip to acquire just eighty acres. At five dollars an acre, that would come to just $400, far cheaper than the $2,000 he'd offered the university trustees for the claim, he noted with some satisfaction.

Then, however, Holland talked it over with two of his own trustees at the museum in Pittsburgh. They agreed it would be wiser—and quieter—to buy scrip for the whole section in which the desired land was located, that is, a 640-acre square mile of land. Sections were already surveyed, while sending out a survey party to mark out a smaller tract incurred the risk of attracting unwanted attention. "You would become owner of a farm," Holland wrote, showing how poorly as yet he had imagined the arid slopes of the Freezeouts. But buying the whole section would cost substantially more, and Holland requested that Carnegie raise his budget for the project from $7,000 to $10,000. For that, "we will get His Imperial Majesty, the Prince of Lizards, and a collection of remains which will rival, if not excel" Marsh's collection at Yale and Henry Fairfield Osborn's at the American Museum of Natural History in New York, Holland wrote. He was a very competitive man: "I believe the wisest thing for you would be . . . seize the whole tract, and then the Regents [trustees] might whistle for the wind . . . My blood is up and I do not wish to be beaten by the Regents of the University of Wyoming and have them crow over us as unequal to the task of getting what we want." Carnegie, too, was a man who hated to lose.

Chapter 6

UNCLE SAM'S LAND

*B*ack in Pittsburgh, as March moved into April, Holland was eager to secure a clear title to the land where the dinosaur lay. Until that happened, there were too many risks for him to remain comfortable. Experienced American Museum of Natural History crews would soon be starting their third field season in southeast Wyoming. Worse, Wilbur Knight, professor of geology and Reed's boss at the University of Wyoming, knew exactly where to find the dinosaur and conceivably could round up student helpers and go get it whenever he wanted. The university might not have owned much of a claim to the land, but its trustees had powerful political motives for getting the dinosaur for themselves. If Holland were honest with himself, he would have had to admit those motives were personal now, too. His conversations with the trustees had most likely turned them into active enemies. And they were out there, near the bones, and he was not.

In response to Holland's cable reporting on the trustees' intransigence, Carnegie quickly wired back, urging Holland "not to antagonize the state of Wyoming." Even if the museum won title to the land, the political cost of antagonizing local interests would be too great: "Must take other policy." But Holland continued to press for purchase, authorizing Downey to buy up to eighty acres worth of scrip, even though buying less than a full 640-acre section meant that a survey would be required, and the main reason for paying the

higher scrip prices had been the chance to close a deal quietly. Perhaps on second thought the idea of spending nearly twice Reed's
annual salary—$3,600 for a whole section at scrip prices—seemed
too extravagant. Perhaps Holland still didn't understand the law very
well. In any case, he made it clear to Reed and Downey that he
wanted a survey, in fact that he hoped it had already begun. In letters to both men, Holland said he assumed Reed had already passed
on to Downey "that minute information"—location of the dinosaur
by township and range on the public-land grid—which would allow
a surveyor to locate the spot on the ground and to provide a legal
description.

News came back shortly that everything was going wrong. The
information Reed had given Downey was off by an entire township—a full six miles, six sections on the public-range grid. About a
week later Reed confessed to Holland that the error was his—and
then went on to say that his attempt to file a mineral claim on the
land may also have failed. He'd sent a copy of the notice to the clerk
of Carbon County, in Rawlins, but he'd never heard back, and so an
official record of the mineral claim might never have been made.

"You do not tell me how in the world you came to make the
error in the township," Holland wrote back. "I would like that explained to me fully." As soon as the museum was in possession of
clear title to the land, Holland noted, he would send Reed his employment contract, "as I wrote you in my last." Holland had not
earlier mentioned a quid pro quo—an employment contract in exchange for a good land claim. As uncertainty rose, it must have occurred to him that he could hold Reed's job hostage.

Shortly after arriving back in Pittsburgh from Wyoming, Holland made two quick trips further east. First he went to New York
City, then to Harrisburg, probably to seek funds for his university at
the state legislature. In New York, Holland conferred with Carnegie,
who expressed some doubts whether scrip purchases would hold up
against more conventional mineral claims under federal mining law.
"Let there be no error in locating [the claim] this time," Holland
wrote Downey.

At this point, Reed wrote to explain that, out in the field without a map, he had taken the township number from the north side of a marker stone when he should have taken it from the south side. He also now could say for sure that Carbon County had no record of the mineral claim he had sent in, although he had included the three-dollar fee in cash in the envelope. Probably it had been stolen, Reed concluded. Holland must have begun to suspect Reed was incompetent, at least when it came to paperwork. But Reed went on to note that the coast was now clear of competition: "there is no claim to contend with except the notice at the quarry and that was put up in August and would only hold for 60 days."

Federal and state law made acquiring clear title to a mining claim complicated but cheap and—at least compared to the five years it took for a farmer or rancher to "prove up" on agricultural land under the Homestead Act—fairly speedy. Two kinds of mineral claims were distinguished: lode claims, for valuable veins going into the earth, and placer claims, for anything valuable, from gravel to gold, that might be lying on the surface. There was a certain logic in assuming that a fossil quarry could be claimed under the placer provisions of the law.

Placer claims could be up to twenty acres in size. For a forty-acre claim, two claimants would have to be listed; for an eighty-acre claim, four claimants; up to a maximum of 160 acres and eight owners. Claims could be held initially by posting a notice prominently at the site, but to remain valid they had to be recorded within sixty days at the county seat, in this case, Rawlins, seventy-five miles from the dinosaur by road and rail.

A miner could maintain a claim and work it more or less indefinitely, as long as he paid an annual fee and could prove that he'd done work of a minimum value each year. Alternatively, he could patent the land and thereby acquire actual ownership of the surface and the minerals underneath. To patent a claim, the miner had to have the land surveyed, had to post a notice of his intent to patent it at the site and to publish a similar notice in a local newspaper for sixty days, and had to pay an application fee. He also had to show that the claim was not contested—that is, that no counterclaimant had emerged during the sixty-day notification period—and that a valuable mineral was present. Finally, he had to demonstrate that a certain amount of work already had been done, or improvements made, on the claim. Once these requirements were met, the miner could purchase the claim for $2.50 per acre.

Thus, when Reed refers to a notice posted the previous August as a potential but minor problem, it seems likely that it was a notice posted *on behalf of the University of Wyoming*—either by Reed or Knight. If Reed had posted a notice in his own name, there wouldn't have been a problem. The term "grub stake claim" Reed had used in correspondence with Holland the previous winter also implies a claim filed on behalf of a distant client or backer. Before Holland came on the scene, the only other likely client in the picture was the university. Carbon County ledgers contain no records of any mineral claims ever recorded for the dinosaur site. Though various claims apparently were posted, none were ever filed, and no patents were ever taken up on the land in the Freezeouts, but Reed and Holland did not know that. It's no wonder, then, that both men's anxiety mounted through April as the survey was delayed and delayed, and more and more bone-hunting competitors appeared likely to turn up any week.

There was another area of concern. By the second week in April, Reed still had not approached his employers about quitting his job. That made it awkward when Holland demanded help against the university with the land claim.

"I wil help you in this business so far as I can but I want it done as soon as possible," Reed wrote. And if Holland was going to hold Reed's job hostage to a good land claim, Reed had another card to play: the Union Pacific Railroad was offering free rail passage to Wyoming to any geologists or paleontologists interested in hunting bones in "these fossil fields." Railroad officials expected to bring in two hundred or more collectors in the summer, and Reed guessed that they planned to make money on the project by shipping big bones from Wyoming back to the collectors' colleges and museums. Knight had worked closely with the UP passenger department on a brochure advertising the expedition, and, as a result, was "in hot water with the Board" at the university, Reed wrote. The actions Reed himself was contemplating would be likely to heat that water a great deal more.

Holland had decided, he wrote Carnegie, that he'd have to go back to Wyoming and accompany the surveyor himself to "make sure by the seeing of the eye and the touch of the hand that there is no error made in our case." But gathering the troops was like herding cats. Downey was in Canada. The surveyor he had recommended, his brother-in-law William O. "Billy" Owen, had little flexibility in his schedule as he, too, was about to change jobs. A trip to the Freezeouts would take a few days at least—more if the weather was bad. If he was to go at all, Owen wrote to Holland, he needed to go right away.

Holland's impatience mounted, as he mentioned in letters to Reed and Downey. More revealing is a note Downey wrote Holland in response to a letter that has not survived. If the whole affair were to end up in court, Downey wrote, there was no guarantee he could keep Carnegie's name out of it: newspapers are always eager to go after "the great names of the country like Mr. Carnegie's." Downey said he could protect Holland's interests, but added, "you must assume the responsibility of the action taken." Downey had grit; Holland's was an overbearing personality, and people who dealt with him seldom had the nerve to point it out. But Carnegie noticed it, too. About to sail for Scotland, he wrote Holland one last letter to urge on him a gentler approach:

You know that I do not believe in antagonizing the state authorities.

We see what a war policy does in the Phillipines [sic] I hope you will repress your pugnacious tendencies and see what a little conciliation will do. You could be willing and gracious if you tried I honestly believe. Do try hard. We want no quarrel with the State authorities remember, or anybody in the State. . .

As for Reed, having divided his loyalties, he was now feeling pulled in two. Headaches plagued him, and sleepless nights. "I was nearly insane with a gathering in my head when I wrote last," he noted to Holland the morning of April 23. Once he gave the trustees his notice, however, he felt better. He'd had a hot time with the board, mostly with Smiley, the university president, he said. Henry Stevens, the trustee who had shown some sympathy to Holland in March, had finally let Reed know five days after the hot meeting that his resignation, effective May 1, would be accepted. The university only asked, Reed noted, to send a man with him to the dinosaur quarry to get the tools and supplies, and "also the claims belonging to the university," apparently a reference to the posted-but-not-recorded August claim.

Reed still didn't have a contract from Holland. He planned to head out to the dinosaur quarry about May 5, he told Holland, whether working "for you or someone else." Then, shrewdly, he asked Holland to write out for him "a letter that wil inform me of what you have done and how you did it. Something that I can show to any one who may accuse me of treachery. Wil you kindly do this for me, whether we finish ower bargain or not, not that I have any doubt as to ower agreement but it is quite important that I should have such a letter for if I do not I may loose some of my oldest and best friends." He mailed the letter that morning. In the afternoon he received Holland's April 20 letter saying he hoped the survey could be arranged for the coming week and he very much hoped Reed could come along.

Reed was stunned to hear that the survey had *not* been completed. Once he'd given the information to Downey, he'd assumed that the survey would proceed, especially as the weather had recently been good. Had he known the survey was still incomplete and Holland's route to a patent that much less secure, Reed implied in a reply sent the same day, he might not have resigned so soon. One reason he may have waited as long as he did to resign was to give Holland time to get the survey done—taking seriously Holland's threat of no land title, no job.

As it was, Reed could feel the vise of circumstances tightening down on him even further. When he resigned, he now told Holland, "I gave my word of honor that I would not give any information or myself do anything to jepordise the interests of the university either before or after the first of May and you can plainly see in what kind of boat I am sailing . . ." A boat with two bows, apparently, navigating in a two-way wind:

My word has been given and it must stand you will remember that you told me after you obtained your clew [to the whereabouts of the dinosaur, apparently] that all I had to do was to keep my mouth shut but then you write me I must give Downey and yourself some information I have done this but I cannot go any farther so you see it wil be impossible for me to go out with the surveying party one thing that I would advise is that as soon as you arive at the old quarry <u>tear</u> <u>down</u> <u>the</u> <u>old</u> <u>notice</u> <u>and</u> <u>put</u> <u>up</u> <u>a</u> <u>new</u> <u>one</u> the blank I sent you will do and Mr. Owen knows the form this business is something new for me and I want it setled quickly so I can get a good nights sleep.

About the end of the third week in April, Holland again boarded a train for Laramie.

Spring in Wyoming is often difficult to locate between snow, mud, and high water on the one hand, and hot summer on the other. The country was still locked in the muddy half of the equation when Holland and Owen stepped off the noon train at Medicine Bow. The name has tugged at lovers of an ideal West ever since Owen Wister opened his novel *The Virginian* on the town's train platform and in its eating house. The narrator meticulously counts the buildings, just as Wister himself had when he described the town to his diary in 1885. When the novel was published in 1902, it locked in the stereotype of the laconic, competent, secretly humorous cowboy the world has ever since found so easy to admire:

"Town, as they called it, pleased me the less, the longer I saw it," Wister's narrator remarks. "But

until our language stretches itself and takes in a new world of closer fit, town will have to do for the name of such a place as was Medicine Bow. I have seen and slept in many like it since. Scattered wide, they littered the frontier from the Columbia to the Rio Grande, from the Missouri to the Sierras. They lay stark, dotted over a planet of treeless dust, like soiled packs of cards. Each was similar to the next, as one old five spot of clubs resembles another. Houses, empty bottles and garbage, they were forever of the same shapeless pattern. More forlorn they were than stale bones. They seemed to have been strewn there by the wind and to be waiting till the wind should come again and blow them away. Yet serene above their foulness swam a pure and quiet light, such as the East never sees; they might be bathing in the air of creation's first morning. Beneath sun and stars their days and nights were immaculate and wonderful.

Holland's memories of the place were more matter of fact. Later he recalled that there were a depot, a water tank and round-house for the locomotives, three saloons, about twenty houses, and stockyards big enough to hold thousands of sheep or cattle waiting to be shipped. The whole town was bursting with men. The Union Pacific, recently rescued from receivership by E. H. Harriman, was pouring in capital and straightening its route all across southern Wyoming. It had changed the towns. "'We have no law here,'" Holland's landlady told him later that summer when he passed through Medicine Bow a second time. In the story she told, law seems especially scarce for people who weren't white:

"If you will stay over Sunday, you can sit in the door of the house and enjoy the free fights going on at the saloons on the other side of the street. We have them every Sunday. You remember the man who sat next to you at breakfast this morning. That was D—— K——. A Chinaman came to town day before yesterday and K—— took his revolver and amused him-self by shooting to see how close he could come to the Chinaman with-out hittin' him. You never seen such a scared Chinaman. He left on the next train."

Vicious or not, there was plenty of labor around. Holland and Owen found no shortage of hands to help them with a little construction job of their own.

Four miles north of town, the Little Medicine Bow River, on its way to the North Platte from the Laramie Range to the northeast, was running high, and out of its banks. All bridges were out. Thou-sands of sheep and their herders were stranded on the north bank. In Medicine Bow empty railroad cars were standing on the sidings, waiting to receive the stock for shipment to Omaha and Chicago. The water might take weeks to recede. It also blocked the road north, to the dinosaur quarry.

Owen and Holland rode out to the river for a look. They found a deep, narrow spot, forty yards across, and decided it could be spanned by "a bridge of rafts." Owen had noticed a pile of telegraph poles near the railroad station and figured other lumber and materi-als could be procured from the railroaders. Wyoming law allowed for condemnation of private property to repair roads when mail routes were blocked, with the county eventually to repay citizens for any damage. That night Holland and Owen met with the locals in one of the saloons. Owen ran the show. Everyone seemed to know and like him. He'd won a statewide election for state auditor five years earlier; he would have been on a first-name basis with many of the men in the room. Holland offered to pay for food from the railroad restaurant for anyone who would help. Soon men were volunteering their teams and wagons to haul the poles and half a railroad car's load of heavy planks out to the river.

With Owen in charge, the caravan left town the next morning and spent two days building a temporary floating bridge. On the morning of their fourth day in Medicine Bow, Holland later recalled, the survey party was "away for the north country, the land of the antelope and sage chicken." Herds of sheep filed past them. The bridge was narrow, with no rails. They unhitched the horses, led them across one by one, and pulled the wagon across by hand. By nightfall, snow covered the ground. They reached the ranch of State Senator J. D. Dyer, on the flank of the Freezeouts.

The next morning, with Dyer guiding them, they crossed a ridge and into a wide valley on the far side—apparently the same "Happy Holow" where Reed had built his cabin in the 1880s. A driver took the wagon around the mountain spur and met them at noon. At the quarry, Holland noted, "the big femur was exposed to view, and some of the large bones." Without delay, Owen found the section corner, ran the boundary lines, and they staked the placer claim. All that was left was to load the bones: "Over the tailboard of the waggon went so much of the big femur as it was safe for us to think of loading into the vehicle. It required the strength of three men to lift the fragment. Then we were off," Holland wrote. He headed east again. He could only have felt triumphant, returning this time with stories to tell, a land claim, and, finally, a piece of the dinosaur. It was the first dinosaur bone ever collected for the Carnegie Museum. On May 2, Owen billed Holland for six days' surveying and expenses: $75.90.

Chapter 7

HEWN INTO
FRAGMENTS

*T*wo things had become clear to Holland. First, though Reed was a veteran fossil collector, he was not the man to run an ambitious new museum program in vertebrate paleontology. That would require an educated scientist with administrative experience and a sound reputation among his peers. Second, ownership of the dinosaur was murky, and unsolvable by simple outlays of cash.

The best vertebrate paleontologists in the nation at the time were beginning to gather around Henry Fairfield Osborn at the American Museum of Natural History in New York. Holland headed there late in March, within days of his return to Pittsburgh after his first trip to Laramie. When he checked with the experts in New York, they told him what he wanted to hear: his $2,000 offer to Gramm for the dinosaur had been far too high, and the Wyoming trustees had been foolish to reject it. "The offer," Holland wrote Gramm redundantly, "is altogether and unconditionally withdrawn."

Next, he called on Carnegie. The tycoon almost certainly tried to impress on his museum director a clear if politically delicate idea: Don't make enemies, but get the dinosaur. It's similar to the message Carnegie left with Frick in the spring of 1892, before the Homestead Strike: Don't make enemies, but break the union. Like Frick, Holland would find the second half of the directive easier to obey than the first.

Finally, Holland took a cab from his hotel on Madison Square up to the American Museum at 77th Street and Central Park West to talk to a certain staff member there who was not too happy in his job. Physician-naturalist Jacob L. Wortman had led American Museum bone-collecting parties in Wyoming and the West every summer since 1891. He'd been born in Oregon in 1856, making him eight years younger than Reed and Holland. As a young man Wortman had studied at universities in Oregon, where his interest in geology began. Before he was twenty-two, he was assisting Cope's great collector, Charles Sternberg, in the fossil beds of the John Day River country in eastern Oregon. Sternberg trusted Wortman's skill and initiative enough that he had left the younger man to work the fossil quarry alone for weeks at a time.

When Cope was no longer able to finance field parties, Sternberg went to Washington in the early 1880s, and Wortman went with him, working first as a curator at the Army and Navy Medical Museum, then obtaining a medical degree at Georgetown Medical College. He then went to work for Cope as a fossil preparator in Philadelphia, at the Academy of Natural Sciences. Many of the fossils Wortman worked on in Philadelphia were ones he and Sternberg had collected in the West. But Cope gave Wortman no chances to publish, and he returned to the medical museum in Washington briefly. Finally, Osborn recruited Wortman to work at the American Museum in New York. Wortman supervised all the museum's field work in paleontology for the next eight summers. Osborn, who had succeeded Cope and Marsh as the driving personality in the advancement of American paleontology, did allow Wortman to publish, sometimes as joint author with himself and sometimes on his own.

Wortman seems seldom or never to have practiced medicine, but was always known to his colleagues as "the Doctor," a term they used with jocular respect. His medical training had given him a solid knowledge of anatomy and osteology—and he was generous with it. After Wortman's death, Osborn and Holland both wrote long obituaries in their respective museums' publications. Each director recalled Wortman's company after a day in the field. "It was indeed a rare bit of one's education as a paleontologist," Osborn wrote, "to see him return to camp on a cold night after a hard day's fossil hunt,

Paleontologist Jacob L. Wortman was hired away from the American
Museum of Natural History in 1899. Courtesy of Library Services, American
Museum of Natural History photo, negative number 311591.

roll a cigarette, huddle as close to the fire as possible, and tell glow-
ingly of the day's discovery or lament bitterly the fatigue and exhaustion of fruitless search. After a large draught of hot coffee and perhaps a good supper, the casualties of the day were forgotten and the
Doctor would begin to philosophize or discuss some favorite hobby
of his in comparative anatomy or to expound some theory of mam-

malian descent, stimulated perhaps by some outstanding 'find' of the season."

Holland noted that "the younger men who were associated with [Wortman] at that time, derived great benefit from the instruction which he voluntarily gave them in the science of comparative anatomy. . . . Dr. Wortman in the evenings gathered 'the boys' about him and, using the skull of a coyote, a bison, or a horse, which had been picked up on the prairie, imparted to them a thorough knowledge of mammalian craniology. When these parties returned to the Museum in the winter months, Dr. Wortman, as a labor of love, formed a class, composed of the young men associated with him, and regularly gave them instruction in mammalian anatomy."

Years later, after the automobile changed the range and techniques of fossil hunting, paleontologists would remember the early years of North American exploration with a nostalgia for its pace and strenuousness that glossed over its true difficulties. Wortman and American Museum collector O. A. Peterson in the 1890s hunted fossils in Wyoming, Utah, South Dakota, and New Mexico. They and others like them traveled with a saddle horse or two, a team and wagon loaded with tent, camp stove, groceries for the men and oats for the horses, and a bedroll with a big canvas tarp for each man. They camped near good grass and water, then prospected outward during the day. The routine would continue until all likely exposures within range of camp—a five-mile radius on foot, ten on horseback—had been checked out. Discovery of fossils worth collecting would mean a delay of a few hours to an entire season or more. Often the most barren country—the gully-gouged badlands, where plants are few but bones weather out of the steep, soft slopes—made for the best success.

Osborn at that time was building up the American Museum's paleontology program dramatically. He was the son of the president of the Illinois Central Railroad and a nephew of J. P. Morgan. He came from Princeton to the American Museum in 1891, bringing with him great personal wealth, influential connections, a knack for public relations, and a feel for audience. From his first years at the museum, he made it clear to Wortman, Peterson, and others that he wanted mountable specimens: skeletons suited for public display. He hired artists to paint diorama backgrounds and sculpt models. For most of the 1890s Osborn and his collectors concentrated on Tertiary fossils—mammals from the times since the dinosaur disappeared.

The focus shifted, however, in 1897, when Osborn hired a recent University of Kansas graduate, Barnum Brown, and sent him to Como Bluff to look for Jurassic mammals—the little ones that had been contemporary with dinosaurs. Brown kept finding big dinosaur bones, instead. Realizing the dinosaurs' potential popular appeal, Osborn directed other American Museum collectors in Colorado, South Dakota, and Kansas to join Brown in Wyoming.

Twenty years after the first one, the second great dinosaur rush was on at Como Bluff. American Museum crews discovered even richer diggings in 1898, at the Bone Cabin Quarry, a dozen miles to the north. Wortman was in charge, but Brown was the rising star. Tension between the two men is palpable in Wortman's letters from the field. Late in 1898, Osborn arranged for his banker uncle, Morgan, to pay Brown's expenses to accompany the last of three Princeton expeditions to hunt fossils in Patagonia. Wortman must have felt some intellectual ownership of the issues the expedition would investigate. As early as 1896, he had published papers on evolutionary connections between ancient North and South American mammals, based on Tertiary fossils he had discovered in New Mexico. He almost certainly felt passed over when Osborn backed Brown for the trip instead.

When O. C. Marsh, the grand old man of North American paleontology, died unexpectedly in March 1899, Wortman was in for far greater disappointment. He had believed that he was the logical successor to Marsh's position at Yale—a nonteaching professorship which included supervision of the Peabody Museum and the vast collection of vertebrate fossils Marsh had assembled there. Wortman may have inferred promises from Marsh that had not been made. Osborn, a Cope loyalist, may have been unable or unwilling to use his influence to help Wortman move to a job on Marsh turf at Yale. But in the end, there simply were no funds to keep the position going. Holland learned later that spring that Marsh's estate was bankrupt, and Yale could come up with no other money to pay Wortman a salary.

Wortman was ripe for recruiting, therefore, when Holland visited him at the American Museum on March 29, 1899. Holland was impressed both by the man and by the museum he worked in. Here was a person with an education, administrative experience, and a sound reputation among his peers. Wortman also knew Reed well, from working at Como, and liked him. What could go wrong? "I was led to feel that if I could obtain the services of a man like Wortman in addition to the services of Reed," Holland wrote Carnegie two days later, "I would probably have a force that would enable us to do something at our museum that would be of the highest importance to science and something of which we all should be excessively proud."

Wortman apparently took the train to Pittsburgh for an interview the weekend of April 15 and 16, and stayed at Holland's house two blocks from the museum. On April 20, in the same week he was impatiently finalizing plans for his second Wyoming trip, Holland wrote Wortman directing his attention to recent news reports that Carnegie had just announced plans to give $1.75 million to expand his institute in Pittsburgh. The natural history museum would continue to be one of the most important departments, and "some competent man" would be needed to direct the museum's efforts in paleontology, Holland wrote. It wasn't a direct job offer, but nearly so. By May 15, Wortman and twenty-five-year-old Arthur Coggeshall, one of the American Museum's most skilled fossil preparators, had given their notices to Osborn, who was sorry to see them go. The following weekend, friends threw a farewell dinner at which all the curators made speeches and drank Wortman's health, soothing the bitterness he felt toward Osborn over the failure to get the Yale job. On May 22, Wortman and Coggeshall boarded a train for Pittsburgh and the West.

Holland now had in place as skilled and seasoned a field crew as he could have assembled anywhere, especially on such short notice. That left time for addressing the trickier question—how legally to get the dinosaur without making enemies of the trustees of the

University of Wyoming or of the citizens of the state. Diplomacy was never Holland's strength. Over the next six weeks he would bully and beg, wheedle and scheme, until impatience and bottled-up rage made it nearly impossible for him to see what was going on. Downey and Carnegie had already advised him politely to keep a tight rein on his belligerence. Things would get worse before Holland could hear their advice.

On his way out of Wyoming after the bridge-building and bone-grabbing trip to the Freezeouts, Holland stopped in Cheyenne long enough to write a long letter to Otto Gramm of the university trustees. With Owen's survey complete, Holland wrote confidently, it was clear that Reed's error—his erroneous numbering of the township on the claim notice posted at the quarry site the previous August—meant the claim was not valid, and therefore "the ground is open to location by anyone."

Holland informed Gramm that Reed had been asked to file a new claim. Besides paying for the survey, Holland offered also, now, to pay for the land and to get clear title to it *for the benefit of the university*. He said he hoped Gramm would "accept the offer in the spirit in which it is made." Saying he was confident there were plenty of bones for both institutions, Holland swore "to generously aid you in any way in my power, and to establish relations of confidence with a view to the exchange of duplicate material which we may severally secure." Such exchanges were common enough among scientists who did not feel the need to compete with each other. In Holland's mind, however, there was still only one dinosaur, and he had every intention that it would one day stand in the halls of his own museum.

Downey quickly proved worthy of his fees by arranging a meeting with Wyoming's power elite. The new governor, DeForest Richards, had the power to appoint new university trustees when a vacancy came up and was an ex officio trustee himself. Also present were a handful of other politicians and newspaper editors, U.S. Attorney and university trustee T. G. Burke, and U.S. Senator Francis E. Warren, already for more than a decade the most powerful politician—perhaps the most powerful man—in Wyoming and destined to remain so for another thirty years. Holland was confident these men could solve his problems. "After we had swapped stories for a while and everybody was in charmingly good humor, Downey spoke of my errand to Wyoming and the little gathering broke up with hearty assurances from the Governor and all the rest that they would use their best efforts to accomplish my wishes," Holland wrote Carnegie a few days later. Politics seemed simple enough. To get things done you just went to the men at the top: "The Governor went so far as to speak of the action of the regents in refusing to grant what I wished in extremely uncomplimentary terms, pronouncing them in strong Western parlance d—— f—— [damned fools, apparently]. He also said that as the appointments of these regents is with him and it will be his duty shortly to make some reappointments, he will look into the matter and see what matter of men these are."

Downey, Holland went on to report, had high hopes the maneuver would work. Holland's letter announcing his plan to turn the land claim over to the university would be published in the Wyoming papers. For the trustees to show "in the face of such generosity . . . an ugly spirit" would surely backfire. And if it didn't work out, Holland went on, he himself had found nearby "the remains of another beast of the same sort . . . which gives promise of being perhaps quite as good as the first one found, and I suspect that we shall find before long that it is not going to be as difficult, as we were at first inclined to think, to get one of these huge saurians exceeding in size the largest specimen found by Prof. Marsh."

This second specimen appeared to be as big as the one whose femur piece he and Owen and an assistant had brought to the railroad from the Freezeouts. That prize, still on its way to Pittsburgh, was twenty-eight inches in diameter, two and a half feet long, and weighed five hundred pounds—"a very large soupbone," Holland reported.

A veteran like Wortman would have responded that nothing was certain in paleontology, that a collector never knew what he had until digging was finished. Still, high hopes were contagious, even among the most seasoned diggers. The bone trade attracted men who could not subdue their hopes for long. Reed still had them, every time he dug. It's not surprising that Holland also would quickly discover the thrill of finding bones in the dirt, and would suppose his own find was as big as the biggest. It gave him a feeling of power. And it blinded him to his own bad faith.

"Your kindness in making it possible to do these things is very aptly appreciated," Holland went on to Carnegie. "Your advice to adopt pacific measures I realize to have been extremely sagacious, and I believe that we have so heaped coals of fire upon the head of the little President of the University of Wyoming and his narrow minded compatriots, and have so thoroughly enlisted the good will of men who are very much more potent in State affairs than they are, that we shall have very little to fear from that quarter."

Gramm, meanwhile, chose to read the offer of the land claim as including an offer of the dinosaur fossil itself. And he brought up another reason for the trustees' refusal of Holland's $2,000 offer "for the Fossil discovered by Mr. W. H. Reed while in our employ"—one that hadn't come up in the initial meeting. Even if Holland had offered ten times as much, the trustees would still have had to turn him down, Gramm wrote, because the executive committee "had no power or authority whatsoever to dispose of or sell the State's property." The trustees had only one alternative: to offer the Carnegie Museum first crack at buying the fossil if it ever did go on the market. That being said, Gramm added that the university "fully realizes the importance of having *scientific* parties exhume the bones," and the university further "has no desire whatsoever to be selfish in this matter." Gramm added that he desired on behalf of the university "to accept your gift of the Jurassic Fossil located [that is, claimed under the placer law] by you, and I do this in the same spirit in which it is made." Each man seems to have understood perfectly the true spirit of the other's remarks. They distrusted each other profoundly.

Holland was back in Pittsburgh by Friday, May 5, when he wrote Carnegie about his trip and about his meeting with the governor. On May 6 a mostly accurate version of events so far ran in the *Laramie Republican*—making the supposed deal public and thereby pressuring Holland and Gramm to get what they wanted out of it quickly. On May 10 Holland urged Downey to continue at the trustees' June meeting to pull strings to get the dinosaur. The best plan would be to have a motion introduced to give the quarry claim *back* to the Carnegie Museum. Such a move would establish "terms of reciprocal kindness for Mr. Carnegie" at a crucial time, Holland wrote, just when Carnegie was cashing in all his steel interests. The law, Holland went on, would have allowed the Carnegie Museum to hold a claim "against all comers," but he added, once again, that he found a conciliatory approach preferable. "We have, however, acted kindly upon the premises and thrown ourselves wholly on the mercy of the Regents."

At the same time, Holland continued to profess good will toward Gramm, while completely ignoring Gramm's specific thanks for the "Jurassic Fossil." Three days later, Holland tried to enlist Owen, too, in his efforts to pull Wyoming strings. He asked Owen to remind the governor to remind the trustees it would be in the university's best interest to please Carnegie by allowing his museum to "take up the dinosaur lying on the forty acres which we have bought for them." The scheme seemed to be working; Carnegie was pleased at least. "My Dear Lord Chancellor," the steel king wrote from Skibo, "Your report of May 5th is worthy of you. It is another proof that genius, always imperious in any line it undertakes, is yet capable of playing many parts. Believe me nothing becomes your Grace more than the role of an angel of peace. Should the interests of science or any other interest bring you Skiboward, we will agree to change the subject for you, from bones." Carnegie used the word "genius" liberally when referring to his partners and top managers. It made them like him.

As Holland and Gramm drifted in mutual, intentional misunderstanding, the Carnegie Museum's new field crew assembled in Wyoming. Reed left Laramie for the Freezeouts May 6, probably glad to get away from his former boss and former loyalties. Holland wrote Reed a week later, reminding him of his promises to scout a variety of far-flung prospects: Rock Creek, east of Medicine Bow; Muddy Creek, north of Medicine Bow; and "to mouse around your 'Happy Valley'" in the Freezeouts "in which lie the 'bones of contention.'" This was a total of thirty or forty square miles in three different locations. Reed was also to look for bones as close to the railroad as possible, Holland noted, and to stay as close to Medicine Bow as possible, in order to be able to connect with Wortman on short notice when he arrived. Wortman, Holland made clear, was to be in charge; Reed should "cooperate with him as I should expect you to cooperate with me were I myself personally present and in the field with you."

Coggeshall arrived in Medicine Bow on May 27, a Saturday; Reed met him there with a team and wagon. Wortman had stopped in Chicago for an extra tent, two more tarps, and photographic chemicals with which to develop glass negatives in the field. Holland had arranged for separate shipment of a camera and a case for five dozen five-by-seven-inch plates. Wortman stopped again in Omaha to finalize Holland's arrangements for free passage over the Union Pacific for himself and Coggeshall, then stopped for another day in Laramie, probably for groceries, as the men expected to be in the field through fall.

The competition was gathering forces, too. Knight was already back in the Freezeouts by mid-May. American Museum crews by then had returned to the Bone Cabin Quarry which would prove so productive in dinosaur bones in the coming five seasons. And everyone was aware that the country would be flooded with bone seekers in July. The Union Pacific Railroad, with Knight as planner and trip captain, had sent out a circular in April offering free railroad passage over its lines to any geologists and their assistants or any other scientists who wanted to prospect in "Wyoming's fossil fields." There was no point wasting time.

More than fifty years later, Coggeshall recalled vividly the loads that he, the most junior member of the three-man field party, was expected to carry. Holland's and Owen's pontoon bridge across the Little Medicine Bow River was still the only way north to the Freezeouts. The bridge, Coggeshall wrote, was "just flat timbers tied together and held up by oil barrels. As the bridge had no sides, the horses had to be unhitched and led across, then the wagon unloaded and pushed over." Much of the load was made up of burlap and hundred-pound sacks of plaster for wrapping the bones for eventual shipment. In a method that would remain unchanged for decades to come, the men would cut the burlap into strips, dunk the strips

Fossil preparator Arthur Coggeshall was also hired away from the American Museum. Courtesy of Carnegie Museum of Natural History, Pittsburgh, Pennsylvania.

into wet plaster, then wrap them around the excavated bones. The plaster would harden, like a cast, and the bones would then be safe during long wagon and railroad rides. The older men led the horses, pushed the wagon, and carried the other gear across: tents, bedrolls, a camp stove, digging tools, food. Coggeshall got to carry the 100-pound sacks of dry plaster. Every relationship was part of a hierarchy.

As soon as they reached the high swale west of Dyer's ranch—the area where Reed had found parts of the big dinosaur the previous August, where Holland and Owen had grabbed half a femur, and where Knight and some assistants had already been at work for a few weeks—the Carnegie crew made camp and started working. Wortman reported June 6, a week after he'd left Medicine Bow, that "All of Reed's prospects proved disappointing and we proceeded to locate others." Disappointing as the prospects may have been, Wortman does not sound worried. Coggeshall, on the other hand, took quite a different tone. Writing fifty years later, he noted,

After a few days of digging, Reed had to admit, as we suspected, that the piece of leg bone which was in Pittsburgh was all he had ever found there, and the whole story of the 'Most Colossal Animal Ever Found' was based on that fragment.

Discouraging? Yes, it was, but bone hunters, like prospectors for gold and silver, have to take discouragement in their stride.

Whether "All of Reed's prospects," as Wortman called them, included the supposedly huge Brontosaurus on which the hopes of so many people, Holland especially, were by now based is not entirely clear. In his June 6 letter Wortman went on to detail six other prospects the Carnegie crew had by then checked out, despite bad weather. The best included a femur, tibia and fibula, hip and pubic bones, a neck bone, and several ribs of a sauropod—either a large *Morosaurus*, Wortman guessed, or a small *Brontosaurus* (now called *Camarasaurus* and *Apatosaurus*, respectively.) The other five prospects were still unexcavated but looked good; they included parts of a *Stegosaurus*.

But with the summer's likely influx of other fossil hunters, Wortman decided it would be wise to prospect more widely before settling in to work on the specimens at hand. After a few more days at the site west of Dyer's ranch in the Freezeouts, Wortman and Reed left on a long swing southwest to the head of Troublesome and Difficulty creeks. When prospects there proved disappointing, they swung north again, coming back on the north side of the Freezeouts

as far as the T. B. Ranch. Then they went west again to a small exposure at the western end of the Little Medicine Anticline, where they
found three or four good prospects.

Of them, the best was the sauropod Wortman now confidently
identified as a "Brontosaurus" (that is, *Apatosaurus*). They had a femur five and one half feet long and the other leg and hip bones he'd
described earlier. Now there also were about a dozen ribs and four
or five vertebrae exposed. Prospects looked good, though the work
was slow, as the bones were tangled together. So far, about two
wagon loads of bones had been excavated, Wortman guessed, "and
as soon as Bill [Reed] and I get at it we will snatch things out at a
lively rate."

The second best prospect was a sauropod Wortman judged to be
a *Diplodocus*, with a femur five feet long and neck vertebrae and a toe
bone in sight. Not much was out of the ground yet, but the specimen could turn out to be very good. At the head of Troublesome
Creek they'd found three or four Ichthyosaur fossils—marine reptiles, of which the best was a *Baptanodon*. Fair results might come
from the sites at the west end of the Little Medicine Anticline,
Wortman noted, but the *Stegosaurus* "appears to be 'n.g.' [no good]".

"We have labeled all our quarries [apparently this meant posting
notices on site in the first of the steps of making a placer claim], and
I do not apprehend any difficulty in holding them until we can get
around to work them out." It was already on the whole a "fine collection," Wortman wrote, "and a really good start in our vertebrate
paleontology department."

Subsequent correspondence appears to show that Holland, out
of Pittsburgh the last week or ten days of June, did not see this letter until the end of the month or afterward, along with another letter Wortman wrote later. There's no record, therefore, of any reaction he might have had to Wortman's news that there was no single,
perfect dinosaur, such as Holland had told Downey in May that
Carnegie "has his heart set on obtaining."

Meanwhile, Wortman had nothing but praise for Reed. Wortman's enthusiasm recalls Arthur Lakes's enthusiasm for Reed from
the early days at Como Bluff, twenty years before:

We have been hustling from daylight to dark ever since we struck the field and I feel well satisfied that you made no mistake in employing Reed. He is earnest energetic and thoroughly interested in the welfare of our undertaking. He is an agreeable fellow to be with in camp and everything goes on pleasantly and smoothly.

Late in June, something happened to the bones at the quarry in the Freezeouts where Reed had found the bones of a large sauropod the previous August. Unfortunately, because a letter Wortman wrote to Holland has not survived, actual events are unclear. Holland's response to Wortman's lost letter does survive, but by then he was so angry that his anger clouds the facts.

By mid or late May, Holland had been making openly contemptuous remarks about the university to his correspondents. "It will do the University in Wyoming a great deal more good to have this skeleton taken up and mounted and exhibited in the Museum at Pittsburg [sic]," he wrote Owen, "where three or four hundred thousand people will see it every year, having attached to it the label stating that it was presented to the Museum by the University of Wyoming, than it will if they should have some bone butcher go in and grub the thing up, as bones in their museum have been grubbed up, and piled away in their cellar. A pile of old broken bones in the cellar of a university cannot be compared to a skeleton, skillfully exhumed from the matrix and set up. They have the chance of their lives now [to turn the dinosaur over to the Carnegie Museum] if they only knew it." And to Wortman he wrote, more ominously, "I only hope that Knight will not have torn the whole thing to pieces before such action [a university choice to turn the land back to the Carnegie Museum] takes place."

Downey was working hard to set up a meeting between Gramm and Holland, to settle once and for all just who owned what. The university trustees at their meeting June 22 appointed Gramm, Governor Richards, and President Smiley to a committee to meet with Holland on his expected return to Wyoming that summer. Earlier, Downey had thought Gramm might be able to make a trip to Pittsburgh, but the two men's schedules prevented it.

Knight, meanwhile, had been making various trips to the

Freezeouts since May 15 or earlier. Reed wrote Holland on May 26 to say that Knight had an assistant digging "on the bluff just above Dyer's ranch. . . . I found the same bones last summer but they are very poor and badly decayed. They have not disturbed anything else." What Reed reported as plain fact, Holland would have taken as threat. Faced as they were with the daily labor of finding fossils, digging them out and preparing them for shipment, the field crews were less concerned with competition and ownership than were Holland and Osborn back east. Not long afterwards, Holland received an unusual letter:

Flagstaff Arazona [sic]
June 5th 1899

Dr. W. J. Holland C.B.B.
Dear Doc;—

We want you eastern chaps to understand that the farmers up in Wyoming are not the only fellers that can put bones on the market. The concern which I belong to is called the Arazona Fossiliferous Manufacturing Co & is ready to supply anything that is wanted in the skeleton line. Our process is fully protected by patents & if anyone is caught trying to imitate us he is very liable to become a genuine sample of what he is trying to imitate much sooner than he otherwise would. Dont take anything in this line unless stamped with our secret trade mark which we'll tell you about & where to look for it if you are willing to deal

We have two ways of doing business the direct and the indirect. The first way we ship Co. D. to your address from the factory. The second way we bury the beasts ordered at any place you want & you C.O.D. (ceep on digging) until you find them. The last sceme seems to have the call now as we planted some big orders lately for swell museums in the East who have sent out their own parties to dig them up.

Our plant is able to turn out anything you want in the bone line anything from the smallest fossil insect to the biggest elephant or snake The workmanship is garunteeded in every respect & the finish is warranted to be natural & to be weathered according to the exposure the bones are supposed to have had.

We stick strictly to specifications & working drawings & can furnish you skeletons with anything left out or added on as you think they ought to be & we can make them aggree with anything you may have said or written about them before hand.

Orders should be sent in early to avoid the rush & to give us time to set up your designs & plant them in the fall ready for next summers digging.

Your confidential Friend
Jack Bowie

The offer to make the bogus bones "agree with anything you may have said or written about them beforehand" shows a writer who understands the scientist's occasional wish for compliant evidence. Regardless of who Jack Bowie was, or how kindly his jokes were intended, they can only have increased Holland's already mounting fears that westerners soon would make him appear a fool.

Holland was back in his office July 3, after a late June trip to his alma mater at Amherst, Massachusetts. On his desk he found two letters from Wortman—probably the long one from June 18 specifying the prospects at hand, as well as a later one that has not survived. They filled Holland with what he called "a feeling of disappointment," though soon enough in his reply, disappointment sounds more like rage.

Everything has turned out badly. The last letter, in which you inform me of what has been done by Professor Knight, caps the climax. I had no idea Knight could act in such a way. After arranging to buy the land for the university, to discover that the specimen which makes it alone valuable has been utterly destroyed, is a profound mortification . . . We want as quickly as possible to extricate ourselves from all relations with these people at Laramie and [from the] President of the University down I have a very poor opinion of the whole blooming outfit: they apparently do not know how to meet manly men in a manly way, but are as full of little narrow, petty jealousies as an egg is of meat.

Holland was more specific about his complaints when he wrote Downey that day to tell him to abandon the museum's land claim, as there now was no point in acquiring the title:

I am in receipt of a letter informing me that Prof Knight has removed the notice of the filing of the claim which I had placed upon the ground and has substituted one of his own bearing the date of May the 11th; that he has furthermore dug a trench 15 feet long and 10 feet wide through the remains of this dinosaur, working with the utmost carelessness and practically ruining the specimen for all scientific purposes. My informant in regard to these matters is Dr. Wortman, who, at my request, visited the locality to report.

The dimensions of the trench and the replacing of the Carnegie claim with a university one are probably accurate. Harder to judge without Wortman's account is the charge of "utmost carelessness," as Holland by now had bound so much of his pride up with his hopes for the fossil. His heart was as set as Carnegie's, perhaps more so, on finding one big, perfect specimen.

His pride had also led him to continue maneuvering for the dinosaur the entire time he was trumpeting his "gift" of the land to the university. Surely he could have both the peace Carnegie wanted and the biggest dinosaur in the world. He saw no contradiction between the two. All the failure "to meet manly men in a manly way" was the university's, as far as Holland was concerned.

Knight's actions are harder to trace. Holland's letter announcing the land gift had appeared in the Laramie papers May 6. It would have been perfectly reasonable if, after Holland's offer became public, University President Elmer Smiley, or perhaps Trustee Otto Gramm, had made it clear to Knight that now was the time to go get the bones from what was about to become the university's land. But exactly when he got to the quarry, replaced Holland's claim on the post with one of his own, and dug the big trench is hard to say. If he did so as early as May 11, as the new date on the post indicated, Wortman would almost certainly have reported the change in his letter to Holland on June 6.

Wortman reported nothing of the kind, however, so a mid- or late-June visit while Wortman and Reed were off prospecting other sites seems much more likely. Knight may have botched, or partly botched, the job. He was primarily a mining engineer; fossil expertise he left to Reed. Now Knight was on his own, and probably in a hurry.

Holland on July 3 gave strict orders to Wortman and Downey to say absolutely nothing to anyone about Knight's removal—perhaps smashing—of the bones. Reed was not to go to Cheyenne to the federal land office "to prove up our claim to the land." Holland still planned to meet the university's negotiating committee when he came to Wyoming in a few weeks, but only for the sake of appearances. It was clear where the blame lay, he wrote Downey:

I appreciate all the interest and kindness that you have shown in this matter, but it is quite plain that the fates have decreed that the whole thing shall end in nothing so far as this particular specimen is concerned. It is another added to the long list of valuable and interesting specimens which have been hewn into fragments by the hands of incompetent men, leaving nothing to science except a few broken bits of bone which utterly fail to tell the story which would have been told had slow and patient fingers been allowed to do their work.

While Holland was cooking in his anger, Reed, Wortman, Coggeshall, and Reed's seventeen-year-old son, Willie, who by now had joined the party, patiently left the Freezeouts and headed for another outcrop of the Morrison Formation, twenty or more miles away. Earlier in the spring, Reed had found dinosaur bones there, weathering out of the ground. He buried them to guard against discovery by rival parties, then marked the spot by building cairns fifty paces away. The place lay near the banks of Sheep Creek, a tributary of the Little Medicine Bow River, east of the Freezeouts and north of Medicine Bow. The bone hunters were there by the second of July.

Chapter 8

SOME GOOD LUCK
AT LAST

On the evening of July 2, Wortman, Reed, Willie Reed, and Coggeshall came up from the south over the brow of a hill and found a shallow valley spread below them. Lined with willows, Sheep Creek made a green thread across the dry plains. Mountains rimmed the northern and eastern horizons. Upstream to the right, they spotted a rim of Dakota sandstone with the telltale Morrison clays sloping out below it—a familiar combination from so many other Jurassic sites they'd prospected before. They camped, and next morning they strolled up the creek toward the outcrop, probably guided to the spot by cairns Reed had left there when he scouted the place in May. First they found miscellaneous bone fragments scattered on the surface, and then Wortman spotted a line of huge vertebrae—most of an entire backbone—showing among the sagebrush through the clays. At nearly the same moment, Reed shouted from a rise nearby. He, too, had found bones, apparently those of an even larger dinosaur.

After digging for the better part of two days, Wortman wrote Holland, "very happy to report some good luck at last. We have two good prospects . . . on which we are now working." The better of the two was a "small Brontosaur," of which a five-feet, four-inch femur had already been exposed, also "many vertebrae, pelvic and limb bones. . . . The bones are in fine preservation and the prospect looks better every day." Second was a "very large Brontosaur," with many bones in sight and the likelihood of many more, though the bones of the larger specimen were somewhat fragile and required more care. Still, Wortman had high hopes that it would make a "superb mount"—apparently because of its size. He expected to spend the rest of the season at the spot, though as always his curiosity ranged outward to prospects he hadn't gotten to as yet: "The Douglass region," apparently a reference to prospects near Douglas, Wyoming, on the North Platte north of the Laramie Range, "is only two days [wagon] drive across the range and if possible we will find the time to give it a whirl before the season closes." Regardless, he was sure of results worthy of exhibition. "When you come out," he added, "you will find us here 35 miles north of Medicine Bow."

Holland arrived in Laramie on July 19. About eighty other scientists and students had converged on the town for the field trip Knight and the Union Pacific had engineered. Holland was happy to turn out some oratory at a reception that night for academics and townspeople on the university campus. But on July 21, when the field trippers all rolled off in wagons for their adventure, Holland and the three young men he'd brought with him—a museum staffer, the son of a museum trustee, and the son's friend—instead took the train for Medicine Bow. There they waited a day for their groceries and gear to catch up with them. The young men seized the opportunity for some natural history, gathering fish, plants, and insect specimens for the museum while Holland sat in the depot and wrote a description of Medicine Bow and an account of the field trip's opening festivities for the *Pittsburg Dispatch*. On Saturday afternoon, July 22, they left for the Sheep Creek quarries.

South-central Wyoming was crowded with scientists that summer. Besides the eighty or so professors and students touring with Knight, representatives of four other institutions had already found good fossil prospects: an American Museum party near Bone Cabin Quarry, the Carnegie Museum at Sheep Creek, and parties from the University of Kansas and the Field Columbia Museum of Chicago in the Freezeouts. The more established parties felt no need to spend time with Knight's expedition. The patrician Henry Osborn, in particular, was eager to avoid the bigger crowd and arrived in Medicine Bow the same day Holland did. There, Osborn was met by members of the American Museum staff who'd been in the field since May. Osborn left that afternoon, but not before passing on to Holland his congratulations on the brand-new "splendid discoveries" at Sheep Creek, news of which Osborn had just received.

By now it was clear that the "small Brontosaur" Wortman had mentioned earlier was a *Diplodocus,* a genus named and described first by Marsh from fragments, and known somewhat better from a good series of back, hip, and tail bones discovered by American Museum crews near Como Bluff two years before. But Reed and Wortman's new find looked far more complete than any of the earlier ones, Holland wrote to the newspaper. "Of the nature of the discovery it is not time now to speak at length, but it suffices to say, that from the present prospects it appears that we shall become in all probability the possessors of one of the largest and possibly the most perfect skeleton hitherto found of a colossal dinosaur belonging to the genus Diplodocus, 'a rare bird' indeed, something which no museum in Europe possesses, and of which only fragments exist in American collections." Holland was happy to publish his speculations before he'd even had a chance to see the specimen or talk it over with Wortman face to face.

Holland's arrival at the Sheep Creek diggings brought the party at Camp Carnegie, as it began to be called, to at least nine: Wortman, Reed, Coggeshall, Willie Reed, a cook, Holland, and the three young men from Pittsburgh. They built a flat-roofed, board-and-bat shack with a cook tent attached, pitched three big canvas wall tents for sleeping and a fourth for eating, and dug a well near the creek to ensure a good water supply. Holland was stimulated by the physical, social, and culinary labors of camp life. He was particularly amused by the cook, whom he never names in his newspaper article, but whose career he delighted to recount. After stints as an oiler and then a fireman on two steam voyages around Cape Horn, the man got a job in a circus sideshow imitating a raw meat–devouring Fiji Islander.

"The thing went all right for a while and we made money," the cook had said. "But one day an old gentleman stuck his gold-headed cane through the bars of the cage and hit me a swipe on the top of the head. That was too much for me, I made the air blue for a

The Carnegie Museum bone collectors camped near the *Diplodocus carnegii* quarry in 1899 and dubbed their living quarters Camp Carnegie. Courtesy of Carnegie Museum of Natural History, Pittsburgh, Pennsylvania.

William J. Holland, *at left in armchair*, eats dinner at Camp Carnegie with the bone diggers. Jacob Wortman, *with cup*, is seated at Holland's left. Courtesy of Carnegie Museum of Natural History, Pittsburgh, Pennsylvania.

minute, while the old gentleman stood back and grinned and said, 'I knowed you was no more a Fiji than I am.' . . . That was at Peoria, Illinois." The man cooked well, regardless of his previous enthusiasm for raw meat: "The rattle of the tin baking-pan, which takes the place of a gong, and which he thumps thrice a day as only a Fiji Islander rattles his shield," brought quick responses from all members of the party. The fare was potatoes, fried or stewed sage chickens, and dough gods and larrup—lumps of bread dough spitted and toasted over the coals, then covered with maple syrup. The air was clear; the work was hard and full of promise.

Twice, at least, Osborn and others from the American Museum crew traveled the ten or so miles from Bone Cabin up to Sheep Creek for a visit. A photo survives of the American and Carnegie museum parties assembled at the quarry. So many of them went on to notable careers that modern paleontologists have called the group a dream team.

Reed sits on a rock on the left, at ease. To his left, Albert Thomson, American Museum fossil collector and preparator, sits in a bowler hat and holds a butterfly net. Holland, in dark suit and tie, short-brimmed hat pushed back on his head, leans against an outcrop with his arms folded. Next to him, Osborn, in cowboy hat, shirtsleeves, tie, fancy knee-high moccasins and general posture of command, dominates the group. Osborn at that time was Dean of Pure Science at Columbia University and curator of paleontology for the American Museum. Soon he would be named government paleontologist for the U.S. Geological Survey: Marsh's old position exhumed. These positions—combined with his wealth, charisma, and political skills—made him one of the two or three most powerful men in American science.

William Diller Matthew and Walter Granger sit on a rock behind Osborn's left shoulder. Both were just beginning long careers at the American Museum. Matthew developed a statistical understanding of prehistoric animals' diversity and geographic distribution, which eventually brought him into conflict with Osborn, whose approach was always to find a species' most splendid example. Granger would act as lead scientist in the American Museum's headline-grabbing expeditions to the Gobi Desert of Mongolia in the 1920s, where he

Paleontologists from the American Museum of Natural History visited
their Carnegie Museum counterparts at the *Diplodocus* quarry near Sheep
Creek, Wyoming, in the summer of 1899—a gathering of great dinosaur
collectors from the late nineteenth and early twentieth centuries. *Left to
right*, William H. Reed, CMNH collector; Albert Thompson, AMNH fossil
preparator; William J. Holland, CMNH director; Henry Fairfield Osborn,
AMNH curator of vertebrate paleontology; William Diller Matthew,
AMNH paleontologist; Jacob Wortman, CMNH paleontologist, *squatting in
foreground*; Walter Granger, AMNH paleontologist; Richard Swann Lull,
AMNH paleontologist, later curator of vertebrate paleontology at Yale
Peabody Museum. Courtesy of Carnegie Museum of Natural History, Pittsburgh,
Pennsylvania.

discovered the first dinosaur eggs known. Richard Swann Lull stands
to Granger's left. Lull had been one of Osborn's first Ph.D. students
at Columbia and currently held a position at the Massachusetts State
Agricultural College in Amherst. Osborn continued to invite him
on American Museum expeditions. Within a few years Lull moved
to Yale, where in the 1920s he became a principal architect of the
dinosaur mounts still on display at the Peabody Museum and where
he spent a long and distinguished career. At the right, squats Wort-

man, closest to the camera, his left foot near a big sauropod limb. Holland gazes down at Wortman. The sagebrush stretches off behind them all.

"Our success in fact has been simply phenomenal and will not I fear be duplicated," Wortman wrote the third week in August. "I was talking with some of the Amer. Mus. party and they cannot get over the wonderful 'luck' as they call it that has attended our efforts."

Holland, meanwhile, left the bone camp and, with two wagons, the three young men from Pittsburgh, and the cook, headed into the Laramie Range for an idyllic week of camping and feasting on fresh trout, grouse, and sage hens. They visited a sheepherder and admired his dogs and wagon, stopped at two ranches where no one was home but the doors were ajar for any travelers who might need shelter, admired the irrigation ditch and hay meadow at one of the ranches, thrilled to hailstorms, wandered in mountain parks and by willow-shaded streams, and between meals found time to collect an unspecified miscellany for the museum: probably butterflies, fossils, wildflowers, and the skins of animals and birds.

Within a day or two of his return to the bone quarry, however, Holland's personal luck plunged. On the night of Wednesday, August 9, he was attacked by abdominal pain so severe he realized the following day he had to leave camp. Suffering "almost mortal agony" as the wagon jolted over the rocky road, Holland urged more speed on S. Sage, the driver. Sage responded with "a volley of oaths, he informing me that he was doing the driving and he guessed he knew how to do it better than I did," a behavior, Holland later wrote, that he found "simply brutal." He realized that he must have appendicitis, and, apparently without seeing a doctor, caught an eastbound train in Medicine Bow on Friday morning.

In too much pain to stop and file some federal land claims in Cheyenne, as he had planned, he traveled straight through to Pittsburgh. There "three of the most eminent members of the medical profession hereabouts" confirmed his diagnosis. By the following Tuesday, he was well enough to sit up in bed and write, or at least dictate, letters about how angry he was.

He demanded that Wortman fire Sage, as well as a man named Hoggshead, who apparently had worked at the quarry, or hauling

The American Museum and Carnegie Museum crews posed for a second photo nearer camp the same summer. *Standing, left to right*: W. D. Matthew, R. S. Lull, H. F. Osborn, W. J. Holland (*with rifle and cartridge belt*), unknown (*on wagon*), Jacob Wortman (*with pipe*), W. H. Reed (*gesturing to dog*). *Seated, left to right*: Walter Granger, George Mellor, Ira Schallenberger, and Arthur Coggeshall, CMNH preparator and collector. Mellor and Schallenberger were young men from Pittsburgh who accompanied Holland into the field. Courtesy of Carnegie Museum of Natural History, Pittsburgh, Pennsylvania.

bones to the railroad. Hoggshead "turned up at the railroad station on Friday morning to bid me good-by," Holland wrote, "almost too drunk to stand straight. He was full as a tick."

A week later, he was still in bed, his abdomen packed with ice, and under orders to lie perfectly still lest the appendix burst and kill him. Surgery was too dangerous to be anything but a last resort. Lying under ice around the clock, he wrote, had completely numbed his abdomen and allowed him to sympathize with Mother Earth during the ice age, "when she was poulticed with frozen snow from the pole to Long Island."

Work on the dinosaurs, meanwhile, progressed well. Coggeshall and Willie Reed worked on the *Apatosaurus* (that is, the specimen they'd first identified as the "larger Brontosaur") while Wortman and the senior Reed stayed with the *Diplodocus*, an indication of its greater value. Nearly all the neck and back vertebrae down to the base of the tail had turned up, as well as a complete set of shoulder bones—coracoid and scapula for both sides. Coggeshall planned to return to Pittsburgh before Wortman and Reed, in order to set up the fossil-preparation lab for the winter's work. Wortman would hire a man to cut hay for padding the bones in shipment.

On August 24 the doctors operated on Holland. Two days later he was still "hovering between life and death," a museum associate reported to Carnegie. Six days later he was out of danger, though it would be more than a month before he was up and around, and mid-November before he was back to work full time at full vigor. The illness changed him. He would remain a man who was difficult to work for, who loved to speak in public, who wrote most vividly when angry. But mountainous rages like the one that filled him in July when he felt thwarted by Knight seem not to have returned. He kept the appendix as a souvenir, pickled in a jar of alcohol.

Back at Sheep Creek, Wortman, Reed, Willie Reed, Coggeshall, and Paul Miller, a big laborer from Laramie with a feel for bones, proceeded with end-of-the-season chores.

Standard procedure was to saturate the excavated fossils in gum arabic to make them stronger and harder. Then the men pasted tissue paper on the bones to prevent the next layer, plaster-soaked burlap, from sticking—so that it could be more easily removed once back in the lab. If the bones were long, sticks might be laid next to them when the plaster bandages were wrapped around, to act as splints for protection in transport. The fossils in their plaster casts would be numbered according to a code that revealed what they contained and would be photographed in place in the quarry. With lumber hauled out from the railroad, they built stout boxes, lined them with hay, and laid the bones inside. Last, probably with a tripod of poles, block and tackle, and winches, they slung the boxes into the air and loaded them into the bed of a wagon. Boxes of fossils excavated in the turn-of-the-century West may still be seen in the basement of the Carnegie Museum, hay still poking out through the slats. Full of fossil bones, these boxes each weigh perhaps five hundred pounds.

The hard work at the Sheep Creek quarry in the summer of 1899 was done by, *left to right*, laborer Paul Miller, Jacob Wortman, W. H. Reed, and Reed's son, Willie. Courtesy of Carnegie Museum of Natural History, Pittsburgh, Pennsylvania.

A two-horse team could pull a wagon loaded with a ton of goods and a driver at three miles an hour. Depending on the quality of horses and road, the trip to Medicine Bow might have taken more than a day. By September 11, the diggers had taken up all of the *Diplodocus* in sight—from the top of the neck all the way down the backbone to vertebrae above the hips. Only a scrap of the lower jaw had turned up, suggesting it was unlikely they'd ever find a skull. They had also dug out most of a *Stegosaurus* and the *Apatosaurus*. Everything was packed and boxed; twenty-five boxes had already been hauled to the railroad. Z. H. Fales, of Medicine Bow, charged $7.50 per ton to make the trip. Wortman complained to Holland that the price was high, but there was no alternative unless the museum bought a team and wagon of its own. Wortman estimated the total haul would weigh 50,000 pounds—twenty-five tons—and planned to

The Carnegie crew builds bone crates at the end of the 1899 field season at Sheep Creek. *Left to right*, Willie Reed, Jacob Wortman, Paul Miller, W. H. Reed. The bones were wrapped in plaster-soaked burlap, then packed in hay in the crates. Courtesy of Carnegie Museum of Natural History, Pittsburgh, Pennsylvania.

leave anything over that amount in the shack for the winter. Fales's final bill of $92.60, however, indicates that only a little over twelve tons were shipped.

Wortman had also hoped the Union Pacific would allow a freight car to stand on a siding at Medicine Bow for ten days, so the bones could be loaded directly from wagon to boxcar as each new load arrived from the quarry. That proved impossible, however; the bones had to be handled twice. By September 27 Coggeshall was already back in Pittsburgh, and the freight car in Wyoming was loaded and ready to go. Wortman wrote Holland that his plan, before leaving southeast Wyoming for the winter, was to visit the head of Troublesome Creek once more "to collect a Baptanodon or so" and take some photographs. Then he planned to travel back by the Sheep Creek quarry one last time to locate—that is, post the placer claims on—the diggings. Aparently Wortman never got around to the paperwork, however. Albany County and Carbon County record books of those years show no evidence of any claims having been filed on behalf of the Carnegie Museum, of individual paleontologists, of any other museums, or of the University of Wyoming.

During his illness, Holland had fallen behind on his requests for free shipment of the fossils back to Pittsburgh. He wrote appeal after appeal to the railroad presidents in September and October and managed to get the bones shipped free the whole way. The freight car arrived in Pittsburgh in mid-October. Wortman and Reed arrived about the same time. Filled with a new energy from their work in the field, they were uncomfortable when confined to the museum's prep lab. By early November, before Holland was even back at work full time, Wortman was disenchanted with him.

Chapter 9

THE AMPLE
FOSSIL FIELDS

At about 2:15 a.m. on June 2, 1899, three bandits held up a Union Pacific train near Wilcox, the next station east of Como. They stopped the train just after it crossed a bridge over a draw, then blew up the bridge, so that the next train, expected soon, would not be able to come to the first train's aid. The timing allowed the robbers several hours' night riding before anyone could put together a posse, let alone think about where they might have gone.

Or there may have been six bandits; reports conflict. Most of the major facts of the crime—who the bandits were, how many there were, where they went, how much loot they got—were unclear. Long afterward the robbery became the West's most famous, thanks to writer William Goldman and actors Paul Newman and Robert Redford. But at the time, no one seems to have heard of Butch Cassidy or the Sundance Kid. Not the staff of the *Laramie Boomerang*, in any case, which after six weeks decided the culprits must be George Curry and the quarter-Cherokee Roberts brothers, also known as Dave Putty and Bud Nolan.

Later on June 2, a big posse lost the bandits' trail six miles from where it began. That evening, sixteen or eighteen hours after the holdup and eighty air miles away, three men were spotted crossing the North Platte River at Casper. A second posse left from Casper next morning. Twice during the next few days, the bandits ambushed their pursuers. The first time, newspaperman E. T. Payton

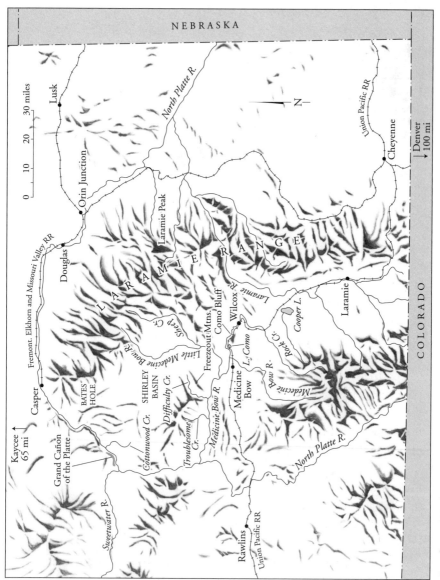

Southeast Wyoming, 1899

of Thermopolis, Wyoming, had his horse shot out from under him. The second time, Converse County Sheriff Joe Hazen was mortally wounded. The bandits were heading north toward the country on the Middle and Red forks of the Powder River in the southern Bighorn Mountains—the Hole-in-the-Wall country. The area had been popular among thieves for fifteen years or more. It was still very far from railroads or police. A third posse started out from Buffalo, 110 miles north of Casper. Bloodhounds were shipped in, but by then the trail was cold. The *Boomerang* published stories on the chase almost daily for two weeks, grabbing at whatever scraps of information floated past:

The Union Pacific officials and others of the officers think that there were only three in the gang who did the work. It was at first supposed that the three men were Hank O'Day, Bob Taylor, and a Mexican, or, if not the Mexican then a gambler named Cavanaugh. But this idea seems to have been abandoned and George Curry and the Roberts brothers charged with the crime.

Whoever they were, it seems plausible the bandits were in fact surprised by the number and persistence of their pursuers, as Goldman's script indicated. At some points that month as many as two hundred possemen joined the chase, at least according to *Boomerang* reports. And they were well paid. Pursuers could apply for reimbursement as soon as they left the field. The railroad paid up promptly, at five dollars a day. Laborers and cowboys at the time earned about a dollar a day. The bandits, if they did feel pressed, were feeling the new power of the Union Pacific Railroad.

Under the leadership of Edward H. Harriman, the Union Pacific in 1899 was emerging from years of receivership with money to spend. Like many other railroads and businesses across America, it had overextended and it then went bankrupt when revenues plummeted in the Depression of 1893. Private and public plans to rescue the railroad failed. Late in 1897 the U.S. government, the railroad's biggest creditor, finally foreclosed, Congress having failed to come up with a refinance plan. Harriman emerged as lead player in a consortium that bought the railroad at the foreclosure sale. He brought with him the resources and credit of the Illinois Central Railroad, of which he was finance manager. He also brought with him a bold, simple, and expensive plan: invest enormous amounts of money at the right time, and you'll eventually make enormous profits.

When railroads in the 1880s had overexpanded, the resulting competition forced them all to keep rates low. That, in turn, meant there was never enough money to maintain tracks and trains in good repair. But the Union Pacific, protected from its creditors in the 1890s during five years of receivership, did not have to pay interest on its debt, and could therefore apply more money to maintenance and improvements. Harriman's insight was to understand that this fairly comfortable status quo was not enough. A physically sound railroad still would need to be overhauled if it were to profit fully from booming new demand. The way to make more money was to reduce the cost per ton of transport. This meant longer trains and heavier locomotives, which in turn demanded straighter track, lower grades, and stronger bridges. Late in 1898, the executive committee of the Union Pacific approved a $9 million construction campaign. Work began in the spring of 1899.

Only now, as Harriman passed fifty, was he making the bold moves that brought him power and attention on a national scale. He was a shy and brilliant man, born in 1848—the same year as Holland and Reed. He rose through the ranks of New York finance selling securities on Wall Street and did not begin managing railroads until he was thirty-five.

But in the spring of 1899, wanting a break from hard work he decided that a trip to Alaska would be both relaxing and invigorating. A private vacation was not enough, however. He ordered a special train, had a steamboat refitted, and invited twenty-five scientists to accompany him and his family. He began planning the trip only in March; the train left New York on May 23 and passed through Wyoming unnoticed—at least by the *Boomerang*—on its way to Seattle. Fifty passengers boarded the steamer there, including the twenty-five scientists from a dozen fields, three artists, two photographers, two stenographers, a chaplain, a physician and his assistant, Harriman's immediate family, close relatives, a friend, and servants. Together with sixty-five officers and crew, and eleven hunters, packers, and camp hands, the human population on the steamer *George W. Elder* totaled 126.

Probably the best known of the scientific party were the naturalist-writers John Muir and John Burroughs; probably the most brilliant was the geologist G. K. Gilbert, and probably the best known to posterity was the photographer Edward Curtis, who later gained wide fame for his nostalgic photos of American Indians. Also along was the writer, editor, and conservationist George Bird Grinnell, who had first gone West with Marsh to collect fossils in 1870 and had briefly gone into the sheep business with Reed in 1883.

Many of the scientists were recruited through connections with the elite Cosmos Club in Washington, D.C. Their credentials were impeccable, and included affiliations with the U.S. Geological Survey, the biological survey of the U.S. Department of Agriculture, the U.S. National Museum, the Field Columbia Museum, the California Academy of Sciences, Harvard, Yale, and Cornell. Only two of the nation's newer universities were represented: the University of Washington and the University of South Dakota. They divided themselves into committees and heard a lecture nearly every night of the two-month voyage. They saw themselves as a "floating university."

The voyagers hugged the coast all the way to Port Clarence on the Bering Strait, with a stop at Plover Bay on the Siberian side. Harriman shot a bear on Kodiak Island. The scientists were absorbed by land, ice, sea, and weather. During the boat's numerous stops, they collected adventures and specimens, including totem poles, grave monuments, and other ceremonial artwork from an unoccupied Indian village north of Cape Fox, in southeast Alaska.

They returned to Seattle July 31. The *Boomerang* did notice the special train this time on its return through Laramie, but incorrectly assumed Harriman was aboard. In fact he took a different route east, inspecting rival railroads across northern Idaho and Montana.

The same month Harriman began planning his Alaska trip, Wilbur Knight in Laramie and E. L. Lomax in Omaha, chief of the Union Pacific's passenger department, were already planning a bigger, less luxurious scientific expedition closer to home. Knight's close work with Lomax on the text and illustrations for the UP advertis-

Wilbur C. Knight, professor of geology at the University of Wyoming, who organized the Fossil Fields Expedition for the Union Pacific Railroad in the summer of 1899. Courtesy of S. H. Knight Collection, American Heritage Center, University of Wyoming.

ing brochure "Some of Wyoming's Vertebrate Fossils" had ruffled some feathers among the university trustees. Such UP brochures were common at the time; many featured sights travelers could look forward to as they rode the railroad, or scenes of destinations as far away as Hawaii.

But, from its opening sentences, "Some of Wyoming's Vertebrate Fossils" trumpets the discovery of a specific fossil, then goes on to imply that any college, museum, or university willing to expend a modest amount of effort in Wyoming's "fossil fields" might reasonably expect a similar return on the labor: "After already bequeathing to geological science the rarest of fossil treasures, the State is again writing a strange chapter in the world's geological history by unearthing the petrified bones of the most colossal animal ever taken from the earth's strata." The brochure goes on to repeat the hyperbolic dimensions reported first in the *St. Louis Globe-Democrat* the previous November, then in the *New York Post* and the *New York Journal and Advertiser*: a monster 130 feet long, 35 feet high at the hips, 25 feet at the shoulders, an animal that in life weighed 120,000 pounds.

Reed wins high praise as discoverer. Knight wins similar praise in the brochure for having assembled a collection of Jurassic vertebrate fossils second only to Marsh's collection at Yale. Wyoming itself, of course, deserves most of the credit, Knight notes, as "no State or Territory in the United States, and indeed, no equal area in the world, has done so much for the theory of evolution and comparative anatomy as this State."

Finally, Knight, in quotes that run several pages, gets around to mentioning the brochure's target audience. So far, he notes, work in Wyoming's fossil fields has been done "only by institutions having ample means, or by private parties especially interested in the work." As a result, most colleges and universities are unaware of these fossil resources unless they happen to review the scientific publications, and local students and average citizens have never seen the fossils because they are spirited off to large museums in the East.

"The fields are ample for all who wish to avail themselves of the opportunity to collect and create museums as large, if not larger than any that have been built up during the last quarter of a century," Knight says in the brochure. Though most universities and colleges did not have collections or museums to match the ones at Yale, Harvard, and Princeton—or even the ones at the universities of Kansas, Nebraska, Wyoming, and California—many hoped to gather similar collections, and Knight knew enough to tap that desire for science and adventure. He goes on to note that the work is as exciting as gold hunting, that any geologist will have his skills further honed by field work, and that camp life itself produces unpredictable events which will only be recalled with pleasure afterwards.

The brochure includes a good map of Wyoming, with the Union Pacific route prominently marked. It also includes eleven photos and ten drawings of fossils from the collections at Yale, the University of Wyoming, and the American Museum of Natural History—all collected in Wyoming. In the spring of 1899 the railroad sent hundreds of copies of the brochure to colleges and universities around the nation, along with an invitation to pay the railroad fare for any scientists and assistants wishing to explore Wyoming's fossil fields for the summer. Then, as now, the principal cost of such an expedition was getting there.

The *Wall Street Journal*, already a Harriman admirer, missed the point that fossil hunting was the trip's main object but thoroughly understood the business advantages of appearing liberal and enlightened: "Union Pacific Progresses," the paper noted on its April 4 front page:

The offer of the Union Pacific to give free transportation to scientists to investigate the mineral wealth of Wyoming is attracting widespread attention. A circular letter of invitation is to be issued immediately, which shows that the Union Pacific is wide awake to its opportunities and progressive in its methods of taking advantage of them. It also indicates a liberal policy where the interests of its communities are involved. The advantages of this unique scheme are many, not the least being that of advertising. If Wyoming has mineral resources, [as the] Union Pacific evidently thinks it has, the scientists will soon discover them and a rush must inevitably follow. In any case the attention of settlers and investors will be attracted to a section of the country that has wide opportunities and which needs to be more densely populated.

At this time, when he was expanding the railroad's power and wealth, Harriman understood that it would be in the company's interest to appear magnanimous. His invitation to join him on the Alaska expedition went out privately to the elite of the scientific world. Knight's and Lomax's far more public invitation was taken up by the scientific middle class. Nearly four times as many scientists would end up touring Wyoming by wagon that summer as accompanied Harriman on the *Elder* up the Alaskan coast.

While the scientists were planning their summer trips, an influx of railroad construction workers was about to change the social fabric of southern Wyoming in a hurry, and some of its prominent citizens were nervous. The *Boomerang* predicted March 24 that there would soon be two thousand laborers moving dirt and laying track between Laramie and Medicine Bow. The population of Laramie at the time was only about eight thousand at best; the total population of all the towns strung along the UP across southern Wyoming was only four times that much. The railroad was also building new roundhouses,

Railroad construction workers swarmed to southeast Wyoming in the summer of 1899 when the Union Pacific rebuilt and straightened its tracks. Here, horse-drawn scrapers move dirt for a fill at the site of the Dale Creek trestle. Courtesy of Grace Raymond Hebard Collection, American Heritage Center, University of Wyoming.

section houses, and depots. It was boom time again—a boom such as southern Wyoming had not seen since the tracks were laid the first time, thirty years before.

Newspaper reports sound familiar to anyone who lived through Wyoming booms in later decades. The *Boomerang* that summer carried stories of the death of two graders, who, after being paid one Saturday, mixed wood alcohol with their moonshine; of fights and mayhem crashing through Laramie saloons, streets, and a restaurant in the wake of "a big grader" named Monroe Tarrant; of the theft near Sheep Creek of a revolver and surveying equipment from two prospectors by a seventeen-year-old boy who was driving the wagon they rented; of a strong-armed robbery at night in downtown Laramie; and of a fatal shooting during a drunken spree early on a Sunday morning in Rawlins, as a dance was letting out. Five men were arrested for the shooting. "The prisoners . . . are strangers here, having lately come to work on the new round house," the *Boomerang* noted. News of distant troubles, too, ran in the Laramie paper, from a bloody trolley strike in Cleveland to guerrilla war against American troops in the Philippines, to approaching war between the British and the Boers in South Africa. And from time to time, locally, hoboes or just working men trying to save the railroad fare were mangled or killed trying to hop freights.

Violence even touched the university campus. On the June morning after baccalaureate services, the juniors woke to find a four-by-seven-foot flag in the sophomore colors—purple and white—floating from the campus's main pole. A junior named Ross Moudy climbed the pole to haul it down. But sophomores attacked him "with sticks with sharp nails in the ends and beat Moudy about the legs until he was forced to come down and a physician was called to dress his wounds. It was found that he had fifteen or twenty deep wounds on the legs . . . one of the most serious affairs that has occurred at the university for some time," the *Boomerang* reported.

Stephen Downey, the local prosecutor as well as a lawyer in private practice, appears to have had a good deal of criminal work that summer. He decided it was time for the town to protect itself. On August 1 he tried to persuade the Albany County commissioners to invest in an arsenal sufficient to arm the sheriff and any deputies he might need for his assistance. "Calling attention to the presence within easy reach of this city of 1,800 graders, an army recruited from all classes and conditions of men and brought together from all points of the compass, Col. Downey predicted that, driven by discharge or otherwise to face the stern question of where they were to get something to eat, there are going to be many robberies between now and the time the snow flies," the *Boomerang* reported.

It would be simple enough, Downey said, for five or six bandits to ride into town, loot a bank and ride out again, and no one would be able to stop them. A certain Jack Martin, who had served on "that fatal and futile ride" chasing train robbers north of Casper, reported that the bandits' guns could shoot twice as far as their pursuers', Downey told the commission. Clearly, he went on, it was the duty of the commission to provide a store of arms and ammunition at the courthouse enough to arm "any posse sufficiently to cope with a body of desperate men in the field." Noncommittal, the board agreed to take the matter under advisement.

Downey's graver fears proved groundless, though he was right in predicting danger when the weather changed. In October the onset of snow and cold weather convinced the leaders among sixty Italian graders from Chicago that it was time to quit. They demanded railroad passes from Hutton Junction, west of Laramie, back to Chicago. Deputy sheriffs arrived, cracked one man on the head, and threatened the rest with violence and death. The workers were subdued, and the "ringleaders," as the paper called them, accepted free passes to Laramie.

But along with crime and labor jitters, the boom brought high hopes. Big gold nuggets from a mine in southern Albany County excited one "expert" enough to predict that the mine would be able to produce $1 million a year for twenty years—as soon as capital could be raised for fifteen steam shovels. Knight and a university colleague, chemistry professor Edwin Slosson, wrote papers for scientific publications and industry bulletins that drew the attention of investors from out of state. Knight also appears to have acted as an unofficial information center for anyone interested in mining and mineral development. Oil and gold prospects were prominent in the news. But the professor's time and resources were limited. A number of prospectors and their financial backers appear to have complained bitterly that Wyoming had no state geologist or state mining bureau to meet their needs.

In June Knight had been busy, taking mining students on field trips, protecting university bone quarries, planning the Union Pacific field trip, and, most likely, fielding queries about mineral prospects from all directions. By the third week in June he was ill with the measles, and seeing no one. He recovered in July. On July 19 eighty scientists from universities as far apart as Berkeley, California, and Chapel Hill, North Carolina, descended on Laramie in a convivial invasion. They walked through town from the depot to the campus.

About eighty geologists, mostly professors from colleges and universities as far apart as Berkeley, California, and Chapel Hill, North Carolina, were lured to Laramie in the summer of 1899 by the Union Pacific's offer of free railroad fare to anyone wishing to explore Wyoming's fossil fields. A number of them gathered on the steps of Old Main at the University of Wyoming before the field trip began. From *Wyoming Geological Association Guidebook*, 1949, p. 8; used by permission.

In their broad-brimmed hats and field clothes, one little girl complained, they looked just like anyone else: a parade of professors and not a single silk hat among them.

What followed was more like a traveling summer camp than a field trip with scientific objectives. Most of the scientists arrived on the mid-morning train from Omaha. As soon as they got to the campus, they met to establish a mini-government. How they must have loved the parliamentary forms! First they elected a pair of temporary officers, who appointed a committee on nominations, which presented a slate of permanent officers for approval by the group. Knight was elected president and director of the expedition. Three secretaries were elected, also "referees" for each of the academic divisions represented. Osborn of the American Museum was elected referee for vertebrate paleontology, though he appears to have stopped in Laramie only briefly.

That evening a public reception in the university auditorium drew two hundred people from the town, most of them women curious about the influx of professional men. Speech followed speech. Downey welcomed the scientists, and thanked Union Pacific executives E. L. Lomax and A. Darlow, who were present. The newspaper described Holland's lengthy remarks as "witty, patriotic and altogether eloquent." Most of the scientists slept in the university armory that night because the tents were a day late in arriving. As latecomers straggled in the next day, the men organized themselves into messes and loaded their groceries and gear. With a few exceptions—paleontologist Charles Schuchert of the Smithsonian's U.S. National Museum and a couple of journalists—the professional men were all academics. Even Holland and the three young men he arrived with were listed as representing the Western University of Pennsylvania instead of the Carnegie Museum. They camped a second night on campus, building fires on the gravel drives and boiling big pots of coffee. More slept in tents than the night before. During the night some students shot off a cannon, and when that failed to get much of a reaction, they wheeled it closer to the tents and shot it off again.

The next morning, Friday, July 21, the first wagons rolled west out of Laramie around 9:30, with stragglers not underway until three in the afternoon. They had organized themselves into eleven messes of six to ten scientists each. Each mess was attached to a chuck wagon with a cook, supplemented usually by a lighter spring wagon and a saddle horse or two. Men from the same college usually traveled together in the same mess. In addition to the cook, each mess included one or two drivers, who would have acted also as horse wranglers and camp attendants. Cooks and drivers were all local men, the horses and wagons were all rented locally, and most of the provisions had been bought in local stores. Laramie's merchants, watching the wagons leave, must have hoped the expedition would become an annual event.

By lunchtime of the second day out they reached Cooper Creek, west of Laramie. After eating, they armed themselves with sacks and digging tools and hurried across the little valley to a red sandstone

The Fossil Fields Expedition on the march near Cooper Creek, west of Laramie. Courtesy Wyoming State Archives.

Fossil Fields Expedition members, some in pith helmets, in camp on Rock Creek, northwest of Laramie. Courtesy Wyoming State Archives.

bluff half a mile away, eager for a chance at fossils at last. The Cretaceous Fox Hills formation yielded fossil deciduous leaves and coral, and the party stayed another night to allow for a day of wildflower picking, a snowball fight, and visits to nearby mines. By Monday evening, July 24, the expedition had camped at Rock Creek, back on the U.P. line, where they stayed two days to work another Fox Hills outcrop and the shales of the Cretaceous Fort Pierre formation.

Still, they had only found fossil palms, pines, seashells, and coral, when nearly all the scientists were eager for stuff with backbones. By Thursday evening, July 27, the wagons reached Como Bluff: dinosaur fields at last. They expected little in the way of bones, as the Marsh and Cope crews in the 1870s and 1880s had so thoroughly exploited the area. The interest was primarily historical and geological. And the *Boomerang*, for once, got the geology exactly right: Como Bluff, it reported, "is on a huge anticlinal fold whose summit has been removed by erosion and the different layers of rock left exposed."

They found that new bones had weathered out. Geologists from Gustavus Adolphus College of Saint Peter, Minnesota, spotted a big dinosaur, and two professors stayed behind to dig further. Two professors from Baylor University in Waco, Texas, had what the *Boomerang* hoped would be equal luck. Finally, Knight himself found "one of those large saurians"—initially unidentifiable. At Como station, some expedition members boarded a train for home while others took the opportunity to ship fossils, a hoard already of thirty forty-pound boxes, back to their universities. Friday most continued northward toward the Freezeouts, stopping to visit with the American Museum paleontologists digging near the Nine Mile Crossing of the Little Medicine Bow River.

Osborn had by then been there a week, having ducked quickly through Laramie while the main expedition was first gathering. The professors stopped with the New Yorkers at the quarry site long enough to photograph bones already jacketed in plaster. But the visit appears to have been short. Osborn and his staff—Granger, Matthew, and Lull—were cool to "that great crowd of curiosity and bone hunters" with its "miscellaneous scrambling for Dinosaurs," as Osborn termed it. Inside those plaster jackets were the bones of a promising *Apatosaurus*. The New York paleontologists would have known all the other likely prospects in the vicinity and would have been happy to see the big group move on.

Heavy snows had made for a well-watered summer in the hills, short cliffs, and creek bottoms of the country north of Medicine Bow. In July it continued to rain frequently, and the bluestem grass was so thick in the little valleys it could have been cut for hay. Mosquitoes swarmed. By August 1, a Tuesday, the wagons had reached the Freezeouts. Here the professors were hoping for the best results, for here it was that Reed had found the colossal dinosaur described in the railroad brochure they'd all received with their invitations. The scramble began in earnest.

"Men could be seen everywhere," the *Boomerang* reported, "struggling down the hill to the wagons with a piece of a great femur or a long rib bone. . .. No complete animals were unearthed. It was due to the fact that excavation was not made, for the remainder of the bones could not have been dug out in time. Nearly everybody was content with securing one or two fine bones for souvenirs, for they were not prepared for taking up the entire remains of an animal." A similar exhilaration must have swept through the scientists on the Harriman expedition when they appropriated the totem poles at Cape Fox, and must have swept Reed, too, as he looted the grebes' nests in the cattails at Lake Como, twenty years before. In the face of such abundance, what could one do but take?

Three more days' travel to the north brought the wagons to a campsite on Cottonwood Creek. From there it was just an hour's walk to the rim of the Grand Cañon of the Platte, known today as Fremont Canyon. The scientists could hear the roar of the water from a mile away. Many had brought cameras, and this was expected to be the most scenic spot of the trip. From the edge, granite walls dropped straight down five hundred feet in some places to boulder-frothed rapids in a channel only fifty feet wide, shrouded in near-permanent shadow. Pieces of driftwood stranded on the canyon walls showed the water in spring sometimes reached a depth of one hundred feet, though by late July the river would have been much lower. The canyon ran eight miles along the northward-flowing Platte, from the confluence of the Platte and Sweetwater Rivers down to a spot near the head of present-day Alcova Reservoir, where the stream widened out again and the walls lowered. The men took five hundred photographs. The canyon was so majestic that Knight was convinced it was "determined in the near future to be one of the famous resorts of the Rocky Mountains."

The scientists spent four days camped at Cottonwood Creek, exploring up and down the main canyon, prospecting for dinosaurs in the nearby Morrison beds, and bathing in the hot springs further downstream. It was the most time the expedition spent in any one place—and the fact that the men spent so long in a spot with more Romantic than scientific appeal sends a clear message about their priorities. They knew they were on the trip of a lifetime, and now, camp-hardened and exalted, they were determined to enjoy it.

On Monday, August 7, about half the party started back for Medicine Bow. The rest headed eastward from the river through Bates Hole, an area rimmed with badlands of Tertiary rock eroded into fantastic forms and potentially rich in mammal fossils. Soon most of the rest also headed back, leaving only one mess to continue east and south inside the arc of the Laramie Range, stopping to climb Laramie Peak before returning finally to the tracks at Rock Creek station.

The effort deserves to be called an expedition more for its size than for its goals or achievements. The Army surveys of western railroad routes in the 1850s and the government surveys mapping the West in the 1870s never numbered more than a few dozen men per party. Scarcity of water and grass in arid country made traveling in large groups impractical. Yet the Fossil Fields Expedition was huge, especially the first week—twenty-three tents, eighteen heavy wagons and many more lighter ones, two dozen cooks and drivers, and seventy-five or eighty scientists representing two museums, two state geological surveys, and at least twenty-seven colleges.

Unlike the Army and government surveys of earlier decades, however, and unlike the parties digging all summer in the Freezeouts and north of Como, the expedition was out to solve no specific topographic, geographic, geological, or paleontological questions. They did little or no prospecting for commercially valuable minerals. The country they traversed was well known. And, unlike the

Army surveys, the government surveys, or Harriman's expedition to Alaska, they had no plans or financing to publish findings or reports.

Ten years later, however, the Union Pacific did report on the endeavor. The railroad's passenger department in 1909 published a second booklet on Wyoming fossils and geology, titled "Fossil Discoveries in Wyoming" on its cover and "The Fossil Fields of Wyoming" on its title page. Newspaper reports, of which the *Boomerang's* were the most detailed, had run at the time of the expedition, and Knight had written an article which was published, with photographs, sixteen months later in the *National Geographic*. But the Union Pacific's 1909 brochure was the first attempt to gather any specific results under a single cover. Mostly the articles describe the topography and geology, with brief accounts of the route. Between the lines, the expedition's true virtues emerge. These men were not explorers, not research scientists, not even museum curators and collectors hunting new material for display. Primarily, they were teachers, and nearly all were from the wet and vegetated parts of the nation—parts where rocks are obscured from view by soil, forests, pastures, and cities. The earth's structure is much easier to read in arid climates, as easy sometimes as a book to one who has learned the alphabet.

Expedition member George L. Collie of Beloit College in Wisconsin described the topography of central Wyoming: "The hard rocks have not been reduced to the general levels of the country, but stand up as rampart-like walls which sweep about as they pass from anticline to syncline, in great curves, forming the most conspicuous topography to be seen on the Piedmont plains. No vegetation obscures them; there is nothing in this country of magnificent distances to hide the sweep of these natural ramparts as they wind back and forth across the country."

To an eye accustomed to trees wherever it looks, arid landscapes are thrillingly naked. Prof. J. A. Yates, professor of natural sciences at Ottawa University in eastern Kansas, could hardly contain himself:

The most sublime sight I ever beheld was to stand on the edge of this cañon [of the Platte] and see the tilted strata, the Archaean [i.e., Precambrian] to the left and below, and look to the right and see the great number of strata through the series to the characteristic red beds of the Triassic and above these the Jurassic. The scene impresses one in a way that words meagerly describe, but the feeling that comes here is an epitome of Nature's records inviting one to read the history of these formations, see the principles of structural geology here unfolded, and conceive the great length of time necessary for their consummation.

Uplift, faulting, erosion, and deposition are much easier to understand when you can see their records plainly. Many of these men, as new to the West as they were to camp life, must have been stricken by how ideal a classroom for the teaching of geology these great, treeless landscapes would be. Stephen Downey, in his welcoming speech to the scientists before they set out, proposed that the University of Wyoming establish a permanent summer school in geology and paleontology. By the 1920s that idea had taken hold and began spreading as more and more eastern and midwestern colleges and universities established summer field camps in Wyoming. Most have continued down to the present, and thousands of students have benefited. Wyoming is still an open book.

Chapter 10

NOBLE CHAMPIONS
OF TRUTH

Andrew Carnegie had much larger matters than dinosaurs on his mind in the fall of 1899. He was convinced his longtime partner and manager, Henry Clay Frick, had cheated him. By October the two were locked in a struggle that each week became more intense. The summer before, Frick and another partner had brought to Carnegie a pair of speculators—William H. Moore and John W. "Bet-a-Million" Gates—offering to buy out the newly reorganized Carnegie Steel Company. They proved unable to raise the capital, however, and when the deal disintegrated, Carnegie discovered Frick and the other partner had been promised what amounted to a kickback—$2.5 million in stock, each, in the new company that would have been formed out of the old. Furious, Carnegie refused to return to Frick and the other man the partners' shares of $170,000 each had put up towards the Carnegie Steel Company's pot of earnest money on the deal. Instead, he declared Frick's and the other partner's contributions forfeit and kept the money.

Frick retaliated with an attempt to raise the price the Frick Coke Company would charge to Carnegie Steel for coke, the refined coal crucial to making steel. Carnegie owned 58.5 percent and Frick 6 percent of both companies, but Frick had brought the coke interests with him when he came into the firm in 1882 and always felt more proprietary toward them than toward the company's other interests. Carnegie refused to pay the higher price. In December, from the distance of New York, Carnegie maneuvered Frick into resigning as board chairman, relieving him of his managerial duties.

Dinosaurs, meanwhile, appear to have gone out of Carnegie's mind almost completely. He sent Holland a note of sympathy when he was recovering from his appendectomy, but otherwise Holland received no answer to any of the letters he sent Carnegie in the summer and fall. "You know I am a creature which feeds upon encouragement, but starves on neglect," Holland wrote on New Year's Day 1900, "and your failure to reply to two or three recent letters of mine, which no doubt was due to the pressure of business cares, was just a little discouraging."

Carnegie's and Frick's struggles were not yet public; Holland had no idea how pressing those business cares were. The plans and hopes Holland went on to detail for the museum must have seemed small change to Carnegie—perhaps delightfully minor compared to the mutual death grip in which he and his old ally, turned foe, were holding each other. Holland reported that he had recovered from his illness. The museum would do well, he went on, to buttress its own strengths, rather than try to duplicate others'. The museum could be great both scientifically and "as an instrument for popular instruction" in ways other museums hadn't yet achieved. The trustees backed his ideas. Carnegie's support and recommendations, Holland added, would help a great deal.

He suggested they meet and talk over matters further. To his surprise, Carnegie appeared in Pittsburgh just a week later and sent word to Holland that he had arrived. In fact, the old Scot had come out for a final showdown with Frick. Their famous last meeting took place in Frick's office January 8, 1900. The ostensible subject was coke prices; the real subject was power.

When Frick threatened to get a court order preventing him from delivering coke at the low price demanded by Carnegie's newly stacked board, Carnegie threatened to invoke an old agreement allowing him to buy out Frick's interests at a price far below their true value. Frick jumped from his chair. "For years I have been convinced that there is not an honest bone in your body. Now I know that you are a god damned thief. We will have a judge and a jury of Allegheny County decide what you are to pay me." Then Frick, fists clenched, advanced around his desk toward Carnegie, and Carnegie retreated out the office door. Frick slammed it behind him. They never spoke again.

Details of Holland and Carnegie's meeting two days later have not survived. But Carnegie about then began urging Holland to quit his chancellorship of the Western University of Pennsylvania and assume the museum directorship full time. Rising need for the university's services had meant fast growth during the previous nine years, yet Holland was steadily frustrated that the wealthy people in one of America's wealthiest cities could come up with no more than they did to support their university. Carnegie himself was on the board but never gave any money. Within a year Holland would yield to Carnegie's pressure, and resign the university post. He always remembered it as a decision made in a moment of weakness.

Wortman, meanwhile, had begun to feel that Holland was more hot air than scientist. His letters from the field during the *Diplodocus* summer of 1899 had been professional and efficient. But in November, writing back to Osborn, his former boss, in New York, Wortman passed along a joke Holland often told about a Scotsman at dinner declining his hostess's offer of baked beans. He found them a "'verry windy vegetable.' What applies to the baked beans," Wortman noted, "may sometimes also be said of the remarks of our good Doctor—they are a trifle windy." But, if Holland was not expert in paleontology or the earth sciences, at least he was spending money for a good purpose. "It looks very much as if they mean business," Wortman reported, "and will endeavor to establish a first class department. Their knowledge of the subject however is very crude at present but they are willing to listen to wise suggestions."

"Crude," of course, refers to Holland's understanding; the "wise suggestions" were Wortman's own. Most likely he continued making them; most likely Holland's resentment at being told what to do grew as his health returned. At the same time, Wortman's true intellectual interests lay elsewhere. More than anything else he longed for a chance to study and describe for science the huge collection of Tertiary fossils at Yale that Marsh and his fieldworkers had amassed beginning thirty years before. At Marsh's death they were still largely undescribed. Wortman, with his thorough knowledge of Tertiary fossils from sites as far flung as New Mexico, Oregon, Utah, and Nebraska, was just the man to do it, and he knew it. He hoped Osborn would support his effort by allowing him to inspect the American Museum's Tertiary collection for comparison and by advising him on publication. He was much more interested in the big mammals of the Tertiary than he was in dinosaurs. Matters came to a head January 30, 1900, when Wortman brought Holland the proofs of an article that was about to appear in *Science*.

Wortman's article contained "one or two expressions which I thought were likely to offend members of his own force and friends of the institution," Holland wrote museum Trustee C. C. Mellor the next day. "I courteously suggested to him a modification of the paragraph in the interests of peace." At Holland's suggestions, Wortman "became very angry; told me to 'go to hell' covered me with uncomplimentary epithets." The account is similar to Holland's version of his quarrel with Sage, the wagon driver, the previous August: calm, critical words spark an unexpected explosion. Wortman "acted altogether in so ungentlemanly a manner that I felt compelled then and there to demand his resignation."

That was that, Holland must have thought. But it wasn't. Wortman's article in *Science* was published February 2. Purporting to describe the "New Department of Vertebrate Paleontology at the Carnegie Museum," Wortman announced the museum's plans to build "a general collection illustrative of extinct life from its very earliest period." He detailed the previous summer's discoveries at Sheep Creek, then went on to suggest that the most interesting bones might belong not to a *Diplodocus*, but to a *Barosaurus*, another sauropod with an extremely long neck only scantily known at the time from a few tail bones in Marsh's collection.

This question—whether the bones were part of a *Diplodocus*, as Holland had announced loudly in Pittsburgh and New York newspapers the previous summer and fall, or part of a *Barosaurus*—appears to have been the true heart of Wortman and Holland's dispute. Wortman had already resigned and headed for a new job at Yale when a New York newspaper published a garbled version of the breakup a few days later: "The disagreement arose because one of them, it is said, maintained that certain bones dug from the fossil beds of Wyoming were those of the Brontosaurus, while the other insisted they belonged to the Dipsodocus Magnificus."

Carnegie clipped the article and sent it along to Holland with a note meant to be funny. "Onward Ye Braves," the old Scot began. "I like to see great men have great issues for their wars.

This one goes to the root of matters, away deep down. fight it out to the end. Death or Victory.

all hail noble champions of truth. Never mind if you get the world laughing at you—that's nothing—Do or Die

AC

His scorn is palpable, "away deep down."

Within a few days, Frick filed suit, and Carnegie filed a response. For the first time, the true size of their profits was available to the press in public documents. The newspapers, naturally, treated their readers to the bonanza. And the one effort from which Carnegie had hoped to gain public affection and support—his effort to find big dinosaurs—was opening him up to ridicule. His scientists looked like squabbling nits. Holland would have understood the implication: when Carnegie scientists looked foolish, Carnegie looked like a bigger fool than any of them. And Holland had allowed it to happen.

Chapter 11

PATAGONIA

olland filled Wortman's job in nine days with a candidate at
the peak of one of the most remarkable careers in vertebrate
paleontology. John Bell Hatcher, not yet forty, already was recognized as one of the best field collectors of the time. He had collected
widely, for Marsh in the West and for Princeton on three expeditions
to Patagonia for which he himself provided all of the planning and
raised much of the money. Like Wortman, Hatcher was never entirely comfortable with the institutions he worked for, but he understood that he needed their support if he was to be able to ask and
answer the scientific questions that consumed him. He was starting
to ask questions that would dominate earth science for most of the
twentieth century.

Hatcher was born in Illinois and grew up in Iowa, worked in coal
mines as a teenager to finance his education, and ended up at Yale,
where he caught Marsh's attention. In 1884 he began a nine-year
stint collecting for the great paleontologist throughout the West.
From his first summer in the quarries, Hatcher showed little patience
with such older collectors as Sternberg, whose work he considered
careless, and, at the same time, began using methods that improved
the science. He took the novel approach of locating the bones on a
grid map of the quarry before taking them out of the ground. Even
with so much added care, his bone production was prodigious. In
1886 he sent carload after carload of the bones and big skulls of

John Bell Hatcher came to work for the Carnegie Museum in 1900, after three years in Patagonia collecting Tertiary mammal fossils for Princeton. Photo first published in the *American Geologist* 35, no. 3 (March 1905): 130.

Brontotherium—a horned, rhinolike mammal of the Tertiary, eight feet high at the shoulder—from Nebraska back to New Haven. But the hard work flattened him. Only twenty-five years old, he spent weeks that winter in the hospital, with rheumatism so painful he could hardly move. The pattern of work and collapse would repeat in later years.

The fact that he'd paid for his education with his own labor set him apart from the wealthy professors and museum directors he would work for the rest of his life. The fact that he had a formal education at all set him apart from older collectors like Reed, who were self-taught. He was part of a new, professional middle class in American science, and the scientific establishment sometimes had a hard time making room for his talents.

In 1888 he traveled to the Cretaceous badlands in Montana where the Judith River flows into the Missouri, an area Cope had worked before. Hatcher found something Cope had missed, however: enough parts of several huge, horned dinosaur skulls for Marsh to understand roughly what they were and create a new name for them, *Ceratops*. Fragments had been known before and described by both Cope and Marsh, but as yet they were poorly understood. The following year, in eastern Wyoming, Hatcher was guided to a spot on Buck Creek, thirty-five miles north of Lusk. Over the next four years he excavated thirty-one horned dinosaur skulls and several skeletons from the place, along with fossil turtles, fish, birds, mammals, and other dinosaurs. Down to the present, while skulls of the rhino-like ceratopsians have proved relatively common in certain Cretaceous rock formations, skeletons are extremely rare. *Triceratops,* with its three horns and a large frill stretching back over its shoulders, remains the most familiar. Wyoming schoolchildren voted it the state dinosaur in 1994.

Marsh, who admired the small and rare as much as the large and stupendous, also during these years pressed Hatcher for fossils of the tiny mammals that scurried beneath the ceratopsians' elephant feet. Hatcher enlisted the help of the insect world, a shovel, and a flour sifter:

The small mammals are pretty generally distributed but are never abundant, and on account of their small size are seen with difficulty. They will be most frequently found in what are locally known as "blow outs" [wind-eroded pockets in the sandstone] and are almost always associated with garpike scales and teeth, and teeth and bones of other fish, crocodiles, lizards and small dinosaurs. These remains are frequently so abundant in "blow outs" as to easily attract attention, and when such a place is found careful search will almost always be rewarded by the discovery of a few jaws and teeth of mammals. In such places the ant hills, which in this region are quite numerous, should be carefully inspected as they will almost always yield a goodly number of mammal teeth. It is well to be provided with a small flour sifter with which to sift the sand contained in these ant hills, thus freeing it of the finer materials and subjecting the coarser material remaining in the sieve to a thorough inspection for mammals. By this method the writer has frequently secured from 200 to 300 teeth and jaws from one ant hill. In localities where these ants have not yet established themselves, but where mammals are found to be fairly abundant it is well to bring a few shovels full of sand with ants from other ant hills which are sure to be found in the vicinity, and plant them on the mammal locality. They will at once establish new colonies and, if visited in succeeding years, will be found to have done efficient service in collecting mammal teeth and other small fossils, together with small gravels, all used in the construction of their future homes. As an instance of this, I will mention that when spending two days in this region in 1893, I introduced a colony of ants in a mammal locality, and on revisiting the same place last season [1895] I secured in a short time from the exterior of this one hill 33 mammal teeth.

Despite Hatcher's skill, Marsh wouldn't let him publish. In this, Hatcher was treated no differently from Marsh's many other assistants. But it meant that, as long as Hatcher was working for Marsh, he would never be known as a scientist. In 1893, when Marsh was losing his government position and financing, Hatcher went to Princeton to work for William Berryman Scott, a friend of Cope's and a close friend and Princeton classmate of Osborn's.

Hatcher published two articles in the 1890s on the horned dinosaurs and the rocks in which they were found. In the first, he criticizes Marsh only by implication, but in the second he attacks his former employer head on. He goes after Marsh for being not so much inaccurate as self-aggrandizing. Marsh himself had published an article on the horned dinosaurs in 1889 in which he designated as the "Ceratops beds" a wide area that had yielded the fossils, without specifying the precise location and nature of the fossil-bearing rocks. The claim offended Hatcher's sense of detail and order, and we can feel his impatience behind his response:

If we accept literally Marsh's statement that the Ceratops beds have been traced for eight hundred miles along the eastern flank of the Rocky Mountains, it will be necessary to suppose that he includes in the Ceratops beds not only the beds in Converse [now Niobrara] Co[unty], Wyoming, but also the *Bison beds* at Denver, and the *Judith River beds* on the upper Missouri. These are very widely separated localities, and no attempt has ever been made to trace the continuity of the strata from the one to the other, nor is it at all probable that such an attempt would meet with success. Professor Marsh did in the autumn of 1889 spend nearly two days in the Converse Co. locality, and again in 1891 he spent one full day in the same locality; but his time was occupied in visiting a few of the localities in which dinosaur skulls and skeletons and Laramie mammals had been found. No time was taken to determine the upper and lower limits of the beds or to trace the outcrops of the strata. After his visit in 1889 when he spent nearly two days with our party in the Converse Co. locality, he took the train for Denver, and in the company of Mr. George L. Cannon of that city, he spent one-half day examining the *Bison beds* . . . This constitutes Professor Marsh's *field work* in the *Ceratops beds*. In a total of three and one-half days field work he seems to have found sufficient time to "carefully explore" the geological deposits of the Ceratops beds and to trace them for "eight hundred miles along the eastern flank of the Rocky Mountains," besides making numerous other observations of scientific interest.

Marsh in 1896 still commanded enormous prestige. Most scientists, especially young ones with careers to build, wouldn't have been so blunt. But Hatcher, as a friend wrote shortly after his death, "hated pretense of any sort." Marsh simply hadn't explored all the Ceratops beds, carefully or not, and someone needed to set the record straight.

Hatcher's scientific articles began appearing as soon as he left the Yale job, and flowed faster and faster from his pen right up until his death. He was a good sedimentary geologist as well as a paleontologist; the publications show as much affection for rock strata as they do for the fossils themselves. Just as astronomers at the turn of the last century engaged in a coordinated, international effort to map the stars, and botanists on all fronts worked hard to name and usefully classify the plants, geologists found they, too, had great amounts of descriptive work to do before they could proceed on to analysis and experiment.

Fossils were fascinating in themselves and for what they revealed about the evolution of life. But they were also extremely useful—the only reliable tool—for determining whether rock layers hundreds or thousands of miles apart had been laid down at the same time. Scientists as yet had no good way to date past geologic events. They were getting better, however, at understanding their sequence—the layers' temporal relationships with each other. Sorting the Tertiary from the Cretaceous, the Cretaceous from the Jurassic is still no easy task: layers get turned upside down or sideways, or are eroded away altogether; catastrophes move blocks of rock tens or hundreds of miles from their origins.

But as more became known, even more could be known, and faster. The best geologists knew they had big questions to get to: How do mountains rise? Why do they so often rise along the edges of continents? Are oceans and continents permanent? How is it that nearly identical animals could have evolved simultaneously half a world apart, while oddly different animals evolved relatively nearby? To ask the best questions you first had to understand the sequence of rock layers worldwide.

As new information came in, often it didn't fit with earlier discoveries. Hatcher, in his first article, complains that dinosaur fossils found by one scientist turned up in beds another described as Tertiary, that is, decidedly post-dinosaur. "Regions affording such contradictory evidences should be thoroughly examined," he wrote, "and, where possible, their actual stratigraphical relations should be determined. Results thus attained there might be sufficient to harmonize observations now in apparent opposition." That is, when in doubt, get back out there and look at the rocks.

Some new and disturbing claims, far out of harmony with the emerging European and North American consensus on geological time, may already have been in Hatcher's mind at this point. Two Argentines, Florentino Ameghino and his younger brother Carlos Ameghino, had been working together since 1887 on the remarkable mammals that had left their remains in the Tertiary rocks of Patagonia. From his base in a bookshop in La Plata, near Buenos Aires, Florentino wrote articles on the fossils Carlos shipped home from the far southern reaches of the nation. Patagonia then (and still) was emptier of human habitation even than Wyoming, and travel was far more difficult. Carlos became an expert wilderness traveler and mule packer, as well as a fossil collector of great range and care. Florentino was the more volatile of the two, accomplishing large volumes of work, yet subject to holding long grudges. The grudge-holding was perhaps connected with a chauvinistic nationalism which colored his thinking about evolution. He came to believe that big mammals had emerged far earlier in South America than anywhere else. He claimed the fossils showed them to have lived all the way back in the Cretaceous, contemporary with dinosaurs. He further believed that all the rest of the mammals in the world, including humans, were descended from these big, supposedly early, South American marsupials.

Hatcher and others found these claims hard to believe:

The discoveries announced by the Ameghinos were of such an interesting nature, and many of the conclusions drawn from them were so extraordinary and so frequently opposed to conclusions believed to be well established by observed facts in the northern hemisphere, that paleontologists everywhere agreed as to the desirability of bringing together a representative collection of fossil vertebrates and invertebrates from that region for study and comparison with collections from North America and Europe, and of making, so far as possible, a detailed study of that region, sufficient at least to determine the exact sequence and relations of the different [stratigraphic] horizons, and of securing all data possible which might prove of use in correlating South American rocks with those of North America and Europe.

The problem was that the Ameghinos' mammals were so different from the ones found in North America and Europe that they could not be used to correlate the strata of the northern and southern hemispheres. The only way to settle the matter was to go there. Hatcher, a bundle of curiosity and ambition, knew just the man for the job:

Since no one else seemed ready to undertake this work, early in the autumn of 1895 the writer decided to attempt it in behalf of the department of paleontology of Princeton University. Dr. W. B. Scott heartily approved of the plan when it was presented to him, and freely gave his energy and influence towards its accomplishment, while from several friends and alumni of the institution came most essential financial assistance. So that by March 1, 1896, I was able to sail with Mr. O. A. Peterson on our first expedition.

And what an expedition it was! Hatcher and his brother-in-law,

Olaf August Peterson, traveled with five horses, two of them pulling a cumbersome cart with two solid wheels. They first explored up the east-flowing Rio Gallegos, just north of the Strait of Magellan; at 51 30' south latitude they were 650 miles further south from the equator than New York is north of it. Coming back down the north bank of the river, they hit their first big fossil bonanza. A second materialized at a cape on the north side of the river's mouth—Cabo Buen Tiempo or, as Hatcher anglicized it, Cape Fairweather. Fossils were exposed all along the Patagonian east coast.

Some of the most dramatic collecting came at a place called Corriguen Aike, where big tides moved over a flat two miles wide or more. The two men would follow the receding tide, pulling up the skulls and skeletons that emerged, then hurry to carry them all ashore before the tide covered them up again. By the end of October—spring in Patagonia—they had collected four tons of fossils and stored them in wool sheds near the mouth of the Gallegos. By good luck, a schooner happened past, and they were able to ship the fossils to Punta Arenas (Hatcher called it "Sandy Point"), the Chilean port on the Strait of Magellan, where the bones could be transferred to a steamer bound for New York.

Leaving Peterson to continue collecting on the coast, Hatcher rode overland to see to the shipments at Punta Arenas and, he hoped, to collect the first mail from home in nearly nine months. Once, after stopping to rest and let the horse graze, he let the reins fall to the ground, as one would do in the American West. The horse's hoofs got tangled, however, and when Hatcher stooped to free them, the startled horse jerked its head up but the reins snubbed it short. Just as Hatcher was beginning to stand, down came the horse's head again, and the bit cut a gash in Hatcher's scalp so large "as to loosen the latter over a considerable area," he wrote later.

Bleeding badly, he continued onward. Twenty-four hours later he reached a sheep ranch. But the "surly Italian" cook, Hatcher wrote, declined to admit the filthy, feverish, exhausted, blood-soaked stranger. Wanting only to wash up and eat, Hatcher finally decided that "this 'dago' should not stand between me and my needs." Making himself "quite at home, after the manner of the frontiersman," he pushed into the kitchen, helped himself to bread and mutton, got the stove fire going, warmed himself, washed, made coffee, and left the cook his card, with a note to the foreman promising to pay on his return trip. The same mix of drive, competence, honor, Anglo chauvinism, and a kind of exhausted desperation fueled Hatcher throughout his three years in Patagonia.

He made three trips; the longest was the first, from March 1896 through mid July 1897. In November 1897 he headed south again and stayed a year. After just a month at home with his wife and children, Hatcher returned a third time in December 1898 for a final nine-month trip. Peterson accompanied him on the first and third trips; on the second trip he was accompanied by A. E. Colburn, a taxidermist. While Hatcher was away on the first trip, his three-year-old son died in November 1896; Hatcher was so far from news that he didn't even hear of the child's death until May of 1897, when he got back to the coast.

They covered territory south of Carlos Ameghino's explorations. Most of the fossils they excavated were of the Santa Cruz formation, named for typical beds near the mouth of the Santa Cruz River on Patagonia's eastern coast. Florentino Ameghino had declared the formation as Eocene in age—from early in the Tertiary, a time now understood to be about fifty million years ago. The Santacrucian fossils are now regarded as Miocene, much more recent, only twenty million years old—and Hatcher's instincts, too, told him that they must be much more recent than Ameghino had claimed. The Eocene date for the Santacrucian layer meant Ameghino had to push the date of a layer below them—a layer he dubbed *Pyrotherium* for its most characteristic large mammal—back even further. All the way back, in fact, to the Cretaceous: Florentino Ameghino had convinced himself scraps of dinosaur bone had been found in the same horizon.

After exploring Santacrucian beds from the coast to the foothills of the Andes on his first trip, Hatcher became obsessed on his second and third trips with finding *Pyrotherium* beds. Once and for all, he hoped, he could test the Cretaceous claim. But Florentino Ameghino never published specific locations of the fossils when he described them. Hatcher had to hunt and hope, relying on his instincts. This led him, on part of the second trip, to travel often with just a saddle horse and a pack horse. His meals were irregular, and shelter was hard to find. He slept without a tent in bad weather and lived on deer and meadowlarks. A snowfall on April 29, 1898, as the southern winter approached, led him to return to camp a final time, and he and Colburn agreed it was time to give up hunting the *Pyrotherium* beds and head for the coast. The weather worsened, and then Hatcher's hard life caught up with him. His knees, then his elbows, began to swell with rheumatism. After the first day he could not walk; they had to make camp.

As the snow piled and swirled outside their tent, Colburn nursed Hatcher through six painful weeks of illness. Finally, with the aid of crutches Colburn made, Hatcher was able to walk again, and they made their way to the coast. Colburn by then was eager for home, and so Hatcher left him with the fossils at the port of Santa Cruz to catch a steamer for New York. Hatcher himself, however, felt the need for more collecting and headed back south along the coast for Gallegos, 125 miles away. Again he encountered brutal weather. Rain turning to snow kept him two nights at the first sheep ranch. Then the muddy pampas froze, and his unshod, tired horses had a terrible time on the snow and iced-over puddles. Still crippled, he found mounting and dismounting extremely painful. The last ninety-five miles took five days; thoughts of mail from home were the only thing that kept him going.

Finally, Hatcher landed in a cold, dirty hotel room in Gallegos, where he had to pay an exorbitant $5 per night. The journey down to Gallegos, one chronicler noted, showed "a persistence that in retrospect seems more maniacal than brave." By now he was out of money. His landlord in Gallegos lent him $50, and a sympathetic sea captain gave him passage to Punta Arenas, where he found a steamship agent willing to take a check on a Princeton bank for the fare back to New York. On the long, warm voyage home, he at last had time to recuperate. He was only back in Princeton a month before he headed south a third and final time, with Peterson again. No record survives of the feelings of Anna Peterson Hatcher toward these long absences of her husband and her brother. She was at home with five children and then, after the death of their son, with four.

Hatcher's final trip lasted nine months. This time, he and Peterson were accompanied by young Barnum Brown, Osborn's rising star from the American Museum of Natural History in New York. Though he seems to have resented Brown's appointment to the expedition, Hatcher was glad to have an extra hand to drive the wagon (by now they were using a light-wheeled North American wagon with springs, which they'd brought south with them), as it gave him more time to prospect for fossils. They revisited the country around Lake Pueyrredon, at the base of the Andes, but still were unable to find *Pyrotherium* beds, though Hatcher found some strata he regarded as Cretaceous.

The *Pyrotherium* beds Carlos Ameghino had worked lay around Lake Colhue-Huapi, farther north than any of the places Hatcher visited. Hatcher apparently made at least one attempt to find out from the Ameghinos where the beds lay, so that he could inspect them and come to his own conclusions. In the southern winter of 1898, he met Carlos in the port of Santa Cruz, and the two agreed they would go together into the field in the coming spring. But Carlos, once he got back to La Plata, changed his mind and wrote to Hatcher not to wait for him. Florentino Ameghino may not have wanted his brother to share information with the North American.

Hatcher's own personality was part of the problem as well. Scott, Hatcher's boss at Princeton, had a subsequent acquaintance with the elder Ameghino which showed that, if approached collegially and cordially, the Argentine was willing to share information. But Hatcher was a man, like so many others of his culture and time, who would call the Italian ranch cook a "dago" and who anglicized Patagonian place names blithely and routinely, as though to do so improved them.

He published scientific and popular articles as soon as he could after his return from each of the trips. They were thorough and clear—but on certain points they were later proven incorrect. Hatcher got the stratigraphic sequences mixed, though he got the ages about right. The Ameghinos got the ages wrong, though Carlos, at least, had the sequences right—and Hatcher unjustly accused him of getting them wrong. The matter was cleared up from an entirely different quarter. Hatcher turned over all the invertebrate marine fossils he'd found—fossil oysters, most notably—to another Princeton paleontologist, Arnold Edward Ortmann. Ortmann published as promptly as Hatcher. The oysters proved to be the Rosetta Stone to the whole situation. They were very similar to fossils well known in the northern hemisphere. In Patagonia they turned up just one layer below, and in some cases intermingling with, the widespread Santacrucian layers. That fact enabled Ortmann to anchor the entire Santacrucian sequence in the late Oligocene and early Miocene, where it belonged.

Eventually, collaboration trumped wrong-headedness and distrust: The Ameghinos brought the fossils to world attention; their claims drew Hatcher south to see for himself. Despite his difficulties with the Ameghinos, he gathered enough fossils to allow new judgments by other scientists, and good evidence drove out previously erroneous conclusions.

After returning from his last trip, Hatcher persuaded Scott that reports on the expeditions should be published in a series, as a cohesive whole, not just in scattered articles. Scott had good connections, and a patron was quickly found: the banker J. P. Morgan. The volumes began appearing in 1903, with Hatcher's vivid 209-page narrative published first. Scott eventually had to take over the editing and much of the writing of the subsequent volumes. While doing so, he traveled to Argentina to compare the Argentine national collection and the Ameghinos' collection with the fossils Hatcher had collected for Princeton. Florentino Ameghino gave Scott complete access, and relations between the men were cordial. Yet even though Scott always admired Ameghino and publicly praised him, it was Scott's close work with the big vertebrates—and Ortmann's on the oysters—that eventually annihilated the Ameghino claims. Florentino Ameghino became a national hero for his work and theories and died in 1911, while Carlos Ameghino lived on into the 1930s, almost completely unknown.

Hatcher, meanwhile, was directing his thoughts further south.

Chapter 12

NO MORE REEDS, NO
MORE WORTMANS

Shortly after Morgan's pledge to support publication of the Princeton reports was secure, Hatcher resigned. He may have come into conflict with Scott over which of the Patagonian fossils he would get to write up and which would fall to Barnum Brown at the American Museum. A document survives giving Brown "first privilege of description" of any fossils he might find. Brown and Osborn had signed it late in 1898, before the expedition began, but Hatcher angrily had refused. In his resignation letter to Scott dated November 17, 1899, Hatcher notes that he would have left earlier but didn't want to jeopardize the financing of the reports. Then he adds that he had hoped "some joint action by yourself and Prof. Osborn might be taken to explain matters and make the action unnecessary." Now, with the money pledged, "there is nothing left to me except either to submit to treatment which I believe I have not merited or resign."

Hatcher had a wife and four children, and his expeditions to Patagonia had almost certainly stripped him of any extra money he may have set by. He told Scott he had no other employment possibilities. Scott, more of a diplomat than either Holland or Osborn, must have persuaded Hatcher to stay on at least until he could line up something else.

Also at the end of 1899, Peterson left Princeton to take a job at the Carnegie Museum, where Holland was continuing to expand the staff. Holland offered him $125 a month, a salary approaching but still below Reed's. Osborn had also had his eye on Peterson when he got back from Patagonia, but Osborn wrote Wortman in Pittsburgh to assure him that the Carnegie Museum's success at landing another veteran collector caused no hard feelings. Thus when Wortman was fired at the end of January 1900, lines of communication between the Carnegie Museum and Princeton paleontology operations were clearly already open and well used. The curatorship of vertebrate paleontology at the Carnegie museum must have looked like the best job in the business—top pay at a rich museum with big plans for expansion and a fast-rising scientific reputation.

When Wortman was fired, Holland contacted Hatcher and Scott almost immediately. By Feb. 7, 1900—just nine days after Wortman's blow-up—Holland was in Princeton, having a long conversation with Hatcher and Scott. That night Holland and Hatcher took the train back to Pittsburgh. Hatcher brought with him a career's worth of letters of recommendation, including testimonials from Marsh; from James Dwight Dana, the eminent Yale geologist and editor of the *American Journal of Science;* and from Scott, who praised Hatcher as "one of the most skillful and successful collectors now living." Hatcher wrote Holland on February 12 that he expected to be on the job by March 2 or 3 and that he had already ordered a dozen geology picks and would send the bill to the Department of Vertebrate Paleontology, Carnegie Museum.

Within two weeks of Hatcher's arrival, he and Holland worked out a three-pronged plan for bone prospecting in Wyoming in the coming summer. Peterson would prospect for Tertiary mammals primarily in the Eocene Bridger formation of southwestern Wyoming—where Cope and Marsh had had some of their earliest successes thirty years before. Reed and Hatcher would go back to Camp Carnegie, as it was now being called, at Sheep Creek, and continue digging Jurassic dinosaur bones where the *Diplodocus* had turned up. Once Hatcher felt the work was going well, he would drive northeast through the Laramie Range to the Cretaceous rocks north of Lusk where he'd found the horned dinosaur skulls and tiny mammal jaws and teeth for Marsh ten years earlier. He was confident he could find many more.

Holland passed this information on to Carnegie, warning him

not to talk about the plans should he encounter any of his "scientific friends." The Field Columbian Museum in Chicago and the American Museum in New York were "red hot after both the Bridger and the Laramie [horned dinosaur] fossils," he reminded Carnegie. He continued, "We have the three ablest bone sharks, so far as work in the field is concerned, in our employment, and the other museums would be very apt, when they found out we were moving in a certain direction, to follow in our footsteps."

Problems during that spring came, not from other museums, however, but from one of the "bone sharks" with ideas of his own. Reed had been hired in the spring of 1899 at $1,800 per year—fully 50 percent more than he'd been making at the University of Wyoming. His initial hire had come under the implication that he would be leading the Carnegie operation to spectacular finds. Soon, however, Holland brought in Wortman—younger than Reed by eight years and far better educated—and placed the younger man in charge in the field. The two got on well that first season, and Reed was willing to learn from Wortman some newer fossil-collecting techniques. By the time Wortman was fired, having worked with Reed for five months in the fossil lab after their first field summer, his opinion of Reed had fallen. Writing to Osborn when he was fresh out of a job and angry about it, Wortman noted that Peterson and Coggeshall would also be happy to leave if any American Museum jobs were open. Reed, Wortman added, "will probably leave in the spring but this would not be a very serious loss since he isn't worth much anyway."

This year, the bone sharks of the Carnegie expedition would be well provided for, all around. Hatcher, coming off his underequipped Patagonian expeditions, now requested the funds from Holland to do everything right. He figured Reed would need two assistants at Sheep Creek, plus a team to pull a wagon and a big dirt scraper. Peterson would need one assistant, a team and wagon to bring back fossils from the Bridger formation, plus a saddle horse, as they would be covering more ground. Hatcher himself would need an assistant and a team, plus an extra man and team at the end of the season to haul the big *Triceratops* skulls, likely to weigh a ton each.

Perhaps eager to prove that he was still valuable to the operation, Reed remembered five skulls of big Tertiary mammals he'd cached way back in 1885 near a place called Picket Lake in the Red Desert, northwest of Rawlins. This must have sounded to Hatcher and Holland like a find that could be picked up easily. Peterson and Reed took the train west from Pittsburgh the first week in April. Hatcher followed a few days later but stopped in Omaha to spend time with Anna and "the bairn"—probably the youngest of their four children—and also to visit with Union Pacific officials about another season of free passage for scientists and free freight for bones. Hatcher arrived in Laramie April 10. Snow was too heavy to allow work to begin, so he stayed with Reed and his family for ten days, probably calling on Knight and inspecting the university fossil collection, as well.

Peterson, meanwhile, seems to have gone on West. Reed met him at Rawlins on April 20, and they took off for the Red Desert to find the skulls. Hatcher left for Sheep Creek a day or two later. Hatcher expected Reed and Peterson back with the skulls by the time a week had gone by. After two weeks he was so eager to get over to the *Triceratops* country that he decided to wait no longer, and hired a man to drive the team and wagon across to Lusk. Hatcher himself took a train all the way down to Cañon City, Colorado, one hundred miles south of Denver, to inspect a Jurassic dinosaur quarry there that Marsh's collectors had worked in the 1870s, then traveled back north to Lusk.

There, a letter from Reed finally caught up with him. The older man confessed he'd found no bones at all at Picket Lake. The lake had turned up, but the skulls in the badlands nearby proved elusive. So Reed had decided to continue prospecting further north—"the field north of the ratle snake hills," he called it. He was sure he could find bones there, he wrote, "for I was colecting bones in the north country whil the place at the picket lake locality I found accidentaly while hunting horses." He noted that if Hatcher needed money before heading off for the Triceratops beds, Mrs. Reed could lend him some. The weather had been bad, roads worse, and Reed had suffered from "a touch of rheumatism" in his hips and back, but he could still walk and work.

Peterson, too, wrote Hatcher, noting Reed's claim that he had

had such good luck years before at the more northern site that he had "'picked up half a bushel of small skulls in half an hour.'" Peterson sounded disgusted, Hatcher reported back to Holland, "from being hauled all over the country for nothing." Hatcher himself had lost nearly all faith in Reed:

I fear the entire story is fiction . . . Now you know as well as I do that <u>Mr. Reed did not</u> tell us the truth regarding his great finds where he said he made his cache. It never costs a man anything to tell the truth & one falsehood often costs much both in time & money. To put it frankly between you and I I am afraid Mr. Reed's veracity is not to be depended upon & for my part I do not like to be needlessly fooled or tricked by one of our own men who should have our own interests at heart.

This trip marked a turning point. Hatcher never would trust Reed again. On Reed's behalf, it should be kept in mind that fifteen years is a long time for any memory to remain reliable and that the country they were prospecting was enormous. High hopes and promises had gotten Reed in trouble in the past, but in the past, when one prospect had not materialized, he'd been able to turn up another of equal value—the Sheep Creek *Diplodocus* is the prime example. This time, however, his anxiety over the slipping confidence of his colleagues led Reed to promise too much. Hatcher was willing to keep Reed on—though unwilling to leave him in charge of a quarry. But when Reed's next report indicated that nothing much had turned up at the northern site, either, and that Peterson had taken the wagon and headed by himself for Tertiary formations on the Henry's Fork of the Green River, far to the southwest, Hatcher knew it was time to do something.

On May 18, he collapsed the three-pronged plan into two segments. Peterson would come in from Tertiary prospecting to supervise Reed at Sheep Creek—an expensive proposition, as both were highly paid, but a necessary one in Hatcher's mind. Hatcher would stay where he was, looking for horned dinosaurs. Reed would probably have to lay off one or both of the assistants he'd hired; that decision would be up to Peterson once he got to Sheep Creek, Hatcher decided.

"I trust you will not take this in an offended spirit," he wrote to

Reed, "as it is done as we think in the best interest of yourself & the
museum & with the approval of Director Holland. I think a year's
work in the field with Mr. Peterson will be of great value to you & I
sincerely trust that your relations will be pleasant." Hatcher enclosed
the letter to Reed in a letter to Peterson, informing Peterson also of
the new plan. The tactic made the two men's niches in the new hierarchy perfectly clear. Peterson rode into the Sheep Creek camp on
Sunday morning, May 27, and handed Reed the letter from Hatcher.

Reed boiled over. The country around the camp and the *Diplodocus* quarry is wide and dry, flanked by hills on the horizon to the
north and east. Wide enough, and dry enough, that even in May it
would quickly have sucked up and muted any words Reed said, there
being no cliffs for echoes. Reed chose not to write Hatcher back but
instead to write Holland, who'd hired him, and with whom Reed felt
he still had a relationship:

You will remember that you told me that you were my friend, and if ever
I had any reason to think I was unjustly treated, to come to you for advice,
and you would deal justly with me. Well, now the injustice has come, and
like a thunderbolt.

He could not obey and keep his self-respect, Reed wrote. When
Hatcher had stayed in his house that snowy April—"and a more
pleasant gentleman I never met"—he had promised Reed full charge
of the Jurassic quarry and had agreed to Reed's hiring a helper, a
man who had quit another job to go dig dinosaurs. Reed had also
hired his son Willie again, and Mrs. Reed had rented their house in
town for six months and come out to the camp to cook for the crew
for no pay at all. "And this is my reward!" Reed wrote Holland. "Oh,
why did you ever come to Laramie? I was fairly contented there, and
would give my last year's salary to be back." Reed promised, "One
thing sure, I will never strike a pick in the ground under Mr.
Peterson—not that he is not a good man and a good collector." And
until matters could be worked out, he would keep prospecting for
bones and would not "trespass on Museum grounds" at the quarry.
Holland forwarded Reed's letter to Hatcher. To Reed himself, he
remained as silent as the sky.

Hatcher left the horned dinosaur country and headed back over to Medicine Bow June 4, ostensibly to persuade Reed to relent but in fact only to tie up the loose ends of his departure. Hatcher was glad, he wrote Holland, to have an excuse to be rid of the older man:

I am very familiar with the work he did for Marsh & looked over carefully that which he did in Laramie & frankly I do not want such work done for us, for in many instances it simply means the distruction [sic], rather than the preservation of rare and important material & we must have the very best work possible for we are paying our collectors the highest wages of any Museum in the country.

In a quiet room they found in Medicine Bow, Hatcher professed toward Reed "the kindliest feelings" and said he was not there to quarrel but to persuade Reed to return to work—but only under Peterson. Reed replied he did not consider himself subject to Hatcher's authority at all: he was responsible to Holland, as Holland had hired him long before Hatcher came on the job. Their discussion continued nearly an hour. Reed at first denied he had quit and demanded Hatcher should fire him, if he believed himself to be Reed's boss. Hatcher countered that a person who considered himself an employee wouldn't have refused to "trespass on Museum grounds," as Reed had written to Holland. At that point Reed appears to have relented. The next morning they drove together in the wagon out to Sheep Creek to pick up the bills and accounts. Their conversation, or lack of it, over those treeless miles can only be imagined.

At Camp Carnegie, Reed turned over the paperwork, then asked for a formal statement from Hatcher for the terms under which he was leaving. Hatcher wrote it out: Reed's refusal in the letter to Holland ever to work under Peterson was a direct repudiation of Hatcher's instructions; further, Reed had said he would never come on "Museum grounds." Hatcher noted that he had reiterated both of these positions when queried in person. Therefore, Hatcher wrote, he could consider Reed's "withdrawal" as dating from his letter to Holland, and wouldn't hold him to the contractual requirement that he give two months' notice before quitting.

With Reed's pay freed up, Hatcher wrote Holland afterwards, they could hire three more men, "any one of which will be of greater service to us than was Mr. Reed, & if we are careful we can get men who are truthful also." Holland congratulated Hatcher on his tact. Reed's departure was a just victory for the museum and for the educated classes: "Reed is afflicted as unfortunately so many partially educated and so-called 'self-made' men are apt to be, with an exaggerated idea of their importance and the value of their attainments. He is one of a long list of those who have fallen victim to the megacephalic disease."

Holland may also have been depressed by what felt like Carnegie's continued neglect that spring. Writing to congratulate his boss in late March on the "rare wisdom" of his decision to settle the lawsuit with Frick, Holland also noted he was sorry to hear, from another source, of Carnegie's disappointment over the size of the *Diplodocus*. Reminding Carnegie that he'd sent him the same news the previous August, at Skibo, Holland went on to recap all the events of the spring and summer of 1899—the land-law minuet with the university, the allegations of Knight's skulking quarry destruction, and finally the end of any dealings with the university trustees by mutual consent. But most important was what had turned up, after all:

Meanwhile our party found and has dug up a skeleton of an even bigger dinosaur, actually the most perfect and the biggest skeleton of its kind ever found, bigger and more perfect than the biggest skeleton ever secured by Marsh or any other paleontologist, and this skeleton we are now working upon and getting ready for exhibition. Besides, we have found other skeletons which cast into the shade "the biggest show on earth" about which the New York newspapers made such a show last spring.

That Reed's pride should outlast his skills and usefulness now made him disposable, in Holland's eyes. It was important that the next person they hire have "a literary course of training in a liberal institution. Such men are far less apt to be conceited and troublesome . . . Docility, willingness, the disposition of the soldier, who obeys orders, are needed in an institution of this character as much as in the army or the navy." This was a veiled warning to Hatcher, too—a man who tended to have ideas of his own. Hierarchy must be maintained:

Men who imagine the holding of a minor position in an institution of this sort entitles them to assume the airs and to talk in the tone of men who have attained to scientific distinction and are leaders in the world of thought, are to be avoided. We have had unfortunate experiences here in the case of one or two men whom we have had with us in the past, who, having published a page or two of their exceedingly insignificant observation, have suddenly blossomed out in their own estimation as full-fledged scientists, capable of criticising the opinions of everybody from a Kelvin to a Cope. We wish no more bumptious, verdant youths in the list of our employes but intelligent, capable, willing men possessed of good common sense. I know such men are somewhat scarce, but I look to you to secure in your department men of such character if you can find them. We wish no more Reeds, and no more Wortmans.

Holland had Wortman's article in *Science* in mind when he wrote of "exceedingly insignificant observation." It can only have been Reed who, though approaching his fifty-second birthday, was guilty of "bumptious, verdant" youth.

Chapter 13

SOUTHERN DREAMS

Within months of his final return from South America, Hatch-er again was longing for the high latitudes. He had already written up the geography and geology he'd found in Patagonia, turning out a scattering of publications during each visit home. The earlier ones he wrote to counter the Ameghinos' theories as fast as he could. Later ones are clearer, and elegantly explain his thoughts on the succeeding processes of subsidence, uplift, and glaciation of the plains and mountains of that empty part of the world. By the time he came to Pittsburgh in March of 1900, Hatcher must already have begun the book-length narrative that would become the first volume of the Princeton reports on the Patagonia expeditions. The writings display his skills as explorer, geographer, geologist, and eth-nologist. Still, above all, he was a vertebrate paleontologist and, like any good scientist, was led by earlier investigations to questions that were more profound. His thinking moved up, from a continental to a global scale:

While there is a striking and universal dissimilarity between this fauna [of Tertiary Patagonia] and that of the northern hemisphere, on the other hand there are many apparently close resemblances between the extinct Patagonian fauna and the recent Australian fauna. The same is also true, though in a more restricted sense, of this fauna and that of South Africa. The explanation of these similarities and dissimilarities in the faunas of the various regions can be best explained by assuming that they indicate in the one case a direct relationship and in the other a totally distinct origin for each. The relations apparently existing between this Patagonian fauna and certain forms now living in Australia and Africa would be the natural result of former land connections between these regions, perhaps by way of an Antarctic continent permitting of an intermigration of species. The dissimilarity in the North American fauna would indicate a long period of isolation of the two Americas, continuing until comparatively recent tertiary times.

Three years in Patagonia had made it quite clear to Hatcher that marsupial mammals were abundant there in the Tertiary, though the opossums alone remained extant in South America. Nearly all the marsupial species in the world now reside only in Australia, Tasmania, or New Guinea. "Former land connections . . . perhaps by way of an Antarctic continent" seemed logical. There was just one way to test the hypothesis, however, and that was to go there and look.

Being Hatcher, he already had a plan. William S. Libbey, professor of physical geography at Princeton, was an arctic explorer himself and well connected in the small, often competitive international circle of polar explorers and scientists. Libbey had made the great Scottish zoologist and polar explorer William S. Bruce aware of Hatcher's interests. By the spring of 1900, Bruce had grown tired of waiting for a position on the British expedition to Antarctica then being planned by the Royal Geographic Society, the Royal Society, and the Royal Navy, and had announced plans for one of his own.

Hatcher hoped to go along with Bruce and look for fossils on the Antarctic Peninsula. Bigger than Italy, it curls northward from the main body of the continent toward Tierra del Fuego. On May 1, 1900, Hatcher was waiting in Medicine Bow—for Reed to show up from the Red Desert with his five promised skulls, and for the snow to melt, so he could travel back out to Sheep Creek for a second week of *Diplodocus* digging. It must have seemed as good a time as any to spring the Antarctic plan on Holland, who, after all, would have to find the money to pay for it:

Now my plan is just this. During three years & more spent in Patagonia & Tierra del Fuego I have been greatly impressed with the great thickness of the late Tertiary rocks that form the great plains of both the mainland and the Island. However these rocks increase in thickness toward the S.E. in which direction they also dip. [That is, the parallel rock layers slope toward the southeast.] On the extreme S.E. of Tierra del Fuego they show a considerable development. As you know the question of a former land connection between S. America and the supposed Antarctic continent is a question which if definitely proven in the affirmative would go far toward . . .the solution of many problems relating to the present and past geographical distribution of animal and vegetable life throughout the world & other biological questions as well. Considering the great thickness of these deposits & their gentle Southeasterly dip I believe that they will be found on the land mass or masses that now constitute Antarctica & that they will be found in places to contain remains of that rich mammalian fauna which so abundantly characterize them in Patagonia. To find only a single one of these mammal skeletons entomed [sic] in the rocks of Antarctica would be ample proof of a former land connection which is only one of the several problems that I should propose to attack in connection with the work.

The existence of an Antarctic continent had been speculated about for centuries but known for only eighty years. Its geographical extent and boundaries were still poorly understood; its geology was unexamined. A Belgian expedition had been the first to winter there when it was caught in the ice in 1897–98, and a British expedition sponsored by a magazine publisher had been the first to winter on land in 1899. The so-called Heroic Age of Antarctic exploration was just beginning. The coming decade would see British, Scottish, French, German, and Swedish expeditions, some privately financed and others paid for with government help. A party under the Norwegian Roald Amundsen, traveling with dogsleds, finally became the first to reach the South Pole in December 1911; a party under the Royal Navy officer Robert Falcon Scott, hauling sleds by hand, reached the pole a month later but perished on the return route. Bruce's effort became the Scottish National Antarctica Expedition of 1902–04. His plans included exploration of the east coast of Graham Land on the Antarctic Peninsula, roughly where Hatcher hoped the Tertiary rock formations that he had seen dipping down under the sea at the southeastern tip of Tierra del Fuego would emerge again, bearing some of the same fossils.

Hatcher hoped to take one or two assistants and sail to South America in the autumn, finish up some fossil prospecting there, then join Bruce's expedition in the spring of 1901. Punta Arenas on the Strait of Magellan would have been a logical port for a rendezvous. Hatcher wrote Holland that he hoped to have two summers to explore "the sedimentary rocks to the right & left of our base of supplies" on Graham Land

in the hope of finding fossil bearing rocks & in making collections along this & other lines of Natural History. I believe our efforts would be entirely successful although in some points & especially the chief one we might meet with failure. At any rate I lay the proposition before you, for you to decide as Director of the Carnegie Museum, whether that institution wishes or is willing to take up this work which I had planned for Princeton had I remained there. If successful you can easily see the great advantages of our having done the work.

He asked Holland to keep the whole idea quiet and out of the papers, to talk it over only with the museum trustees or Carnegie himself, and to reply promptly. In a postscript he needled Holland a little more, noting that he might be able to go as one of Bruce's regular scientific staff, but that, in that case, the results of his work would go to the expedition and not to the Carnegie Museum. There the matter rested for some time. Hatcher brought it up only once more that spring, in a letter to Holland from Lusk. But more immediate problems were pressing him closely: Reed's departure and replacement, reopening an old Marsh dinosaur quarry in the Jurassic rocks near Cañon City, Colorado, and a largely unsuccessful season of prospecting for horned dinosaurs in the Cretaceous beds north of Lusk.

Only John Garrett of Baltimore, a Princeton alumnus and one of Hatcher's patrons for the Patagonian trips, raised the question of whether Hatcher was strong enough to undertake two more field seasons in Antarctica. Garrett seems not only to have been aware of the extent to which in Patagonia Hatcher had been willing to risk his own personal safety, but also to have sympathized with the toll such risks take on a family over time. "I approve most heartily of your scheme . . ." Garrett wrote Hatcher on June 29,

except for one reason—I cannot believe that you are physically up to such an undertaking & I feel very chary of ascenting [sic] in any way to such a precarious experiment, not only on account of yourself, but more particularly because of the state your wife & children would be left in if any accident should befall you. Yet if the matter comes to a head you may count on me to contribute the funds . . . I wish you success, but it is a matter to be thought over very carefully.

Hatcher's candidacy languished for eight more months, near the end of which Libbey, the Princeton professor, must have queried Robert Falcon Scott as well as Bruce on Hatcher's behalf. On March 4, 1901, Scott wrote Libbey that there would be no room for Hatcher on the *Discovery*, the brand-new and only marginally seaworthy vessel Parliament had finally agreed to finance at enormous expense. The *Discovery* would sail in late July. Space for officers and scientists was very limited, Scott wrote, "and appointments have already been made which wholly absorb it."

On March 5, 1901, Bruce wrote Libbey that the Scots were much harder up for funds. They needed £35,000, equivalent to $175,000, for three years' work, of which they'd so far been promised £10,000. With the Antarctic winter approaching, it seemed likely they would not leave for another year. But Bruce apparently still wanted Hatcher to come along, if only for the money he might be able to bring with him to the project: "Do I understand correctly your offer is that you are prepared to pay the sum of £1,000 towards the funds of the Scottish National Antarctic Expedition under my leadership, provided I can see my way to accommodate Mr. T. [sic] B. Hatcher and one or two companions as I have suggested in my letter of April 16th, 1900."

It was not uncommon in the early British polar explorations for young men tied by family or friendship to large contributors to win positions on board. Libbey passed Bruce's letter along to Hatcher, and Hatcher, ever hopeful, took it as an invitation. Always blunt-spoken, he went to talk to Holland about it. But Holland didn't show as much enthusiasm as Hatcher had hoped:

Since my conversation with you last evening regarding the proposed Antarctic Expedition I have thought the whole matter over very carefully & it appears to me that I should abandon the idea of making the trip at the expense & in the interests of this Institution, however much I may have hoped & wished to do so. The chief reason for this conclusion is that you as Director can not lend to the undertaking that hearty support which it seems to me such an undertaking should have if it is to be carried on under the auspices of this Institution. I realize fully the precarious nature of the problem I have had in mind these many years & wish to attempt its solution only with the hearty cooperation & sympathy of all those persons who may be directly interested in it.

I believe Mr. Bruce's offer a reasonable one &, considering the limited time, if he is successful in getting off this year I wish to either accept or reject it in its entirety. I believe I can accomplish the trip in the interests of Princeton University where I know the undertaking is appreciated & has the entire sympathy of all concerned. Thanking you for your conditional offer to me last evening I would request that I be allowed to absent myself from the museum for from three to five days a portion of which time I wish to spend in Washington studying their Diplodocus material at the U.S. National Museum & the remainder in looking up this Antarctic question. I shall of course bear my own expenses.

As always, Hatcher was most eager to move when consumed by a big idea. This was the biggest idea of his career, and, most remarkably, it turns out to have been right, though the evidence was not forthcoming in his lifetime.

The earth sciences around 1900 were tangled in a web of conflicting explanations which it would take more than sixty years and one big theory to unravel. The problem began with a good idea that happened to be wrong. For much of the nineteenth century, scientists assumed Earth was continuing to cool from a fiery beginning. As it cooled, it shrank, and its crust bent down into ocean basins or buckled up into mountains, like the skin of a drying apple. Continents were permanently located, though the presence on dry land of marine fossils made it appear that sometimes land sank under oceans and ocean basins rose to become land. If similar extinct species were found in places far apart, even oceans apart, it must be because land bridges—causeways, they were sometimes called—were from time to time exposed by falling seas, allowing relatively temporary migrations. As for plants, well, their spores could cross oceans on the winds and their seeds on the currents.

Physicists such as Lord Kelvin and others applied thermodynamic theory to the Earth to figure out how fast an object of its size would have cooled to its present state from a temperature as hot as the sun's. Kelvin, who had enormous prestige, first proposed that the earth was only 100 million years old, then shrank his estimate to 20 million. His ideas were widely accepted in the physical sciences, though for decades many geologists, convinced that the processes of uplift, erosion, and deposition must take much longer, were uncomfortable with Kelvin's calculations. With or without Kelvin's additions, the apple-skin model likewise did little to explain why mountains were distributed so unevenly around the earth.

As far back as the 1850s, British engineers in India found that the Himalayas were far less dense, as shown by gravity measurements taken with swinging plumb bobs, than anyone had expected. Gradually this perception led to the concept of *isostasy*, which proposes that continents, their rocks relatively light, follow Archimedes' Principle and bob like huge rafts on a hot, dense, viscous mantle below them. Beginning in the 1890s, the Curies discovered that uranium was unstable and would break down into lead at a consistent rate. Radioactive dating of rocks became possible. The earth's age—geology's great question of the nineteenth century—was becoming measurable at last. Kelvin, it gradually became clear, was wrong, and the whole cooling-earth idea was wrong, too. But for decades, no one had a better idea.

Hatcher was by no means the only paleontologist who was scratching his head about so-called faunal homologies—that is, similarities between animals—continents apart. As early as the 1850s, the British zoologist Philip Sclater had noticed that Madagascar contained almost none of the common African animals—monkeys, elephants or lions, for example—but did have lots of lemurs, which are common in India, 2,500 miles away. In fact, some of the lemurs in Madagascar and India were nearly identical.

The advance of Darwin's theory of evolution by natural selection, beginning in the 1860s, made it clear that the lemurs were too similar to have evolved independently. Biologists began noting similarities between plant and animal fossils on opposite sides of the North Atlantic, the South Atlantic, and around the edges of the Indian Ocean. Hatcher may have been the first to speculate that Antarctica was a logical way station between South America and Africa, and South America and Australia. But, still, there seemed to be no better mechanism than transoceanic causeways to explain former continental connections.

Then, in 1912, a German geophysicist and meteorologist named Alfred Wegener published the first scientific paper on continental drift. Revising and expanding his ideas over the next twenty years, Wegener proposed that the continents, less dense than the ocean basins, floated in a denser, mantle-like, viscous substrate. That meant they could move—and not just bob up and down but also move horizontally. They could come together; they could pull apart again. Collisions and divisions of continents explained mountains, rift valleys, and arcs of ocean islands. Drift solved the question of far-flung faunal and floral homologies, as the similarity of distant species could now be understood to imply the former contiguity of the landmasses on which they were found. The new theory eliminated the need to accept apparently huge climate changes, when fossils from tropical ecosystems were found in very cold parts of the world, for example. And, at last, the visually arresting jigsaw-puzzle appearance of the continents—most notably Brazil's smooth fit into Africa—could be seen not as coincidence but as the result of predictable physical processes.

Wegener, however, was an outsider, a generalist in an age of increasing specialization, and, to English-speaking geologists, a foreigner. Further, no one could yet conceive the mechanics of drift—how it actually worked. He won some early supporters, but after his death in 1930 his ideas were sidelined.

A sequence of technological advances led to the reemergence of continental drift theories. In the 1920s, ships began to use echo-sounding devices to measure and record ocean depths as they traveled. Sonar-equipped German, Danish, and British expeditions found long ridges under the middle of the Atlantic and Indian oceans and later found that these ridges were cleft longitudinally along their tops. After the ridges were mapped and diagrams of worldwide earthquake activity were laid over them, a compelling congruence began to emerge. By the late 1950s, scientists recognized the existence of a global system of seismically active mid-ocean ridges and deep ocean trenches along the borders of some continents and chains of ocean islands. Further, measurements of heat rising from the ocean floor showed it was coming up much faster than would be predicted by simple cooling of the deep interior of the earth. Some scientists began to wonder if there were convection currents in the mantle that were bringing up hot material from below, much as hot water rises over the flame in the center of a bubbling pot of pasta, cools at the top of its ascent and falls back down the sides.

In 1960 a Princeton geologist named Harry Hess began articulating a theory that brought together a whole slew of apparently disconnected observations. He called it sea-floor spreading, and it provided the mechanism Wegener had lacked to explain how the continents move over time. Hot mantle material, Hess proposed, rises by convection to the earth's surface through the clefts along the mid-ocean ridges, then spreads out and away from them. Thus, the ocean floors are covered with relatively young, igneous rocks, which are measurably older the farther they are from the mid-ocean ridges. The moving mantle carries along sea floors and continents alike as though they were great plates. The movement at times brings the plates into collision, as may be seen most clearly along the eastern edge of the Pacific Ocean. There, the Pacific plate, moving eastward, dives under the plate moving westward from the middle of the south Atlantic, causing chronic earthquakes, buckling coast ranges from Alaska to the Andes up in the air, and creating great undersea trenches along the western coasts of the Americas.

It wasn't long after Hatcher began hypothesizing about Antarctica's former land connections that the first fossils were found there. But they were found by accident, along the route of adventure, not the path of science. The Beardmore Glacier flows down out of the Transantarctic Mountains to the Ross Ice Shelf, on the Pacific-facing side of the continent. The early British expeditions based themselves at the edge of the ice shelf. The glacier provided a long ramp up to the high plateau where the South Pole lay, hundreds of miles inland. In December 1908, a party of four men led by Sir Ernest Shackleton ascended the glacier with ponies in an unsuccessful attempt on the Pole. Near the top, Frank Wild found coal outcroppings in some naked rock—about six seams, Shackleton reported, each four to eight inches thick, mixed in with the sandstone. Three years later, Scott's party, reaching the same glacier en route back from the Pole, found coal in about the same place. Despite their exhaustion, they saved beautiful plant fossils from the coal and limestone, hauling thirty-five pounds of rocks with them for several weeks more before all in the party died. The next summer the bodies were found in the tent, the fossils on the sleds nearby.

In London Shackleton's coal and Scott's plant fossils were recognized, correctly, as dating from the Carboniferous period, well before the dinosaurs, when much of the land on earth was covered with lush tropical forests. By that time an early super-continent had split into a northern half, now called Laurasia, and a southern half, Gondwanaland. The scientists who examined Scott's fossils were unable to conceive how such an empty and ice-bound place could once have been lush and warm. Early drift supporters embraced the fossils as evidence of Carboniferous-period land connections between Antarctica and the other southern continents, but skeptics remained unconvinced for decades.

In 1967, near a peak east of Beardmore Glacier, fossils of labyrinthodonts were found. These were amphibians that first evolved in the Devonian period, a time of recurring droughts that preceded the Carboniferous. The discovery prompted more prospecting in the area, and in 1969 scientists discovered the bones of some mammal-like reptiles, *Lysostaurus*, from the Triassic, the same period when dinosaurs first appeared. Labyrinthodonts were known from South Africa and Australia, *Lysostaurus* from South Africa and India. Here at last was sound fossil evidence that Antarctica had been part of Gondwanaland, proof positive of the "former land connections" Hatcher had hypothesized seventy years before. Had the early Antarctic explorers made time to hunt for fossils on the Antarctic peninsula, as Hatcher had wanted to do, his theories might have been vindicated much sooner. In recent years, scraps of Late Cretaceous dinosaurs have turned up there, as well as rare remains of Eocene mammals and birds.

For Holland in 1901, Hatcher's blunt request was a problem. If not crackbrained, the Antarctica scheme at least was likely to prove very expensive, and right or wrong, it offered only a slim chance of producing anything displayable. Dinosaurs, by contrast, must have seemed potentially plentiful. So plentiful, in fact, that an even more splendid specimen than the new *Diplodocus* might turn up any month under the picks of paleontologists from the big museums in Chicago, New York, or Washington, D.C.—all scouring the American West for just such a find. And there remained a great deal of fossil preparation and scientific description to do on the *Diplodocus*. Hatcher was obviously the man to lead the effort, and he couldn't do it if he were scrambling around rocks and ice, risking his health and life at 70 degrees south latitude.

Holland replied to Hatcher's letter the same day, but rather than address these larger matters head on, he stuck, somewhat huffily, to more immediate concerns. He wrote that he could not understand how Hatcher could construe his support as lukewarm, when he had offered him a leave of a year or more for Antarctic work, along with a pledge to find funds to pay expenses. Further, they had agreed that Bruce's letters were vague: it was unclear what was expected from the Carnegie Museum, and a query about whether Hatcher could bring $5,000 to the table was not the same thing as an offer to join the expedition. Further, it seemed very unlikely that Bruce would sail that year, and so the time pressure Hatcher was feeling seemed unjustified. Once they had a clear statement from Bruce of what would be expected of Hatcher, what it would cost, and how long everything would take, Holland wrote, then they could discuss the matter further: "I think my position on the matter has been not only kind but sensible." But he didn't leave the matter there. As so often in the past, when under pressure, he took offense:

It seems to me, however, that no amount of kindness or willingness on my part to aid you and assist you is capable of satisfying you, and I have to inform you that after consulting with the Board of Trustees of the Institution, my reply to your letter is that while we would be very glad to assist you and provide the money that is necessary to carry on your work successfully in connection with this Antarctic enterprise, nevertheless we do not care to be perpetually threatened by the mention of the names of other institutions, which, as you would have us infer, are waiting eagerly to take up all your suggestions while we are proving ourselves in your judgment incompetent to understand the importance of your schemes and unwilling to do what you think ought to be done.

Unlike Wortman, when Holland had pressed him, Hatcher remained calm. Two days later he wrote that he was about to leave for Washington for the reasons he'd mentioned in his earlier letter:

I hope I shall be successful for I am fully convinced of the importance of the matter. However if for financial or other reasons [perhaps he was, after all, thinking about his health and family] I am compelled to abandon it, I shall take my defeat philosophically. At any rate I wish to end one way or the other the suspense I have been in concerning this projected Antarctic trip. If I can not accomplish it now I will drop the matter for all time. One final effort though before I give it up entirely.

He didn't give up. A year later, in April 1902, Hatcher attended scientific meetings in Philadelphia and Washington, D.C., and paid calls at Princeton, the American Museum, and Yale. Antarctica was still very much on his mind as he made the rounds. A number of his colleagues urged him to keep looking for a way to get south, and several promised to use their influence to help him get a grant from the Carnegie Institution in Washington. Promptly Hatcher drew up a proposal, and he, Holland, and trustee C. C. Mellor submitted on behalf of the Carnegie Museum a request for $65,000 to support a Hatcher-led expedition to Antarctica. Its main goal would be to test his hypothesis that South America and Antarctica had once been connected by land. They planned to buy or charter a steam whaler, fit it out with a zoology lab and deep-sea sounding equipment, and staff it with zoologists, paleontologists, and geologists whose salaries would be paid for by the museum. The expedition would depart in August 1904 and would be gone for two years.

Their first priority would be to study the geology, paleontology, and biology of Graham Land, on the east side of the Antarctic Peninsula; the second was to make as complete a collection as possible of local flora and fauna; third, and perhaps most interesting from a modern plate-tectonics viewpoint, was to sound the depths of the ocean between Tierra del Fuego and the Antarctic Peninsula along two routes, one fairly direct, the other curling eastward via South Georgia and the South Orkney Islands.

Such soundings, had they been taken, would have made clear what a map of the region already suggests: the ocean between Cape Horn and the tip of the Antarctic peninsula is deep, but a great loop of undersea ridges and volcanic islands bends far to the east through the South Atlantic before coming back west again to the tip of the Antarctic Peninsula. Some modern scientists see the so-called Scotia Arc as evidence that parts of the Andes, which once ran down the entire west coast of Gondwanaland, were pulled eastward when Gondwanaland broke up. South America and Antarctica, once broken off, moved west, but a piece of the Pacific plate pushed between them, driving an arc of the Andes the opposite way.

Had they been taken, these soundings also would have suggested to Hatcher further good questions. To his first problem, why do we find these similar animals continents apart? he might have added, what produced this long island arc eastward? The theory of continental drift by means of plate tectonics solves both problems at once. How far Hatcher would have proceeded toward that solution, and whether his ideas would have prompted further research by others, it is of course impossible to say.

The Carnegie Institution in Washington was brand new in the spring of 1902. Carnegie had established it just the winter before, endowing it with $10 million, which produced an income of $500,000 per year to support scientific research. Its first trustees included President Theodore Roosevelt and William Frew, president of the board of trustees of the Carnegie Institute in Pittsburgh. Frew's presence on the board, the encouragement Hatcher received from his scientific colleagues, and the novelty and purpose of the new institution in Washington must have made the Antarctic request seem like a sure thing. Nonetheless, Hatcher's group waited a year and a half for an answer. The proposal won the support of the institution's advisory committees on paleontology and zoology, but an executive committee, chaired by Charles Doolittle Walcott of the Smithsonian, found it "inexpedient to recommend" the proposal to the full board of trustees.

Hatcher's reaction is not recorded. His scientific plate by then was full with North American vertebrate fossils, in any case. In fact, he was putting in such long hours it's hard not to wonder if he sensed how short a time he had left on Earth.

Chapter 14

WHEN THE FLAG
DROPS

As it turned out, fortunately, there were parts of two *Dipolodocus* skeletons at the Sheep Creek quarry. Wortman, Reed, and Coggeshall had found and excavated the first in the summer of 1899. It included a splendid vertebral column, lying in sequence all the way from the neck bones just back of the skull, along the neck, down the back, over the hips, and out to the twelfth tail bone. The dinosaur had been resting on its right side, so that was the side in general best preserved; the skeleton also included most of the pelvis, the right shoulder bones and right femur, and eighteen ribs. This was a good haul—the backbone far surpassed that of any *Diplodocus* found before—but by no means was it a complete animal.

The following spring, Hatcher, waiting for Reed to return from the Red Desert, found time between snowstorms in the last week in April to make it out to Sheep Creek himself. He promptly discovered parts of a second, slightly smaller *Diplodocus*, which included many parts the first skeleton had lacked: a left femur; right shin, calf bone, and foot; a complete pelvis; both shoulder bones; more ribs; and forty-seven vertebrae, including many of the smaller tail bones that had been missing from the first specimen. By the end of the 1900 field season, the group could see how exquisitely long-tailed and long-necked a *Diplodocus* really was. Back in the lab, Peterson, Coggeshall, Coggeshall's newly hired brother Louis, and a preparator named A.W. Vankirk promptly began the tedious cleaning and preparation of the bones for study. Hatcher went to work on the scientific description.

Remarkably, he had the text and its illustrations to the printer by mid-May, 1901, even before some of the bones had been cleaned from their matrix. His book-length analysis, *"Diplodocus* Marsh: Its Osteology, Taxonomy, and Probable Habits, With a Restoration of the Skeleton,"* was published in the fall of 1901 as volume 1, number 1 of the *Memoirs of the Carnegie Museum*. It was his first full-length elaborately illustrated monograph, describing important fossils he'd had a hand in collecting, and it had been published by his own institution. No one could dispute that Hatcher the collector was now Hatcher the scientist.

Crucial to the report was its restoration—that is, a detailed drawing of the full skeleton—of the *Diplodocus*. To fill in the gaps in the Carnegie Museum's discovery, Hatcher used Marsh's previously published description and drawings of a *Diplodocus* skull and Osborn's work on tail vertebrae, forelimbs, and feet from two different partial *Diplodocus* specimens at the American Museum of Natural History.

For the first time there was enough information to draw the entire skeleton in extensive detail. Marsh had named his first specimen *Diplodocus longus*; it was the type—that is, the official scientific example—for both the genus and the species. Marsh named a separate species, smaller and with a more slender jaw, *Diplodocus lacustris*. Hatcher argued that size alone was not sufficient for specific distinction. Dinosaurs, like modern crocodiles and other reptiles, most likely grew larger for their entire lives; if one adult was larger than another, that did not necessarily mean it was a separate species.

The new Carnegie find of two specimens did have sufficiently separate characteristics to merit designation as a species, Hatcher announced. First, the long spines rising out of the vertebrae at the base of the tail pointed in a more backwards direction than did the tail spines in Diplodocus longus. Second, the spindly bone extension, called a cervical rib, running backwards at the bottom of each neck vertebrae was much longer on Marsh's *Diplodocus* than were the cervical ribs on the vertebrae found at Sheep Creek. That was enough. Hatcher proclaimed *Diplodocus carnegii*, named, he said, for his

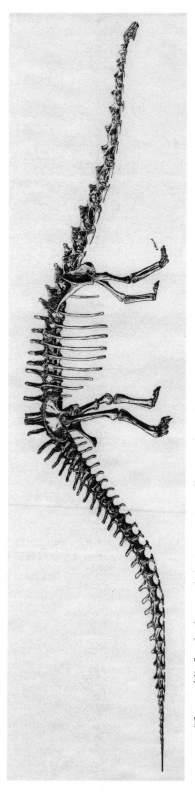

The world's first look at *Diplodocus carnegii*, as illustrated in John Bell Hatcher's 1901 monograph on the dinosaur. Illustration first published in *Memoirs of the Carnegie Museum* 1, no. 1 (July 1901): plate vi.

institution's generous founder "in recognition of his interest in vertebrate paleontology." He named the larger of the two Sheep Creek
skeletons the type specimen; the smaller he named the co-type.

Holland knew even better how to please their patron. He had a
framed copy made of the drawing, captioned it with the dinosaur's
name and dimensions, and sent it to Carnegie at Skibo. *Diplodocus
carnegii* was "unmistakably different in some respects from the species called *longus* by Marsh," Holland wrote. "It is a bigger beast . . .
Now the biggest thing on earth of its kind bears your name; so you
are sure of immortality in the annals of science,—a form of immortality which, I may say, scientific men greatly covet."

Two years later, Hatcher noted, in a short paper updating his
earlier monograph, that the cervical vertebrae with the long cervical rib that Marsh had described had belonged in fact to an
Apatosaurus (at the time still known as *Brontosaurus*). That change, he
added, removed one of the two main points on which he had based
his species designation for the new *Diplodocus*. What he didn't say,
but must have known, was that the now-moot point had been by far
the more compelling of the two. If he had any doubts whether his
museum's *Diplodocus* continued to merit designation as *carnegii*, a
separate species, he had the tact not to say so.

Not long after the monograph was published, Hatcher got a note
from one of Europe's most eminent paleontologists, proposing a
swap. Louis Dollo, in his way, contributed as much to the era's understanding of dinosaurs as did Marsh or Cope—but did it by nar-
rowing his field of inquiry, not broadening it. *Iguanodons*, Cretaceous
plant-eating, duckbilled dinosaurs, had been discovered in a coal
mine near Bernissart, Belgium, beginning in 1878. Many *Iguanodons*.
While Cope and Marsh were sending parties far and wide to find
single examples of as many different species as they could, Dollo
stuck with his *Iguanodons* for twenty-five years, carefully studying
and measuring, noting each specimen's similarities and differences
from the others. Eventually he examined thirty virtually complete
skeletons, gaining a profound understanding of how the animals
moved, their environment, and most important, of the degree of
variety that could exist within a single species. He also was among

the first to erect a dinosaur skeleton that became a permanent exhibit—in a church, at first. Later the *Iguanodons* were mounted at the Royal Museum of Natural History in Brussels, where about thirty of them are still on display.

Writing from his post as curator at the Royal Museum, Dollo thanked Hatcher for the handsome *Diplodocus* monograph, then offered a proposition:

Have you ever thought about casting the bones of this Dinosaurian, so that one could mount them according to the restoration that you have just published?

Or, perhaps, to make a model of your restoration, since [its accuracy] is established by multiple specimens?

This would be an element of exchange against a cast of an Iguanodon. It's an idea which I submit to you.

That sounded good, if unprecedented—to swap one entire dinosaur cast for another. Exchanges were already becoming common among natural history museums. They were handy both for filling in gaps in collections and for raising prestige. Hatcher would shortly report to Holland his pride at being involved in swaps of fossils and services with the best museums in the country—Yale, the American Museum of Natural History, and the U.S. National Museum, just within the space of a few months—at a time when the Carnegie Museum's entire paleontology program was still so new.

Exchanges also enabled curators to mount more dramatic fossil displays. The idea of erecting fleshless fossil skeletons for the public to learn from and admire dates back at least to the South American *Megatherium* mounted in the royal museum in Madrid in 1789. In 1806 Charles Willson Peale, the portrait painter, polymath, and friend of Thomas Jefferson, included the skeleton of a mammoth skeleton among the many displays at his museum in Philadelphia. The first dinosaur skeleton to be displayed was a hadrosaur, a Cretaceous duckbilled dinosaur. It was mounted at the Philadelphia Academy of Natural Sciences in 1868.

The practice gained momentum when Osborn came to the American Museum in 1891. He built a permanent staff of collectors and preparators and hired artists to paint the backgrounds for displays of fossil skeletons in lifelike poses. Marsh, on the other hand, distrusted the display approach, fearing that any inaccuracies in a restoration would be permanently injected into the public consciousness. Nonetheless, he unwittingly contributed to the spread of dinosaur re-creations. In 1895 he published a sheet of illustrations of about a dozen dinosaur skeletons from his collections. Some of the mass-circulation monthlies got hold of it, and commissioned more illustrations by artists who'd already worked for Osborn. Within a few years these images had taken hold of the public's imagination; people seemed mad for dinosaurs. The *New York Journal and Advertiser* story in 1898 on Reed's so-called *Brontosaurus giganteus* was only one of many such sensationalized spreads on monsters from the past to appear as the decade closed.

To satisfy the public's new enthusiasm, permanent mounts of big dinosaur skeletons at the big museums became inevitable—and fossil swaps made them possible. By early 1902 Charles Beecher at the Peabody Museum at Yale had decided to set up Marsh's *Apatosaurus* skeleton—the one Reed had uncovered at Como Bluff back in 1879. Beecher needed casts of some of the limbs to make up for bones he was missing, and he sought help from Hatcher. Hatcher had just what Beecher needed, thanks to an *Apatosaurus* discovered at Sheep Creek the previous summer by a young University of Wyoming graduate named Charles Gilmore. Soon the Carnegie preparators had cast the limbs and sent them on.

Eventually Hatcher's generosity paid off, as he must have expected it would. Beecher, who jealously guarded Marsh's fossils for years against all comers, might have had some sympathy with Hatcher, as they had worked together digging *Triceratops* skulls in eastern Wyoming years before. He allowed Hatcher and his assistants complete access to Yale's horned dinosaurs for a monograph on the *Ceratopsia* commissioned by the U.S. Geological Survey. Gradually, now that Cope and Marsh were dead, cooperation was vying with competition as the way to do business among the big-bone, big-museum paleontologists.

A request from a king for a dinosaur electrified the context of exchange. King Edward VII, the son of Queen Victoria, had to pack away some of his playboy behavior when he finally ascended to the throne in 1901. Early in the fall of 1902, he visited Carnegie at Skibo. The king was drawn to Hatcher's restoration of *Diplodocus carnegii*, nicely framed and hanging on the wall, with the caption that gave the dinosaur's dimensions. It must have seemed astonishingly large, once the king began to think about it. As Holland—who wasn't there—told the story, thirty years later:

The King saw the sketch, and, adjusting his glasses, stepped forward, exclaiming: "I say, Carnegie, what in the world is this?" Mr. Carnegie replied, "The hugest quadruped that ever walked the earth, a namesake of mine" . . . "Oh! I say, Carnegie," replied the King, "we must have one of these in the British Museum."

Carnegie himself was more laconic. "The King was attracted to the Diplodocus when here," he wrote Holland on October 2, 1902. "He wants one for British Museum badly. I read your note which told of the new finds. He is on your track now for duplicates. Maybe you call upon him when you come to us next time . . ." How sweet it must have felt for the rich man to write that note, and how important it must have been that he seem offhand about it.

Work began in earnest late the following winter, after Carnegie made a formal offer of a *Diplodocus* to the trustees of the British Museum, and the trustees accepted it. Holland warned Carnegie that it would be very expensive. Models would have to be sculpted of many of the smaller or more fragile bones. Then molds would be made, either from the models or from the original bones. Finally casts—that is, replicas—could be made from the molds. But good returns could be expected on the investment. For one thing, once the molds were made, it would be simple enough to make more than one reproduction. A dinosaur could be reproduced at least several times over. And gifts to any royal dinosaur recipients—kings or emperors, say—"ought to bring a royal return, more than a thank you," Holland noted. Dollo's desire to swap an *Iguanodon* reproduction for a *Diplodocus* was just a sample of the "fine harvest of paleontological material" they could hope to reap.

In April 1903 the museum hired two skilled Italian modelers at about $100 a month each—artisan's wages, more than most of the men in the fossil lab were making. Meanwhile, the regular fossil

In the fossil lab at the Carnegie Museum in 1903–04, John Bell Hatcher, *seated at right*, directed the preparation and mounting of the first cast of *Diplodocus carnegii*, Carnegie's gift to King Edward VII of England.
Courtesy of Carnegie Museum of Natural History, Pittsburgh, Pennsylvania.

preparators, before heading West again for another summer in the field, finished a complicated and difficult task: preparing the piece of *Diplodocus* skull that had been found at Sheep Creek. They had just the back section—no top, no front of the skull or jaw—but it would prove an important reference point when the time came to assemble the whole animal.

A huge European fossil collection, belonging to Baron Ernest de Bayet of Belgium came on the market in early May for the asking price of 100,000 francs—$25,000. Representatives of the Czar were interested; Osborn was interested; Alexander Agassiz, patron of the Museum of Comparative Zoology at Harvard, was so interested he offered to split the purchase with the Carnegie Museum. The sixty-five-year-old baron had been acquiring fossils for most of his life, but recently he had married a young wife, and she wanted him to buy her a chalet on Lake Como in Italy. Chances like this, Hatcher noted to Holland—and Holland noted to Carnegie—came along once in a hundred years. But there was nothing near the amount of money necessary in the museum budget. Holland asked for help; Carnegie approved the purchase. A paleontologist named C. R. Eastman, from the Museum of Comparative Zoology at Harvard, acted as middleman in the deal. In return, he expected a high salary from the Carnegie Museum to finance a year in Europe studying and writing on the abundant fossil fishes in the collection, many of which had never been analyzed before, and on which he clearly expected to advance his reputation. Hatcher didn't trust Eastman, and Holland picked up some of Hatcher's unease.

Hatcher also, however, was eager to get the Bayet collection back to Pittsburgh, as it would provide the basis for what he was already beginning to see was the next great scientific task before him. Hatcher's experience in Patagonia had made clear that there was a great deal of work left to be done in correlating the rocks of the same relative ages on different continents. Which sediments came from the Triassic period on the continent of Europe? for example; where did they begin, and where did they end? Such questions could be answered only by matching similar fossils; Hatcher knew the Bayet collection was a gold mine for such purposes. As he was already in Montana for another summer's field work, however, Hatcher asked Holland to travel to Brussels himself to oversee the packing of the collection—and to keep an eye on Eastman.

Holland sailed for Europe July 8. Before leaving he had "succeeded in jewing the Baron down to a lower figure," around $23,000, he wrote Carnegie. Holland took his older son, Moorhead, by now a Princeton sophomore, along with him. They joined Eastman in London, where they copied an itemized list of the Bayet fossils given to them by officials at the British Museum who had also had their eye on the collection. Once in Brussels, Holland found the collection immense and thrilling, though the labels were in some disorder. Dollo paid a visit, "very obliging, but a trifle sore that the collection is going to America," Holland wrote back to Hatcher. The Hollands, father and son, dined once with the baron and baroness, and a tableful of other barons and baronesses—"10 kinds of wine and toothpicks at the table"—and lunched with King Leopold II, exploiter of the Congo. Holland decided the king was "a jolly good fellow."

The packed-up collection, ready for shipment, filled more than 250 boxes. Holland rented a warehouse in downtown Pittsburgh to store it, as there would not be room at the museum until the new expansion was complete. Eastman kept some of the fossil fish from the collection and took them to Paris to compare with specimens at the Museum d'Histoire Naturelle at the Jardin des Plantes.

Carnegie, the experienced manufacturer, agreed that it made sense for the preparators and modelers to make additional casts as they went along—five more, in fact. Then when he next called on the monarchs of Belgium, Germany, Russia, or the Netherlands, or on the president of France, he could offhandedly offer them dinosaurs. Great big dinosaurs. None of these nations had yet been informed of his plans—at least not officially. But it seems to have been a fairly open secret that the work was going on. In his annual fall thank-you note for another field season's free passage for bones and their collectors, Holland told Horace Burt of the Union Pacific Railroad that museum staffers were making *Diplodocus* replicas for England, Russia, Germany, and France.

Nor, apparently, had anyone told Eastman or Hatcher that the idea was a secret. In Paris, Eastman mentioned the work to Marcellin Boule at the Museum d'Histoire Naturelle, then turned around and confided to Hatcher Boule's desire for a *D. carnegii* cast. Promptly, Hatcher wrote Boule proposing a swap. In return for a cast, Hatcher politely inquired, could Boule spare "a representative set of the Tertiary mammals of Europe," and "a fairly representative series of such dinosaurian and other reptilian remains from European horizons as it might be possible for you to part with, without injuring your collections." It was a huge request, signifying that Hatcher knew the value of what he had. He made it clear to Boule that he wanted the mammal fossils "not so much for purposes of exhibition as for purposes of study and comparison with forms from American Tertiaries." They would have helped immensely in the great lineup of world rock strata Hatcher hoped to embark on before too much longer. That Carnegie might have preferred to be the first to offer a cast of *Diplodocus carnegii* to the great French nation seems never to have occurred to him. There was science to be done.

In December Boule wrote directly to Carnegie about a replica of *Diplodocus carnegii*. Carnegie passed the letter on to Holland, and Holland had to scramble. First, he informed Boule that any correspondence Boule may have had with anyone at the Carnegie Museum other than himself "has been wholly unauthorized." Then he denied, truthfully enough, that there had been "any definite arrangement" for gifts or swaps made yet with any museums other than the British Museum. Less truthfully, Holland went on to say that no other casts were being made, either: "Of course it may be that at some time or other in the future Mr. Carnegie might instruct us to make another reproduction similar to that which is now being made, but up to this time he has given no such commission, and no one here connected with this Museum has any authority whatever to suggest that such a thing will be done. The matter is wholly in Mr. Carnegie's hands . . ."

To Carnegie himself Holland pretended complete astonishment: "My breath was taken away upon reading the letter." He vowed that he had demanded absolute secrecy of his staff on the subject of making extra replicas, and had himself spoken to no one about it outside the museum. Holland concluded that two staffers whom he declined to name—Eastman and Hatcher, certainly—"impelled by a zeal not coupled with discretion," had corresponded with Boule, "forgetting that these replicas are, strictly speaking, your private property and that they are held here subject to your order and disposition and not as material incorporated in our collections and held to be used in exchange . . ."

Giving was giving and swapping was swapping. It was a useful fiction, anyway. To admit otherwise, to admit that the motives for both often overlapped, would be to imply that somehow Carnegie was less than generous—and how could that be true of such a great man?

While these discussions were taking place, work on the reproductions had doubled. Holland and Hatcher hired two more men for the mold-and-cast crew. By March Holland projected that the reproduction would be finished and set up once for practice by August, and could be erected in England in September. First, however, they needed a place big enough to hold a standing *Diplodocus.* There was no space in the museum that large. In May Holland persuaded the trustees of the Western Pennsylvania Exposition Society to offer free space for that purpose in the society's huge barn of a hall near the Point in downtown Pittsburgh.

On May 13, a Friday, Hatcher reported to Holland that the work of actually putting up the dinosaur cast could begin the following Monday. He would need to move Louis Coggeshall off the fossil-prep crew and over to the mounting crew. He would need to hire a pipefitter and a carpenter. And he would need permission to pay Arthur Coggeshall an extra fee to moonlight after hours modeling the *Diplodocus* foot bones, which still were not complete. If all went as planned, the dinosaur should be up and ready by July 1. They had a lot of work ahead. No one, including Hatcher, yet understood what a toll his work of the previous three years had already taken on him. He was then, in the spring of 1904, forty-two years old.

Hatcher had finished his monograph on the *Diplodocus* in the spring of 1901, just a year after coming to the Carnegie Museum. A year later, he finished his second book, the narrative of the Patagonia expeditions. This would be Hatcher's only contribution to the seven volumes on the Patagonia discoveries eventually published by Princeton.

In July 1902 Hatcher took on what amounted to a second full-time job when he agreed to write a monograph on the Ceratopsia— the horned dinosaurs. After Marsh's death, Osborn had been named vertebrate paleontologist for the U.S. Geological Survey. In that capacity he had taken over four great monographs Marsh had left in various stages of incompletion: one each on the Sauropods, the Ceratopsia, the Stegosaurs, and the Brontotheres, big Tertiary mammals. Marsh had seen to the preparation of hundreds of illustrations but had written no text. Osborn asked F. A. Lucas at the U.S. National Museum to take over the Stegosaurs, gave the Ceratopsia to Hatcher, and kept the Sauropods and the Brontotheres as his own projects. The great majority of the horned dinosaurs known to sci-

ence at the time had been collected by Hatcher himself, most notably the thirty-one skulls he'd found in the Lance Creek formation of
eastern Wyoming between 1889 and 1893. Blocked by circumstances
from the opportunity to write up the Patagonian mammals for
Princeton, Hatcher must have jumped at the chance to take on the
ceratopsians when it came along. Because some of the original collecting had been done under USGS auspices, and some directly for
Marsh, the Ceratopsia specimens by 1902 were divided between the
U.S. National Museum and the Peabody Museum at Yale. Although
Hatcher arranged for assistance in preparing the bones and illustrat-
ing them at both places, he still had to make frequent trips to Washington and New Haven. For the next two years, except for occasional
months in the field, he would work an average of seven hours a day
on the project.

Other scientific questions pulled him in still other directions. As
early as 1896, Hatcher had concluded that the Judith River beds in
Montana, where he'd found Cretaceous dinosaurs, were older than
the Wyoming formations that had proved so rich in *Triceratops* skulls.
This conclusion was hotly disputed by other high-status geologists.
By early 1903 the question had narrowed to whether the Cretaceous
Pierre shales and Fox Hills sandstones were stratigraphically above
or below the Judith River beds. Publications on the argument
crowded the scientific journals that spring. Hatcher seemed completely outnumbered. After reviewing the contrary positions of a
number of other geologists, O. P. Hay of the U.S. National Museum
wrote that "Hatcher has indeed told us that in his work in that region
he saw no Pierre deposits beneath the Judith River beds, but did see
deposits resembling the Pierre overlying the Judith beds. It will, however, not be insisted that this statement shakes the positive observations of many other geologists." That is, just because Hatcher says
it's true doesn't make it so, especially with so much opinion ranked
against him.

Thanks to Osborn's influence, Hatcher won U.S. Geological
Survey support to go back to the field with T. W. Stanton—a USGS
geologist who profoundly disagreed with him on the subject—and
to work out the answer on the ground. They spent two months in
Montana and southern Alberta in June and July 1903. The answer

they discovered was complex: the Judith River beds and the Pierre shales turned out to be interbedded—but Hatcher nonetheless felt vindicated. Stanton also came around to his point of view, once again proving what Hatcher called "that axiom so often disregarded in paleontology, namely, that one observed fact is worth any amount of expert opinion." Reconciliation with Hay was a rougher matter; Hatcher's letters try but fail to conceal his bitterness.

His quarrel with Florentino Ameghino over the sequence of the strata in Patagonia—a similar problem, in its way, to the one in Montana—was turning bitter as well. Ameghino wrote Hatcher in the spring of 1903 to say that he had (for once) accompanied his brother Carlos on a recent trip to Patagonia and there, because of the evidence they found, "we were able to assure ourselves that your observations are completely erroneous, and to continue to support them would be nothing on your part but a simple question of caprice which won't have much weight in the final solution . . ." Hatcher took a milder tone when he answered, sticking with his position but expressing the hope for more dialogue on the subject when next he got back to Buenos Aires. His experience with Stanton had convinced him that the best thing to do was for opponents to work out their differences on the spot, where the rocks were. He had proposed just such a solution to Carlos Ameghino in 1898. In 1904 he again proposed a joint field trip with the Ameghinos, saying he could leave the U.S. in October in time to spend the entire Southern summer working out their differences. His letter went unanswered. Other events intervened, in any case.

All along he was writing, writing, writing. His bibliography lists sixteen publications during the time he simultaneously was working on the Ceratopsia and running the Carnegie Museum's department of vertebrate paleontology. Some of these publications were short, some substantial. He wrote papers reinterpreting the sediments that underlie the American Great Plains and describing the Oligocene carnivores his staff had excavated in Nebraska. He published three different items on the age and stratigraphy of the Judith River beds. At the same time he published a memoir on a sauropod entirely new to science, *Haplocanthosaurus*, an early Jurassic dinosaur that Carnegie crews had uncovered when they reopened the Marsh quarry near

Cañon City, Colorado. The paper was equal in size and scope to his monograph on *Diplodocus carnegii*.

In October 1903, the Carnegie Institution in Washington finally rejected Hatcher's and Holland's request for support for a Carnegie Museum expedition to Antarctica. In December the Hatchers' youngest child died of a fever. Two-year-old Ruth had been born since they came to Pittsburgh, and was the second of their six children to die. Hatcher kept working. In February he traveled to New Haven for more Ceratopsia work; in late May, confident that the *Diplodocus* mount was safe in the hands of the Coggeshall brothers, he traveled to Washington for still more work on the horned dinosaurs.

Since Hatcher had published his *Diplodocus* monograph, the Carnegie Museum collector W. H. Utterback had found parts of two more *Diplodocus* skeletons in two different quarries west of Kaycee, Wyoming, on the Red Fork of the Powder River. One skeleton included part of the back half of a skull. The second included still more and different tail vertebrae. Now they had a total of seventy-three—producing a far longer sauropod tail than any other then known or imagined. The parts were coming together.

By June 4, 1904, the crews had mounted the long neck, the back vertebrae and the trunk. Arthur Coggeshall, probably independently, had worked out a system similar to ones worked out earlier in Philadelphia and Brussels, whereby the vertebrae were strung like beads on an iron rod along the column where the animal's nerves had gone millions of years before. That meant only one vertical rod was needed to hold up the neck. Rods supporting the skeleton at hips and shoulders were largely concealed from a viewer, and horizontal rods holding the ribs in place were not distracting. "Very little iron-work will be visible, and we will avoid the unsightly and cumbrous mass of scaffolding which appears in the restoration of some of these skeletons," Holland wrote Carnegie.

They still needed the casts of the chevrons—tail attachments—which the American Museum was making for them, and a cast of the American Museum's *Diplodocus* skull. The dinosaur's front feet had been cast from an American Museum specimen thought at the

William Holland with the first *Diplodocus* cast, prior to its shipment to England. It was mounted for practice in 1904, at the Western Pennsylvania Exposition Society in downtown Pittsburgh. Courtesy of Carnegie Museum of Natural History, Pittsburgh, Pennsylvania.

time to be a *Diplodocus* and only much later discovered to belong to a shorter-necked *Camarasaurus*. The material Utterback had found on the Red Fork of the Powder included the front limbs of a slightly smaller *Diplodocus*. With those limbs as models, the skilled workmen

William Holland, *in top hat,* and Arthur Coggeshall, *near Diplodocus' right front foot,* as work nears completion in the Gallery of Reptiles at the British Museum (Natural History). Courtesy of Carnegie Museum of Natural History, Pittsburgh, Pennsylvania.

at the Carnegie Museum sculpted slightly larger versions, from which final molds and then casts could be made.

By the end of the month the skeleton was nearly complete. The vertebral column was up from the top of the neck to the tip of the tail, the ribs were attached, and the fore and hind limbs were up. The skull was left for last and proved to be the greatest problem. The final cast combined characteristics of all four of the partial *Diplodocus* skulls then known—the two Marsh skulls at the U.S. National Museum, one at the American Museum, and the one Utterback had found most recently in Wyoming.

Holland had expected it would fit crocodile-fashion on the neck, with the long axis of the skull in line with the axis of the neck vertebrae, but it proved mechanically impossible to mount in that way. Finally they reached a conclusion Marsh had come to years before, though he'd never set up a skeleton—that the only fit was more bird-like, even almost ostrich-like, with the skull at an angle to the neck.

Because the Hatchers were always careful to filter and boil their water, and because he was ever a Pittsburgh booster, Holland would later believe that Hatcher picked up typhoid fever in Washington, D.C. But Hatcher returned from Washington early in June, and it was not until later in the month that he began to complain of not feeling well. Holland tried to send him home but Hatcher refused, pleading too much work. Again, another day, Holland insisted Hatcher go home and go to bed, and he did, but came back to the museum at night with a temperature of 102 degrees, locked himself in his office, and kept working. He joked about his illness and ignored his doctor's orders. Finally the doctor called an ambulance and demanded that Hatcher go to Mercy Hospital.

Holland had a junket scheduled that week—a free train trip to St. Louis, where the World's Fair and Louisiana Purchase Exposition was under way. The Wabash Line had just instituted a new, through train from Pittsburgh to St. Louis, and Holland had been invited to take the trip as a guest of the railroad's president. He stopped in at the hospital Saturday morning, July 2, to check on Hatcher before he left. The doctor told him Hatcher's condition was serious, but not critical; a crisis could be expected within the next four or five days. Holland left town. He returned the evening of Wednesday, July 6, and was greeted on the front steps of his house in Oakland with the news that he'd missed Hatcher's funeral and burial that afternoon. Hatcher had died Sunday night.

"Wire from Douglas [Stewart, Holland's assistant] tells me of our great loss, Professor Hatcher," Carnegie wrote from Skibo July 11. "I had not heard of his illness and was greatly shocked. I know how you valued him, and how difficult it will be to replace him. But when the flag drops from one, another steps forward and takes it up, and so the good work goes on. All well here, trusting you are also."

After that, there didn't seem to be such a rush to get the dinosaur off to London. It seemed reasonable that there be some modest celebration of the gift. As the letters went back and forth, plans grew more elaborate, and began including the king. But the king and

London cartoonists noticed the *Diplodocus'* trend-setting potential. From the *Sketch*, London. Illustration from Carnegie Museum of Natural History big bone room archives.

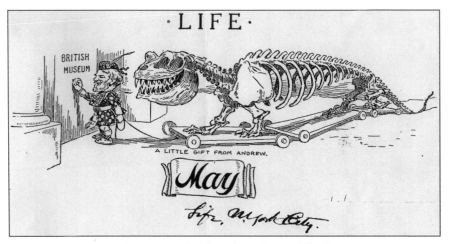

American cartoonists were ambivalent about Carnegie's gift. From the *Milwaukee Sentinel.* Illustration from Carnegie Museum of Natural History big bone room archives.

the museum's trustees were likely to be taking their ease in Scotland or on the continent in the late summer and early fall, and Carnegie always sailed back to New York in October. That made spring a more likely time, and that meant the workmen wouldn't have to hurry to build the bases the dinosaur would stand on, and ship the casts.

Holland named himself curator of vertebrate paleontology and had some trouble, at first, winning the confidence of Peterson and Utterback in the field. He never could seem to remember exactly what combination of horses and wagon they had, nor what condition they were in, nor where they were. Peterson wanted to come back to Pittsburgh to comfort his sister, Anna Hatcher, in her loss, but Holland advised him to stay in the West, so that Carnegie would not be disappointed with a summer with no discoveries at all. Utterback could find nothing of interest, and was severely discouraged. Sprits rose in August, when he finally found two *Triceratops* skulls.

The *Diplodocus* casts were shipped in December. Holland and Coggeshall sailed for England at the end of March 1905, and supervised the erection of the dinosaur that bore their patron's name. Carnegie paid for their passage, and for Coggeshall's expenses while in London. Holland felt obliged to cover his own.

Workmen with *Diplodocus carnegii* vertebrae on scaffolding at the British Museum (Natural History), London, 1905. Holland stands at lower left with arms crossed. Courtesy of Carnegie Museum of Natural History, Pittsburgh, Pennsylvania.

The grand ceremony with Carnegie, the trustees, all the dignitaries, press, and scientists went off without a hitch on May 12. The king did not attend, after all. Holland found Pittsburgh blistering in a grimy heat wave when he returned, and the museum in chaos, with construction of its ambitious new expansion going at full speed.

Carnegie appears to have provided Anna Hatcher with financial assistance after Hatcher's death. In October 1904, Hatcher's policy with the Union Mutual Life Insurance Company paid $3,000. With Stewart's help, Anna Hatcher sold their house. She and the four surviving children—Earl, Harold, Alice and John W.—moved back to Lamont, Iowa, to be near Hatcher's parents. By spring they were settled. "I have rented a better place now," she wrote Stewart, "and will move next week. It is only across the street and it has a barn and more ground so the boys will have some work to do in making a garden and raising chickens. We are all well . . ."

Chapter 15

HEADS AND TAILS

*T*he bones of a *Diplodocus* provide clues to what isn't there: tendons, muscles, organs, blood, and skin—and habits and posture. What did dinosaurs do? What did they eat? What was their gait and how, exactly, did they look when they moved? When Hatcher and Holland chose to mount the *Diplodocus* as they did, with its legs, like those of any large modern land mammal, free to swing forward and back from hip and shoulder sockets, they were following the lead of O. C. Marsh, who had assumed the posture was the natural one in his own early papers on sauropods beginning in the 1880s. But opinions on the subject were by no means unanimous.

Oliver P. Hay, the U.S. National Museum paleontologist who'd argued with Hatcher over the sequence of the Cretaceous rocks in Montana, was the first doubter. In 1905, the same year the *Diplodocus* cast was unveiled in London, a new *Apatosaurus* mount went up at the American Museum of Natural History in New York. Over the next several years, European heads of state sought dinosaurs for their national museums, and Carnegie eagerly complied. Holland and the dinosaur were nearing the peak of their fame. In an article published in 1909, Hay questioned the accuracy of the exhibit.

Scientists, Hay admonished his readers, should be careful to separate what they know from what they assume. In a dinosaur drawing, for instance, there ought to be an indication of which bones came from which specimens, and also of which ones were purely hypothetical. Similarly, in the case of mounts, "beauty ought not to be secured at the expense of truth . . ." That is, the plaster bones ought to be a different color from the real ones. The public then would understand how much the scientists knew and how much they were extrapolating, and would be drawn closer to the scientists' thinking: "The interest of the visitor will thus be excited, he will make the problem of the expert his own problem, and will pass judgment on the work done."

Behind Hay's larger criticisms lay his irritation with Hatcher and Holland for rejecting what seemed to him a more logical conclusion about the posture of *Diplodocus*. He believed the big sauropods moved like modern alligators and crocodiles, or even lizards, with their knees and elbows bent out sideways and bellies often on the ground.

Since dinosaurs were first identified early in the nineteenth century, scientists have tried to understand them by comparing them with modern animals. Richard Owen did it in 1841, in the famous report on British fossil reptiles in which he invented the concept of dinosaurs. He named a big Jurassic specimen *Cetiosaurus*—"whale-lizard"—because its bones seemed whale-like, or cetacean. Scientists make comparisons today, as well, when, for example, they compare sauropods to the big browsers of the Serengeti. Still, it took more discoveries before John Phillips of Oxford, having acquired more *Cetiosaurus* material by 1871, was able to understand better what the big dinosaurs were like. From a tooth, he concluded vegetarianism; from a long femur, he postulated a fairly free-stepping gait and vertical posture. The animal's claws suggested land life to Phillips; still he decided that *Cetiosaurus* was amphibious, living in swamps or on riversides.

Then came the great discoveries of the Cope and Marsh collectors in the Jurassic rocks of Wyoming and Colorado, followed by a flurry of papers by both men. There was considerable overlap in the naming, as often the papers were published while the greater parts of the specimens were still in the ground, but what emerged would eventually be recognized as three of the great sauropod genera:

Camarasaurus, Apatosaurus, and *Diplodocus.* Marsh established the Sauropoda as a new suborder of dinosaurs, and in 1883 published his restoration—that is, a detailed drawing—of *Apatosaurus* (still at the time called "Brontosaurus") *excelsus,* based on the specimen Reed had found at Como in 1879. For the first time, science had a good visual concept of a sauropod. One element, however, relied to a considerable degree on imaginative reconstruction. In sauropods, the connection between the top neck vertebra (the atlas) and the hindmost bone of the skull (the occipital condyle) is a weak joint, and, as a result, sauropod skeletons often lack heads. Reed's specimen was one of these. Marsh based his restoration on two other skulls, neither of which, it would eventually turn out, was very much like a true *Apatosaurus* skull. Marsh's collectors did, however, find a *Diplodocus* skull that was connected to a *Diplodocus* neck, and he published a description of it in 1884.

In the 1890s, the American Museum of Natural History, under Henry Fairfield Osborn's leadership, began scouring the West for vertebrate fossils, an effort that culminated in discovery of the Bone Cabin Quarry near Como in 1898. In 1899 Osborn published three papers on the most complete set of *Diplodocus* bones found to date—a shoulder bone, most of the pelvis, part of a femur, and a very good set of vertebrae, largely complete from halfway down the back out to the thirty-fifth tail bone, all from the Bone Cabin Quarry. They had enough of the spine to understand that the sacrum, that is, the fused vertebrae at the top of the hips, was the high point of the skeleton; Osborn called it "the center of power and motion," and noted with delight how the form wed maximum strength with minimum weight. So smitten was he that he was tempted, he wrote, to discard modern theories of evolution and "to revive the old teleological explanation"—the explanation that sees God in elegance, a divine hand in nature's designs.

The tail showed signs of heavy muscles at its base. Osborn felt it must have been a powerful swimming muscle, aided by a large fin suggested by the row of spines rising out of the vertebrae along the thick part of the tail. He also had in front of him the best set found to date of the smaller, lighter bones attached to the underside of the tail vertebrae. Marsh had called these chevrons; the ones he found first were from a *Diplodocus* tail and were double branched, like one of a set of sergeant's stripes. Marsh even used the idea in his name for the animal: *Diplodocus* means "double-raftered." But now Osborn had enough tail vertebrae to see that the earlier chevrons in the tail sequence had only one member; the double-branched effect began occurring only after the twelfth vertebra back. This was nearing the place where the tail itself might be expected to reach the ground. From that insight Osborn proposed that the double-branched, longitudinal chevrons might have been useful to help support the animal's weight on land, skidlike, when it propped itself back on a tripod formed of its hind feet and tail. The big bipedal carnivores were then and long afterward supposed to stand the same way. Osborn went so far as to believe the animal could raise its forequarters *while swimming*, suggesting nothing short of a bowspritted speedboat propelled by that finned and snaky tail.

If the animal was aquatic, its diet most likely was also. Osborn concluded from *Diplodocus'* lack of molars and weak, peglike front teeth that it ate nutritious water plants still soft enough to need no chewing. The claws *Diplodocus* and other sauropods appeared to have on their front feet would be useful in rooting such plants up from a river or swamp bottom. And though he was working from only about a third of a skeleton, Osborn understood correctly how the animal was different from its thicker-boned cousin: "In contrast with Brontosaurus it was essentially long and light-limbed and agile." He had roughed out the main points of a *Diplodocus* discussion that continues one hundred years later.

Hatcher, of course, had nearly a complete skeleton to work from when he published his 1901 paper on the Sheep Creek *Diplodocus* skeletons and then updated it in light of Utterback's finds. His conclusions follow Osborn's, right down to his description of the sacrum in the same words Osborn used, as "the center of power and motion." Hatcher describes an animal buoyant in water, clumsy on land, living on a diet of soft water plants. And it now was clear the tail stretched—amazingly—to seventy vertebrae or more. Hatcher echoed Osborn's suggestions that it was used for swimming power and as a tripod base—and added the idea that the tail would have been handy for whipping foes away. He contrasted the animal's relatively short, deep back and torso with its long neck and longer tail. In his restoration, and later in the cast mounted for Carnegie's gift to the king, Hatcher maintained the same long-legged, upright walking posture he'd learned from Marsh, and from the bones themselves.

The American Museum's *Apatosaurus*, mounted in 1905, lacked a head, as had the Reed-Marsh skeleton discovered twenty-five years earlier. Admitting the decision was "largely conjectural," Osborn nevertheless followed Marsh's restoration and attached a cast of a skull of what he then called a "Morosaurus," later understood to be the same as *Camarasaurus*, from the Bone Cabin Quarry. Perhaps obliquely registering discomfort with Marsh's conclusion on the heads, Osborn went out of his way to note the difference between the only two sauropod skulls then known, *Diplodocus* and *Camarasaurus*. A *Camarasaurus* skull, Osborn noted, was much boxier, with a high forehead, nostrils facing more forward than up, and "great cropping teeth," much larger and extending farther back along the upper and lower jaws than the "slender, pencil-like teeth" of *Diplodocus*, which were confined to the jaws' front end.

The American Museum's *Apatosaurus* was also lacking both forelimbs, from the shoulder down, so Osborn modeled the missing limbs on the example of Marsh's type specimen at Yale. For the sake of a better understanding of the animal's front end, Osborn had paleontologists Walter Granger and William D. Matthew dissect an alligator and a lizard, to learn how the *Apatosaurus'* muscles connected neck, backbone, and shoulder bones. By analogy to the modern animals, they came up with two important features for the mount. The *Apatosaurus'* shoulder blades were pushed lower, below the level of the back, and the front limbs were cocked outward at the elbow—not as much as an alligator, but still, as Osborn noted, "considerably everted." But he was too cagey to take a strong position on the animal's gait:

There is still room for wide differences of opinion as regards the habits and means of locomotion of these gigantic animals. Some hold the opinion that the limbs were far more flexed at the knee and elbow than they are in the present mount, that on land at least the animal had rather the attitude of the alligator, and that only while submerged beneath the water were the limbs straightened for the purposes of walking along the bottom, the claws serving to keep the feet from slipping in the mud.

Back in Pittsburgh, Holland published a large monograph in 1906. In the wake of Hatcher's death and all the ceremony in London, he may have been eager to consolidate his own reputation as a paleontologist. But he also had genuine news. He and Hatcher had learned things in mounting the *Diplodocus* that they would have encountered no other way.

Holland first describes the structure of the skull, then notes his and Hatcher's surprise that the skull did not fit onto the neck in the fashion they had expected it would. Instead of meeting in crocodile fashion, the configurations of atlas and occipital condyle would only allow the skull to fit at an angle. Holland compared the angle to the setting on the neck of a camel's or an ostrich's head—though the angle on the actual mount was broader, closer to 120 than 90 degrees.

The rake-like teeth suggested a soft diet to Holland, as they had to Osborn, though they seemed to him better adapted to tearing soft algae from shoreline rocks than any other purpose. The tail, now numbering seventy-three vertebrae, Holland compared in relative length to the tails of some modern lizards, including the iguana's, with sixty tail vertebrae, and the monitor's, with nearly one hundred. In the two specimens from the Sheep Creek quarry Holland found some fusing together of pairs of tail bones. He attributed this to injuries, either from being walked on or from being used as a flail, "giving blows to the right and left." The newly mounted partial *Cetiosaurus* in London—the *Cetiosaurus leedsi* Prof. E. Ray Lankester had referred to in his opening remarks at the Diplodocus ceremony—also showed signs of injury to its tail vertebrae, Holland noted. Osborn had found similar fusing in the tail bones of the American Museum's *Diplodocus*, and had attributed the condition to use of the tail as part of a tripod when the animal reared back. The implications of the fused tail bones would still be in dispute nearly a century later. Holland remained silent on the subject of *Diplodocus carnegii's* gait and posture. The mount itself makes it clear what he thought.

Hay entered the dispute in October 1908, cranking up the heat on the gait-and-posture question. If the sauropods, especially *Diplodocus*, walked, he asked rhetorically, "was it on all four legs or on the hinder ones only? If on all four, did they carry their bodies high above the ground, after the manner of the ox and the horse? Or did they carry them low down, like the crocodiles, perhaps dragging their bellies on the ground?" Decidedly he favored the second option. He complained that Marsh's long-limbed restoration "has been almost slavishly followed ever since," yet, a page later, cites Osborn and the American Museum's new *Apatosaurus* mount to demonstrate room for argument.

Instead of reading the sauropod claws as evidence of river-bottom food grabbing, however, Hay saw them as reminiscent of crocodile feet. He concluded that, like crocodiles, the sauropods used their claws to push from the back legs and pull from front. Walking upright in the "mud and muck where they lived," the great sauropods would have gotten their feet stuck.

Hay rejected the walking and tree-browsing habits, and suggested the animal could only creep on land "with perhaps laborious effort," but it swam easily and, because of its long neck, could feed on plants some distance under water or on foliage hanging above. Museums should take heed; a crocodile posture could be equally imposing as the upright stance, "while the long neck, as flexible as that of an ostrich, might be placed in a variety of graceful positions."

In a second paper the same month, Hay got more personal. Holland had loaned Hay the back part of the *Diplodocus* skull Utterback had found in Wyoming, on which much of the skull discussion in Holland's most recent paper had been based. Unfortunately, Holland had mislabeled and misunderstood the function of many of the small bones of the skull. Hay noted other errors: Holland had implied that the *Diplodocus* had three pairs of nostrils and that some modern reptiles have visible ears on the outside of their heads, and he had mixed up the numbers of certain specimens from the U.S. National Museum and from the American Museum.

Holland was stung. He was glad to accept criticism if well founded, but Hay's, he wrote, was not. Hay might be well known for his work on tortoises, but he was a newcomer to dinosaurs. Hay intentionally must have misunderstood his remarks on the *Diplodocus'* nostrils and reptiles' ears, Holland huffed, in the latter remarks even trying to be funny. Holland didn't think it was a bit funny: "He ought first to be sure that he understands what he is talking about."

When, ten months later, Hay called for real bones and plaster bones to be different colors and when he upbraided museums for not being more frank about separating what they know from what they assume, it is hard not to read his remarks as a personal counterattack on Holland, the self-proclaimed paleontologist for a millionaire patron:

The plain indication of the restored parts of fossil animals is likewise a matter of common honesty. Emperors, grand dukes and millionaires may found museums, and they secure recognition for their munificence; but right at hand are the masses of the people who, in the end, foot the bills, and they have also their rights. . . . The buyer has a right to know what he is getting for his money. The principle applies in all walks of life, however much it may fret those who would secure wealth, position and honors disproportionate to their deserts. . . .

It is the practice sometimes to build up a fossil skeleton out of the bones of various individuals. This can not be condemned in all cases, but . . . [i]n the case of less well-known animals . . . there is likely to result a mixture of species and even of genera. And no hybrids are so fertile as these, inasmuch as they reproduce themselves throughout the world by means of the printing press. And these hybrids are monsters besides, having legs belonging perhaps to two or three distinct animals, the head to another and so on.

The observation still resonates, particularly in light of the subsequent confusion over Marsh's choice for an *Apatosaurus* head. But it was fame's negative effect on good science that was really nettling Hay. Sarcastically, he concludes:

And these plaster casts of the great animals that sojourned on the earth in bygone ages present another advantage that seems to be of the highest importance to the advancement of science. For now and anon some one among us, a paleontologist inchoate as yet but confident, the beneficiary of a favorable environment, bestriding his light-legged, straight-legged gypsiferous steed, perhaps Brontodiplodococamarosaurus, may gallop safely and merrily up the rugged slopes of the Mount of Fame.

By now it was the summer of 1909. Since the unveiling of the first *Diplodocus carnegii* cast in London, the original bones had been mounted in Pittsburgh, two more casts had been delivered to Berlin and Paris, and two more were scheduled to go that fall to Vienna and Bologna. As the cast-shipping continued, Hay still couldn't allow the matter to drop. In February 1910 he published an article pursuing his claim for *Diplodocus'* crocodile-like gait in even greater detail. He continued to maintain that the thigh and upper-foreleg bones—the femur and the humerus—of the animal stuck out sideways from the hip and shoulder sockets, respectively, and moved in horizontal planes. The claws pulled the animal forward in a croc-like creep.

The head of the femur, its shape rounded to a blunt cone by cartilage now missing from all existing skeletons, would fit directly into the hip socket, Hay claimed, and could easily move in and out of the socket, as needed, as the femur swung in its horizontal arc. The big abdomen meant that the animal's back legs had to remain far apart from each other, mandating a side-to-side, body-swinging, tail-switching gait. Hay added that, in any case, the Jurassic was too soon for an animal to be walking like a big, modern mammal.

That winter, Holland's assistants were casting another *Diplodo-cus carnegii*, this one for Czar Nicholas. By now not only Hay had attacked the Carnegie's specimen's posture. Two Germans, Gustav Tornier and Richard Sternfeld, had also joined the fight. Tornier placed *Diplodocus* among the lacertilians, or lizards, a group which includes chameleons, monitors, and their relatives. "It was a bold step" Holland responded, for Tornier "to proceed with the help of a pencil, the powerful tool of the closet naturalist, to reconstruct the skeleton upon the study of which two generations of American paleontologists have expended considerable time and labor, and squeezed the animal into the form which his brilliantly illuminated imagination suggested."

Holland played his trump card. All he had to do was set the cast bones from the Russia-bound *Diplodocus* into the positions Hay and the two Germans claimed were correct—Tornier had given detailed drawings of the hip configurations—and see what there was to see. The result was that nothing fit; nothing worked. Holland illustrated his rebuttal with photographs of the bones positioned according to Tornier's drawings. To stick the femur straight out sideways from the hip socket proved "impossible except by smashing the ilium or breaking the femur to jam the head of the latter into the position demanded for it by the learned professor . . . locking the femur into a position utterly precluding all motion whatsoever."

Supposing, he wrote, the femur of the *Diplodocus* could be positioned like the femur of an iguana or a monitor; the bone would have had to angle up slightly from hip to knee. That would have brought the great barrel of *Diplodocus'* rib cage—far deeper, proportionally, than the rib cage of any modern lizard—so low the animal would have needed a trough in the earth to move forward. Holland included a diagrammatic cross section. "The Diplodocus must have moved in a groove or a rut. This might perhaps account for his early extinction." he deadpanned. "It is physically and mentally bad to 'get in a rut.'" He didn't see how there could remain any doubt about the true posture: "The form of the limbs, long, straight and pillar-like, in this respect differing vastly from the limbs of the creeping lacertilia and crocodilia, suggests that they were intended to support a weight thrown on them from above."

Finally, Holland went back over the well-trodden questions of tails and diet. Tornier may have been partly right to suggest the tail was only dragged full length on the ground, to anchor and stiffen the body, but to claim, as Sternfeld did, that the tail was used in "a wriggling motion . . . is to attribute to the organ properties which it hardly possessed." Probably *Diplodocus* often used its tail as one leg of a tripod, Holland noted. Like Osborn, he thought the stance likely largely because it mirrored a similar pose in carnivorous dinosaurs. Questions of diet were trickier. Hay had approved of Holland's earlier suggestion of an algae diet; Tornier had decided *Diplodocus* was not herbivorous, but ate fish; Sternfeld "pictures it as squatting on the banks of streams and feeding on snails, bivalves [clams and mussels] and amphibians." Cycads were plentiful in the Jurassic, Holland noted. But their buds were "woolly and harsh, and the leaves are as stiff as wires and could not have been masticated by such teeth as the Diplodocus possessed." More likely Diplodocus could claw open the bark to get at the soft stuff inside the stems.

Sauropod footprints discovered in Texas in the 1930s and 1940s would be found to lie quite close to the center line of the animal's direction—clear evidence it walked upright, swinging its legs vertically. Earlier in the century, Hay remained unconvinced, even as consensus was shifting further and further away from his views. He was unconvinced about another generally accepted matter as well—that Diplodocus and the other sauropods lived most of their lives in water. Sauropod feet were clearly meant for dry land, he wrote, regardless of what one surmised about their gait and posture. If they had spent all their time in the water, they would have fins or flippers. But it would be 60 more years before those ideas would get much attention.

In the summer of 1909, Carnegie collector Earl Douglass found three sauropod skeletons in hard Jurassic sandstone in a remote canyon in the northeast corner of Utah, a site that later became Dinosaur National Monument. By 1914 many more sauropod skeletons and skulls had turned up. One of them—narrow, with a low forehead and peglike front teeth—looked very much like a larger version of a Diplodocus skull and lay just twelve feet from the end of the neck of a new and spectacularly complete Apatosaurus. In fact, there were at least eleven skulls, all of a Diplodocus-like shape, but only two of which could be referred with certainty to a nearby Diplodocus skeleton. The rest appeared to be more closely related to Apatosaurus, or to some sauropod still unknown. Finally, Holland could contain his doubts no longer. In 1915 he politely raised the flag of uncertainty. Maybe the great Marsh had been wrong, and maybe Osborn had been wrong to follow Marsh's restoration and mount the boxy, snub-nosed Camarasaurus-like skull on the American Museum's Apatosaurus. The Carnegie mount of its new Apatosaurus from Utah— Apatosaurus louisae, in honor of Carnegie's wife, Louise—was nearing completion, and Holland had to figure out what to do about the head.

Richard Swann Lull at Yale looked back through Marsh's records at Holland's request, and discovered that the skull Marsh had attributed to the *Apatosaurus* was found a full four miles away from where Reed found the rest of the skeleton. That confirmed, Holland reported, what Reed had told him years ago, "that the skull utilized by Marsh did not in the judgment of Mr. Reed belong to the same individual as the rest of the specimen and had nothing to do with it." Charles Gilmore, who'd begun his career with the Carnegie Museum in 1900, wrote Holland from his job at the U.S. National Museum to say that records there showed that the second, *Camarasaurus*-like skull which Marsh had attributed to *Apatosaurus*, from the quarry near Cañon City, Colorado, had not been associated with any other nearby *Apatosaurus* bones. Lull still believed Marsh was correct. He had worked with the American Museum crew excavating the *Apatosaurus* in 1899; though they found no skull they found a *Camarasaurus*-like tooth associated with the skeleton.

Holland was unconvinced. Marsh's decision, he wrote, "was the result of a process of ratiocination, rather than . . . the result of ocular evidence . . . There is no intention in these paragraphs to dogmatize, but to express a doubt founded on observation, as to the correctness of Professor Marsh's surmise, which up to the present time has been unquestionably accepted . . . The two skulls used by Marsh were found, one four miles from the rest of the skeleton, the other four hundred miles from it."

A *Camarasaurus*-like skull had turned up at the new Utah quarry, but some distance away, upstream, and in a rock layer eight feet higher and therefore more recent than the *Apatosaurus* skeleton. There was far less reason to use that skull than the *Diplodocus*-like one that had been found only twelve feet from the atlas of the *Apatosaurus*. If it weren't for Marsh's great authority, even in death, it would have been an easy choice. "My good friend, Dr. Osborn, has in a bantering mood, 'dared' me to mount the head, which we have found associated with our Brontosaurus, on the atlas, which it fits." Holland was tempted to take him up on the dare. But he never had the nerve. *Apatosaurus louisae* was mounted in Pittsburgh with no head at all.

Returning to the less delicate question of the *Diplodocus'* tail, Holland reported that the three new sauropods from the Utah quarry, all seemingly examples of *Apatosaurus*, had whip-like, *Diplodocus*-like tails. One of the specimens, with a complete vertebral column from atlas to tail tip, had a total of eighty-two tail vertebrae. Roughly the rear half or more of the tail vertebrae in the big sauropods are simple rods of bone, convex and rounded at both ends, which allows the tail to swing or curl in all directions: maximum flexibility. "This 'whip-lash,' as it has been styled, recalls the long tail of the Monitors, and must have been a weapon of defence in the case of the colossal reptilia as it is in the case of the Monitors," Holland wrote. An acquaintance in the Philippines had recounted how, for some time, he had a pet monitor he kept in the courtyard of his house. When the dog approached, the lizard tail-whipped it and the dog retreated, yelping, and never came close again. Sauropods probably used a similar tactic, Holland suggested.

Nine years later, when he took a detailed look at a new *Diplodocus* skull from the Utah quarry, Holland's doubts about Marsh's head choice were as strong as ever. But perhaps feeling that he should acknowledge his own errors, Holland at last admitted that Hay's criticisms that in his 1906 paper he had misnamed or misunderstood the function of many of the small bones in the *Diplodocus* skull had been largely justified. The new skull from Utah represented a new species. Holland named it *Diplodocus hayi*.

Still he left *Apatosaurus louisae* headless, and so it remained until after his death, in 1932. When the subsequent curator finally did mount a head, he used a cast of a *Camarasaurus* skull.

For seventy years or more *Diplodocus* and its sauropod cousins remained in the swamps, and stupid. Animals that big, the consensus ran, would have had to spend nearly all their time in the water; only water could buoy such bulk. Osborn and his artist Charles Knight had placed them there, as did Rudolph Zallinger in his wonderful 110-feet-long 1947 mural, *The Age of Reptiles*, still on display at the

Peabody Museum at Yale. Then, in southern Montana in 1964, Yale paleontologist John Ostrom discovered a long, sickle-shaped toe claw from a bipedal, Cretaceous meat-eating dinosaur Ostrom named *Deinonychus*, "terrible claw." It looked fast and mean. From Ostrom's insights, the insights of Robert Bakker, one of his Yale students, and the ideas of others, a shift in the overall understanding of dinosaurs began to spread in the early 1970s.

Near the end of the decade, Luis and Walter Alvarez offered new conclusions on why dinosaurs went extinct. A thin layer of iridium-rich clay had been found in widely separated places around the world, in strata that coincided perfectly with the end of the Cretaceous period. Because asteroids are rich in iridium, while Earth is not, the discovery led to a surprising thesis: that a huge meteor or asteroid hit Earth at that time and scattered dust and debris all over the planet. The impact caused fires and floods; the airborne debris shut out sunlight for years, bringing on prolonged cold and the great die-offs at the end of the Cretaceous. Suddenly, in the popular imagination, dinosaurs seemed no longer responsible for their own demise—no longer doomed for lack of mental equipment. Popular interest in dinosaurs boomed, and dinosaur research boomed too.

By the mid-1970s Bakker was describing dinosaurs as generally agile and warm-blooded. The big sauropods lived in herds for defense and looked out for their young, he maintained. With their tails, they whipped away any predators careless enough to approach. Warm-bloodedness—a high metabolism—meant they had to consume massive amounts of food and move it down their long necks. Therefore the small-headed sauropods, which couldn't really chew at all, must, like birds, have had gizzards in their guts where stones ground the food. Some had big food-fermentation vats as well, Bakker suggested, like the first in the series of cows' stomachs, where the food would soften chemically before moving along for further digestion.

Diplodocus was a high browser, Bakker believes, and spent a great deal of its time reared back tripod-fashion on its tail, eating. Its mouth could reach nearly forty feet above the ground—more than twice as high as a giraffe's can. Bakker was agreeing with Osborn, Hatcher, and Holland on this point, but he had thought more thoroughly through its implications for diet and habitat. The Jurassic conifers and cycads grew slowly, but since few dinosaurs were specialized for feeding at ground level, the plants were mostly safe from browsing pressure when they were young and small, Bakker believes.

Another new argument was that sauropods didn't like swamps. Cretaceous duckbilled, horned, and armored dinosaurs are relatively common on the high plains stretching from Alberta to New Mexico. The sites were once Cretaceous deltas, low, warm and swampy, where rivers flowed eastward into the shallow sea that lay down the middle of North America. But the only Cretaceous sauropods have been found far to the West, in what is now Utah, where the ground was higher and dry, Bakker notes. They "eschewed the soggy terrain and moved their evolutionary centers elsewhere."

By the mid-1970s, two other paleontologists were at last ready to challenge Marsh's authority, seventy-five years after his death. John S. McIntosh, professor of physics at Wesleyan University in Connecticut, was then and now recognized as the world's leading expert on sauropods. David S. Berman was and is a curator of vertebrate paleontology at the Carnegie Museum. The dubiousness of Marsh's conclusions had long been an open secret. After studying Douglass's field notes, his correspondence with Holland, and some cataloguing mixups at the Carnegie museum, McIntosh and Berman were positive Holland's long-ago suspicions were legitimate. The skull Douglass dug up at the Utah quarry just twelve feet from the end of the *Apatosaurus* neck had been an *Apatosaurus* skull. Even leaving the head out of the discussion, *Apatosaurus*, with its extremely long tail, tall back legs and shorter front ones, relatively short back, and long neck was an animal much more like *Diplodocus* than it was like the shorter-tailed, longer-backed *Camarasaurus*.

On Oct. 15, 1979, the curators at the Carnegie Museum replaced the old *Camarasaurus*-like skull on the head of *Apatosaurus louisae* with the correct one. It was slender, with a lower forehead and weak, pencil-like front teeth only in the front of its mouth—a lot like a *Diplodocus* skull, only bigger. Appropriately, the head switch came first at the museum that was the source of the idea in the first place. Other museums followed suit, some more reluctantly than others.

Apatosaurus also was reclassified, moved out of the sauropod family of camarasaurids and in with the diplodocids where it belonged.

Since then, ideas about the diplodocids have continued to evolve. The tails have been compared to whips at least since Osborn's 1899 papers. Hatcher continued the analogy, as did Holland and Bakker. But not until 1997 did a pair of dinosaur scientists distinguish between two kinds of whips. One kind is used like a flail, simply for striking and causing damage; a second kind—a bullwhip—cracks loudly to catch the attention of livestock. A whip crack is actually a sonic boom; when the tip of the whip—just the last few inches—exceeds the speed of sound, it cracks. Nathan P. Myhrvold, a computer scientist with Microsoft in Redmond, Washington, and Philip J. Currie of the Royal Tyrrell Museum in Drumheller, Alberta, decided to find out if the diplodocids' tails indeed were flexible enough to crack like bullwhips.

Working from ten different diplodocid specimens, Myhrvold and Currie found the tails to taper evenly from thick end to thin, like bullwhips. Diplodocids generally have tails of more than eighty vertebrae. A computer-modeled tail, reconstructed from the Carnegie Museum's *Apatosaurus louisae*, showed the center of gravity to be only a short way down the tail, at the seventh vertebra, where the tail is still quite thick. The fusing of vertebrae Holland puzzled over between about the eighteenth and twenty-fifth vertebrae, is not best explained by injury or by strengthening for a tripod-back posture, Myrhvold and Currie maintain. By that point, the tail is already so thin that only three percent of its mass lies in the remaining fifty-five or so vertebrae; rather, the area around the twenty-fifth vertebra would be right about where the tail's "bullwhip" would need a "handle." Actual bullwhips show a great deal of stress and wear at the point where the handle joins the flexible remainder of the whip; it would make sense that there be fusing of the bones for strength at that point if the tail were routinely subjected to whip-like stresses.

Beyond the thirty-fifth vertebra, as noted, the bones are simple rods, convex at both ends for flexibility in all directions. But they have no other parts—no chevrons on the bottom or spines on the top— suggesting significant muscle or tendon attachments. The tail's entire back half or more was so flexible that cracking it took less energy than walking, Myrhvold's and Currie's computer models showed. Bullwhips generally have a "popper" of string or other lighter-than-leather material on the last few inches of their length to make cracking easier. Myrhvold and Currie speculated the diplodocids' tails may have ended similarly, with an extension of skin and tendon beyond the last tail bones. It would have frayed and worn off easily with frequent use and would therefore have needed constant growth to replace itself. At the same time, it would have protected the last vertebra or two from constant whip-end stresses.

Being thin enough to crack, the tails were too thin to inflict any damage when used as a flail. Mindful of Holland's account of the monitor and the dog, Myhrvold and Currie checked with a Seattle zookeeper, who reported that monitors strike hard enough to startle but not hard enough to break human skin. Their tail lashing is not supersonic; and the monitors' tails survive use as weapons because they move more slowly—without the rodlike whiplash vertebrae, or the bi-convex joints that a *Diplodocus* tail would have.

The noise the crack made was probably its rationale. Myrhvold and Currie speculate happily about what the noise might have been good for: predator deterrence, enforcement of herd discipline, or displays of dominance by members of the same or opposite genders. Their calculations on the tails' cracking rate and power, they note, were all made with the assumption that the big animals were standing still. But if *Apatosaurus* were walking, there would be so much added side-to-side momentum from the hindquarters that the animal could have cracked its tail in time with every footfall.

Some scientists now say the engineering of the diplodocids' skeletons also supports the likelihood of the tripod-back, high-browsing position. The front legs, tall spines off the vertebrae at the base of the back, and powerful muscles in the thighs and at the base of the tail all provide the right leverage and center of gravity for the animals to assume the posture easily. Blood pressure, however, would be a problem. A giraffe's blood pressure is two times that of other mammals. To pump blood from the heart all the way up to the head of the longest-necked sauropods would require twice a giraffe's pressure: difficult to construe but not impossible. Some paleontologists have suggested that *Barosaurus*, a diplodocid with an even longer neck than *Diplodocus*, must have had two hearts to pump to so great a height.

To better understand the physical capabilities inherent in the diplodocids' neck, Kent Stevens, a computer scientist from the University of Oregon, and Michael Parrish, a paleontologist from Northern Illinois University used a computer model with twenty-four adjustable parameters for each of the fifteen pairs of neck vertebrae. Basing their work on *Apatosaurus louisae* and *Diplodocus carnegii*, they found that the most neutral pose for the neck was with the spine sloped slightly downward, the head just above ground level. A nuchal ligament, similar to one in modern horses, cows and other ground grazers, may have run along the top of the neck vertebrae, allowing the animals to cantilever the neck out comfortably, without a lot of extra work. In the neutral pose, the angle of the dinosaurs' eye sockets would have allowed them to look forward, perhaps even with some binocular overlap and therefore some depth perception, Stevens and Parrish found.

The computer modeling showed the *Apatosaurus* could curl its neck somewhat more tightly back around and to the sides than *Diplodocus*, but, because *Diplodocus* had a longer neck, it could cover about the same amount of grazing area. The *Apatosaurus* could also bend its neck further upward. Its shorter and more flexible neck could be brought, with some effort, into a high S-curve. *Diplodocus*, however, could barely raise its neck above the height of its back, the model showed.

Perhaps most interesting was the discovery that both genera could reach a considerable distance downward—a meter and a half, or nearly five feet, below the level of their feet. A *Diplodocus* standing on a semi trailer could graze grass or shrubs off the ground at a highway rest stop. In its own time, that downward flexibility may have been most useful when the animal was standing on a lake or river shore, feeding on plants floating on the water or submerged below it.

From a tripod-back position, the *Diplodocus* could feed at heights from twenty to thirty-eight feet above the ground, Stevens and Parrish found. But the gingkoes and conifers available at those elevations would offer a lot more chewing problems than food value.

Softer and more nutritious plants grew close to the ground: ferns, a variety of cycads, horsetails, and algae. If they fed primarily off the ground or out of the water, the blood pressure problem becomes moot. On diet and feeding posture at least, Osborn and Holland may not have been so wrong after all. *Diplodocus* and *Apatosaurus* may have fed not so much like giraffes, elephants, or even swans, as like great, long-necked water buffaloes.

 *Chapter 16*

CELEBRITY

I n Argentina, with time on his hands while yet another *Diplodo-cus carnegii* cast was being mounted in yet another national museum, Holland visited a church in the city of Tucuman, in the foothills of the Andes. Decorated plaster saints and apostles and gilded madonnas filled its niches. He professed a tourist's fatigue: he was tired of churches, tired of museums, tired of travel alto-gether. Closer to the truth would have been a confession of how deeply the splendor unsettled his Protestant soul; it looked gaudy to him. But in any case, he noted, the saints were better back home, lined up in the Pittsburgh workshop of the Italian who so skillfully cast the bones of the *Diplodocus,* and who ran a business making saints on the side.

After the first *Diplodocus* cast was made and shipped to London in 1905, Holland and his employees had concentrated on getting their own, original *Diplodocus carnegii*—made of real bones from the Sheep Creek and Red Fork sites—mounted and ready for the grand reopening of the expanded Carnegie Institute in April 1907. This was not just a bigger museum; it included more library and art gallery space, as well, and the old *campanile* had been removed to make room for a lavish new foyer for the music hall.

Besides a hall for the *Diplodocus* and other dinosaurs soon to be mounted, big spaces in the expanded museum included a Hall of

Sculpture, with plaster copies of Greek and Roman statues, and a Hall of Architecture, with full-sized plaster copies of European cathedral facades and a scale model of the Parthenon. Educating the public with plaster reproductions was not uncommon in turn-of-the-century museums; it was a manufacturer's approach. The showcase of the museum's new spaces was the one-of-a-kind foyer for the music hall. Floor, columns, and gallery were all marble; the columns were of a deep green Vert Tinos marble from Greece. A statue of Carnegie stood at one end, and the ceiling was of elaborately molded plaster covered in gold leaf.

The number of plasterers swelled to a small army. Where it had taken two Italians, together with the regular fossil-preparation crew, to model, mold, and cast the first *Diplodocus* replicas, the halls of sculpture and architecture and the new music hall foyer took the combined labor of eighty-five Italian workers. Carnegie could go all out when he wanted to. The foyer ceiling alone cost $14,000. The entire expansion took eight years to plan and build, and eventually cost $5 million.

Carnegie was giving his money away faster and faster now. He paid for a peace palace at The Hague; the cornerstone was laid in 1907. He had recently founded the Carnegie Hero Fund and a few years earlier had started up the Carnegie Institute in Washington, D.C., to support scientific research. Soon, giving away his fortune for individual projects would become too big a job, and he would establish endowments and corporations to give it away for him. His most cherished hope was to persuade President Theodore Roosevelt and Kaiser Wilhelm II of Germany to sit down with him and hear his program for world peace. He was sure he could charm them into accepting his ideas on the spot. When the Kaiser invited Carnegie to the annual boat races that summer at Kiel, on the Baltic Sea, Carnegie attended with the highest hopes. The Kaiser, also a charming man, promised nothing, but Carnegie left happily, feeling he'd planted the crucial seeds.

Carnegie came to Pittsburgh in April 1907 for the rededication of the expanded building. Also on hand were representatives of the Kaiser and of the French president. They brought Carnegie presents—lavish books, engravings, and photographs. With these gifts in hand, the prince of manufacturers must have felt he could now reciprocate without looking too eager. He instructed Holland to ask the Germans and the French to ask their superiors if they would care to accept a gift in return—*Diplodocus* replicas for their respective national museums. The Kaiser cabled his acceptance the next day. President Fallières followed suit not long afterward.

By fall, Arthur Coggeshall and his assistants had mounted another cast for practice in Pittsburgh and had taken a photo of it. This time they mounted the head and the front of the neck slightly higher, an "attitude . . . far more graceful and lifelike," Holland wrote Marcellin Boule in Paris. Boule, finally about to get the dinosaur Hatcher had promised him four years earlier, replied that his museum was short on space and would need to plan for a wider, shorter rear platform to allow the tail to curl partway back around. Holland, disgruntled, agreed politely. He assured his counterparts in Paris and Berlin that Carnegie would pay for everything but inquired if their railroad systems might be counted on to provide free passage for the cast bones from the docks to the capitals. The crates, thirty-six per dinosaur, were shipped in mid-March 1908. The Germans insisted on being first, so Holland and Coggeshall sailed for Hamburg on April 7.

The German skeleton was successfully mounted in Berlin and ready for the Kaiser's inspection by May 11. Holland was feted at a banquet, but the Kaiser apparently did not put in an appearance. In Paris, however, there was a ceremony on June 15 of equal or greater pomp than the one in London two years before. Parisians of all ranks crowded the Jardin des Plantes outside the Museum d'Histoire Naturelle to watch President Armand Fallières and other dignitaries arrive between two rows of National Guardsmen. Inside, Coggeshall, Holland, and leading French scientists gathered in the paleontologic gallery to hear the president's remarks.

M. Fallières seems not to have had a previous glimpse of the *Diplodocus,* and he was stunned by its size, especially the length of its tail, even curled. He could only remark, *"Quelle queue!"* And again, amazed into inarticulateness, *"Quelle queue!"*—What a tail! But "*queue*" means penis, too—at least it did that year in Paris. For months, cabaret singers lampooned the president's unintentional *double entendre* in song and rhyme. Holland's reaction is not recorded.

In Vienna in September 1909, Emperor Franz Josef accepted the *Diplodocus* replica in person. Again the tail had had to be curled to save space. Holland and Coggeshall traveled on to Bologna the following month to present another replica to King Victor Emmanuel of Italy; this time there was enough space to run the tail out straight. Their dinosaur giving continued. The Czar's uncle, Grand Duke Wladimir, had happened to be in Paris in 1908 when Holland and Coggeshall were setting up the French cast. The duke had asked Holland to tell Carnegie to remember Russia, too. The Americans arrived in St. Petersburg in June 1910, to install a *Diplodocus* in the Imperial Academy of Sciences.

The Russian replica brought to six the number of *Diplodocus* casts Carnegie had given away. College students, who in those days loved to sing, made up a song about it:

> Crowned heads of Europe
> All make a royal fuss
> Over Uncle Andy
> And his old diplodocus.

By now, Holland and Coggeshall were getting efficient at *Diplodocus* mounting. First, workmen built scaffolding with a top crossbeam high off the floor and substantial enough to hold the two-or-three-ton weight of the entire central part of the cast skeleton. Then they assembled the vertebrae on a platform of planks and inserted through them a steel rod shaped to the arch of the spinal column.

Using blocks and tackle suspended from the main beam and steel cables looped under the platform, they raised the backbone assembly to about fifteen feet off the floor. Vertical steel supports were screwed to joints in the longitudinal rods at the pelvis and shoulders, and everything could then be lowered—this was the trickiest part—until the uprights dropped into sockets in the base, where they were bolted securely. Once the central vertebral structure was secure, steel supports for the ribs, limbs, neck, and tail were added. When all the other work was finished, a polished mahogany or walnut top was laid on the base, under the dinosaur's feet.

In St. Petersburg a moment of truth came when the backbone was suspended high in the air, with six "moujiks," as Holland called them, standing at intervals holding guy-ropes to steady the mass. Coggeshall was on a tall step-ladder at the front end, ready to help Holland screw the threaded top of one of the front uprights into its socket when the time came. Holland had lifted the long rod from the floor and was carrying it forward when the door burst open and a company of Imperial Academy dignitaries strode into the room. Holland, long rod in hand, turned to bow to the visitors, and so missed what happened next. The moujiks perhaps felt obliged to bow, themselves. In any case, one or more of them jerked a rope or let go altogether, the spinal column began twisting at the front end until it came loose from the tackle hook, the bones slid from their plank platform and crashed and broke with a roar, the portraits of the Czars and Czarinas trembled on the walls, and the visitors fled, looking as if a bomb had exploded.

Coggeshall's first question, to his credit, was for Holland's safety. Both men were amazed to see that some of the cast bones had broken the exposed oak joists of the base, "as if chopped through with an ax." But what to do? It would take three months to travel back to Pittsburgh, cast new bones, and ship them back to Russia. So they glued it, "with that strong cement, which we know how to prepare," Holland wrote later. As it was June, St. Petersburg's latitude allowed them to work by natural light from early morning to ten at night. With the help of a preparator named Petz, they had the broken bones back together in a week. Next time they swung the vertebrae to set the uprights, they locked the doors.

Holland was tired of traveling when a request came in 1912 for a seventh *Diplodocus* cast, this time from the president of Argentina, Dr. Roque Saenz Pena. When Holland later wrote a book about the voyage, he opened it with a ditty about wanting to be something one was not:

THE DIPLODOCUS

I wish I were an ichthyosaurus
And could swim the Lias ocean
And eat fish. But Oh! I am not.
Alas! I cannot be an ichthyo-
Ichthyosaurus; for I'm a diplo-
Diplodo-do-docus. I can tie
My rubber neck into a knot.
—Song book of the Geological Society of America

The William Holland of *To the River Plate and Back* is a naturalist with time on his hands—time to notice airborne spider webs at sea, to speculate about volcanoes on the moon, to paint ocean sunsets from the deck of his steamer. He's a languorous William Holland, fond as ever of his own turns of phrase but never impatient, never disappointed or betrayed, never eager, never angry—a different man from the one in his letters. He was reluctant, he writes at the beginning of the book, to undertake the trip. He was swamped with work, poor in health, low in spirits. He'd been on long trips abroad at least four out of the previous six years and may himself have begun feeling like a *Dipolodocus* with its rubber neck tied into a knot. Of course he allowed Carnegie to persuade him to go, took Coggeshall and the casts along—and finally swore he was very glad he went. The voyage south took thirty days over calm summer seas. He was restored, he said, by the time he got there.

Not much happened. He went fossil hunting, though he did not meet the Ameghinos. He went sightseeing but much preferred butterfly collecting. He admired the Tertiary mammal fossils in the new National Museum in La Plata, dined with scientists, let Coggeshall supervise another *Diplodocus* mount, and met President Saenz Pena, who asked many questions about the Taft-Roosevelt-Wilson race for the U.S. presidency, then in high gear. A final banquet on October 15, 1912, at the Sportsman's Club in La Plata featured *Canapé Multimillionaire* as an hors d'oeuvre, *Grande pièce Diplodocus à la Holland* as an entrée, and other dishes named after the Argentinian paleontologists on hand, all arranged around a five-foot-long

Diplodocus centerpiece, sculpted by the same Charles Knight who had painted so many murals for Osborn and the *Triceratops* frontispiece for Hatcher's monograph.

Two years later, after war had broken out across Europe, Holland and Coggeshall traveled to neutral Spain to install a *Diplodocus* at the National Museum in Madrid. Holland was granted an audience with King Alphonso XIII and also met the king's mother, Dona Maria Christina. He gave a slide lecture, in Spanish, before the Royal Society in the large audience room of the International Institute for Women. Then, for many years, no more invitations came.

Carnegie died in August 1919, in a mansion in Lenox, Massachusetts, which he had bought after his age and the outbreak of World War I made it impossible to travel to Skibo any longer. Holland visited him in those last months and found his old friend in a good mood. "What are you thinking about?" Holland asked one day. Carnegie replied, "I have been thinking about my mother. I have been thinking about her all the morning. I can feel her moist hand on my forehead now."

In 1922 Holland turned seventy-four and retreated to director emeritus status at the museum. In exchange, he took on the duties of president of the Carnegie Hero Fund, with an office in the Oliver Building in downtown Pittsburgh. He also joined the board of the Carnegie Corporation of New York, the huge charity into which Carnegie had moved the bulk of his fortune. Holland was busy as ever, but, as he grew older, he felt scattered and unsatisfied. Colds laid him low longer, travel took longer to recover from, letters took much longer to answer.

In the summer of 1927 Manuel Tellez, Mexican Ambassador to the United States, passed along to W. M. Gilbert at the Carnegie Institution in Washington, D.C., an inquiry from Professor Alphonso Herrera, director of the National Museum of Natural History in Mexico City. Gilbert passed Tellez's letter to Andrey Avinoff, a Russian emigre and lepidopterist by then director of the Carnegie Museum, and Avinoff passed it to Holland. The question was, Might there be a Carnegie *Diplodocus* available "for museum study in Mexico City?"

Holland appears to have been unaware of the fact that Mexican-

American relations at that moment were at a low ebb. U.S. oil companies with holdings near Veracruz, Tampico, and elsewhere along
the Gulf Coast were openly defying Mexican law by drilling without
permits. When Mexican government authorities closed the valves,
the oil workers simply broke the locks and started drilling again. Finally, in June, Mexican troops surrounded the wells and denied the
companies access. The Hearst newspapers and others howled for
intervention, and for a time the likelihood of a U.S. Marine landing
looked very real. The Mexicans certainly feared it: President Plutarco
Elias Calles put General Lazaro Cardenas in charge of defense along
the Gulf, ordering him to retreat inland and make a stand if the
Marines invaded. But before retreating, he was to fire the wells.
Calles threatened that a conflagration of oil wells in Tampico
"would light up the sky all the way to New Orleans."

Early in July, some of the companies backed off and instructed
their lieutenants not to drill. The rainy season, when drilling was
difficult anyway, was beginning, and the oilmen realized the Mexican government would not for long tolerate the lower revenues that
would result when no new oil was being produced.

Tellez, the Mexican ambassador, was in the thick of these matters, and perhaps was glad to have a more pacific task on hand, in
finding a dinosaur. Holland was game, and he wrote to Louise
Carnegie, the tycoon's widow, for support. She liked the idea, too,
and by the spring of 1928 it was arranged that she would finance yet
another *Diplodocus* gift, this time through the Carnegie Corporation.
There were three partially completed casts stored in the museum in
Pittsburgh, there was $1,950 still in the *Diplodocus* Restoration Fund,
and the men thought that the molds, though old, would hold up
long enough to finish the three casts. Holland drew up a budget one
last time: finish the three casts, fabricate the metal supports for one,
build bases in Mexico City, ship casts, travel there, install the *Diplodocus*. Cost, he told the corporation board, would be around $5,000. It
should be made clear at all times that Mrs. Carnegie was the donor,
not the museum. All the other casts had been Mr. Carnegie's personal gifts, he reminded them, a tradition best continued.

Six more months went by before Holland gave up trying to pass
news of the gift back through Tellez and contacted Alphonso

Herrera directly at the museum in Mexico City. Herrera was delighted, though Holland had to correct his misapprehension that the dinosaur skeleton would be made of bronze and would be displayable outdoors. And that, in turn, meant Herrera had a serious space problem. The government had recently granted the museum a new plot of ground, 16,000 square meters, on which to expand. But there was no building yet, nor any funds. Herrera sent out fundraising letters almost immediately. As had happened in Pittsburgh nearly thirty years before, news of a *Diplodocus* on the way started plans for a hall to hold it. Holland asked F. P. Keppel to let Mrs. Carnegie know that her gift "will be a mighty stimulus toward the erection of new buildings for the museum, which, as I understand it, they are proposing to build at a cost of about $1,000,000." If that bit of information was meant to nudge Mrs. Carnegie toward financing a new museum building in Mexico, she didn't pick up on it.

By the fall of 1928 the Mexican press was writing with enthusiasm about the *Diplodocus*. Herrera compared the gift to aviator Charles Lindbergh's recent goodwill flight to Mexico in its potential for increasing the two nations' mutual regard. Mexican-American relations had in fact done an about face in the fifteen months since Tellez had first passed along Herrera's request. The turnabout was due primarily to President Coolidge's replacement of the bellicose Ambassador James Sheffield with Dwight Morrow—who was shrewd yet respectful, who liked Mexicans and had been instructed to keep the two nations out of war, and who happened to be Lindbergh's father-in-law.

By the end of October, the three *Diplodocus* casts had been completed, along with castings of some extra bones to fill in gaps for a new *Diplodocus* mount at the U.S. National Museum. "Your dear husband once said to me," Holland wrote Louise Carnegie, "'I never got as much pleasure or as much publicity from so small a sum of money as I have through your happy thought of making replicas of the animal, which bears my name.' Of course that naturally pleased me coming from him, but the ball is still rolling." Not rolling quite fast enough, however, to raise the money for a new hall in Mexico. Herrera eventually found floor space for the *Diplodocus* directly underneath a full-scale model of a whale that was suspended from the ceiling.

By March 1929 the casts were packed in their thirty-six crates and ready to ship. Arthur Coggeshall had finally left Pittsburgh to take the directorship of a new museum in St. Paul, Minnesota, and, in his absence, Holland, now eighty years old, had to write all the letters needed to figure out the best way to get the dinosaur to Mexico. Down river to New Orleans, by steamer to Veracruz, and train to the capital? Or train the whole way? Word had reached him, too, of civil war south of the border. "Owing to the disturbed condition of affairs in Mexico," he wrote Herrera in May, "and the statement which was made some time ago that Veracruz was in the hands of the revolutionists I have hesitated a little in making final arrangements for the shipment." In mid-May, Herrera wrote Holland that the war was as much as over, and he need not worry about the *Diplodocus* having to move through Veracruz—or through Brownsville or El Paso, for that matter, should he decide to ship the whole way by rail.

Holland finally shipped the crates late in October 1929, via Cincinnati; New Orleans; Alice, Texas; and Laredo. He was still unsure whether to make the trip himself or to send Louis Coggeshall, who knew no Spanish, on his own.

It must have been a relief to both Holland and Herrera to see the bones at last under way, two and a half years after the initial request. While the bones were en route, however, Herrera quit his job. In a bureaucratic shakeup, probably due to shifting political waters, the museum was removed from the auspices of the national Department of Agriculture and Public Works and became part of the National University. Herrera wrote Holland that he had been "unjustly attacked" and had felt obliged to give his resignation. Once it was accepted and the museum was under new auspices, he no longer had any influence there. He added that he thought he might leave Mexico.

Holland was, of course, far more eager for news of the *Diplodocus* crates than he was worried about Herrera's career. "I am wholly at sea," he wrote. "A few lines from you . . . would be greatly appreciated . . . It is with regret, I repeat, that I find your final relationship to the Museum has terminated by your own act of resignation." In his eagerness for the original Sheep Creek *Diplodocus* years before, Holland had convinced himself Reed's departure was voluntary, too.

Isaac Ochoterena, who had replaced Herrera as director of the museum, wrote to tell Holland that the twenty-six crates of cast bones had arrived. Surely, Holland wrote back, Ochoterena meant thirty-six cases? Yes, Ochoterena telegraphed back, thirty-six. The pedestal under the whale was ready to receive the dinosaur—a highly visible place, a place of honor.

Holland stopped vacillating and decided to go. With Louis Coggeshall, he arrived in Mexico City on April 6, 1930. For once, he saved the letters Carrie Moorhead Holland, his wife, wrote him while he was away. They're filled with cheerful news of lunches, dinner guests, new church members, new wallpaper, a cook who quit because the house lacked an electric refrigerator, and the comings and goings of their two sons. Yet her fear that Holland might not survive is palpable. She hopes he won't stay in Mexico long; the altitude in Mexico City will be hard on his heart. Finally she can hide her fear no longer: "I have not written you for a few days as I am so nervous I could hardly hold my pen. I find it most difficult to read your letters as they are so indistinct. We are all well . . . When do you think you will be able to leave?"

The old man seemed to be enjoying himself at last, perhaps because he had made a real friend. As he had in the other capitals, Holland found plenty of time to socialize and tour while the dinosaur work continued. He socialized with Col. Gordon Johnston, military attache at the U.S. embassy, and his wife Julia, and also with the Austrian-born artist, collector, and curator Rene d'Harnoncourt. But he established a more genuinely affectionate tie with a Mexican lepidopterist named Carlos Hoffman. With Hoffman, his German-speaking wife Anna, and their young daughter, Anita, Holland traveled on holiday to Cuernavaca.

He continued to exchange gifts and letters with the family after he returned to Pittsburgh: "The beautiful roses you brought to the train adorned my room until our arrival in Laredo," where they had to be surrendered to a State of Texas plant and fruit inspector, Holland wrote. Earlier on the return journey, the engine and tender had gone off the track about 9:30 in the evening, near Monterrey. No one was hurt, but it was an all-night delay until another engine could be brought out to them in the desert. "We went to bed and slept the sleep of the unconcerned," Holland wrote back to his new friend, "only waking up now and then to look out upon the dusky landscape where here and there I saw fireflies flitting about and was almost tempted to get up and endeavor to catch them, but as I had no net my longings were in vain." Near the end of his life, his oldest passion of the natural world, butterflies, brought him the most comfort. The *Diplodocus,* on the other hand, was a source of headaches. He left for home before the work was quite complete.

Not long afterward, the polished top of the base was finally laid under the dinosaur's feet, and the *Diplodocus* began to draw admiring crowds. That made a total of nine *Diplodocus* casts in national museums in Europe and the Americas. Ochoterena had a sign put up nearby, giving important dates, and mentioning the gratitude of the university and the museum staff to their kind friend Dr. Holland. In July a forlorn Herrera sent Holland a thank-you note for a pamphlet. But the former director still seemed unreconciled to his exile from his museum, if that's what it was: "Here are nothing new. I am sad as ever." In August Ochoterena erected a permanent bronze plaque which Holland had sent from Pittsburgh, announcing the dinosaur's donor and its North American erectors.

Nearly a year later, a friend told Herrera that his name was not on the plaque, and Herrera wrote to Holland, politely, to complain. Herrera's initiative, after all, had brought the *Diplodocus* to Mexico in the first place, and Herrera apparently had requested that his name be on the permanent sign. Holland was brusque. The plaque, he pointed out, said that Mrs. Carnegie initially made the gift in 1928, "when everybody knows that you were the Director of the Museum." It also said, Holland added, that the dinosaur was installed in May 1930 by Coggeshall and himself, by which time Ochoterena was director—but Ochoterena's name was not on the plaque, either. None of the plaques, on any of the donated dinosaurs, "recite at length all the facts incident to the making of the gift," Holland wrote. Herrera did not reply.

Tireder all the time, Holland still managed to finish a new edition of *The Butterfly Book*. Young Anita Hoffman wrote in April 1932, two years after he'd been in Mexico, to thank him for a book he'd sent her for Easter. "When will you come back to Mexico? My father has some new Butterflies to show you.—I shall never forget our little ride to Cuernavaca and the picture which you painted there.—With this letter I send you my last photograph with my little dog Mullata." His Mexican correspondence ends there. He died of a stroke on December 13, 1932.

After Holland's death, versions of the *Diplodocus* kept going out into the world, almost as if they had a centripetal momentum of their own. One cast was traded, for a large assortment of invertebrate fossils, to the natural history museum in Munich, Germany, in 1934, but it never was erected. Records were lost during World War II, and the cast lay incognito on museum shelves in Munich until it was rediscovered in 1977. In the spring of 1952, Carnegie vertebrate paleontology curator Leroy "Pop" Kay persuaded the trustees of the brand new Utah State Field House of Natural History in Vernal to accept one last *Diplodocus carnegii*. With financing from the Vernal Lion's Club, the original molds were trucked from Pittsburgh to the Utah museum. Kay, a Utahn himself, had begun his bone-digging career as a protegé of Earl Douglass at the Carnegie quarry that later became Dinosaur National Monument, east of Vernal. When Kay retired in 1957, he returned to Utah and, under his supervision, the museum staff made a cement cast of the *Diplodocus*, painted it red, and mounted it on the museum's front lawn—an outdoor setting at last—with the neck rising at a steep 45° angle from the torso.

From Vernal the old molds kept traveling—first, to the Rocky Mount Children's Museum in Rocky Mount, North Carolina, although a cast never was made there. Eventually the molds found their way to the Houston Museum of Science, where they were used to fill in gaps in the *Diplodocus hayi* skeleton that had been swapped from Pittsburgh to Cleveland before ending up in Houston. That mount was completed in 1975.

Back in Vernal, the cement *Diplodocus* was weathering badly by 1989. Dinolab, a Salt Lake City firm, disassembled the dinosaur and made new molds from the old cast. From those molds they cast a new skeleton—in fiberglass and polyester this time—and remounted it indoors, with its tail high and swirling, neck arched and dramatically erect, the last and most lifelike of *Diplodocus carnegii* skeleton mounts, just three hundred miles from its Sheep Creek home.

Finally, in July 1999, one hundred years after Wortman, Reed, and Coggeshall found the bones at Sheep Creek, the Carnegie Museum unveiled a full-sized, outdoor gelcoat-and-fiberglass cast of a fully fleshed *Diplodocus carnegii*, made by Research Casting, International, of Toronto. The dinosaur looms off the museum's northwest corner, and with another high, dramatic neck curve, bends its gaze away from the people crossing Forbes Avenue there, while buses and cars back up at the stoplight.

EPILOGUE

Vertebrate paleontologists are often described as independent, single-minded, self-reliant, or averse to clean clothes, but of course they are more varied than that, as is anyone or any group. Like anyone else, they dream and die. Tycoons do, too, though it's harder to imagine tycoons spending much time under a threatening sky, trying to protect a bone while extracting the rock around it from the earth.

Bill Reed, for example, was a dreamer. After his split with Hatcher, he did some copper mining but sold fossils, too, most notably to the American Museum. Then in 1903, Wilbur Knight died unexpectedly, and Reed was invited back to the University of Wyoming. He and his students continued to find fossils and bring them back to the university collection, now in roomy quarters in the new geology building. At last he had a steady paycheck. Photos show freestanding dinosaur femurs, shoulder-and-front-leg assemblies, even a *Titanothere* skull, all bathed in light through the big windows. But only one skeleton looks to be complete. Some kind of marine reptile, it appears to be, mounted with its spine on a long plank, with the ribs arcing down over the board's edge. But there must be fifty ribs on each side! And the skull, on closer examination, reveals itself to be not a skull at all but some amalgam of fragments assembled into a vaguely crocodilian shape. Reed dreamed the whole thing up, out of available parts. It's so obviously a concoction that he can't

By the time W. H. Reed returned to work for the University of Wyoming, the university had built a new geology building with room for a museum. Courtesy of S. H. Knight Collection, American Heritage Center, University of Wyoming.

have meant it too seriously. But he meant it seriously enough to put a great deal of labor into making it.

His students liked him. He was as magnetic in the field and in the classroom as he had been to Lakes, Wortman, and Holland around campfires years before. Late in his life, he got a Model T Ford, took it bird hunting, lent it to friends. He fished often. One of his students was Wilbur Knight's son, Sam, who later would recall that, on those summer fossil hunts, the cans in the wagon's grub box would lose their labels after a while, and you never knew if you were opening beans, peaches, or peas. You took what you got, regardless. When it came time to break camp, Reed would hit the wooden tent stakes with a hammer, sideways, exactly three times. Then he'd pull out the stake, no matter how far in it had been driven or how hard the ground was. Once he had to pull so hard that, when the stake suddenly came loose, he struck himself full in the chest with both clenched hands—he was in his early sixties by now—and broke some ribs. It was days before he could even raise the arm on the broken-rib side. So he and Sam detoured to a favorite fishing spot and stayed

Among the university museum's exhibits was a chimerical marine reptile, which W. H. Reed had constructed from bones of other specimens. Courtesy of S. H. Knight Collection, American Heritage Center, University of Wyoming.

until they caught the precise number of fish Reed planned they would catch. He died in 1915. Nearly all of the university fossil collection was destroyed by a flood in the 1920s. But remaining on the wall of the geology building is a plaque from the students, dedicated to "this faithful and useful man of science."

Jacob Wortman worked for about two years at the Peabody Museum at Yale after he left Pittsburgh, then ranched in Nebraska in country near the Tertiary fossil beds where he had so much success over the years. He hoped he would be able to make more money prospecting for fossils on his own than he ever had working for museums—he had come to hate the idea of working for a salary for men he didn't respect—but finally he was so disgusted he quit paleontology altogether. In Brownsville, Texas, he ran a drugstore for many years, and in 1912, when he was fifty-three, he married Eugenie Brulay and they had two children. He died there in 1926.

Holland wrote a wistful obituary in the *Annals of the Carnegie Museum* recalling both the great breadth of Wortman's knowledge and the love he brought to the work. Holland completely forgot, of course, the disingenuous role he himself had played in Wortman's

W. H. Reed, *right*, leads a geology field trip about 1912. After his death in 1915, Reed's students dedicated a plaque to "this faithful and useful man of science." Courtesy of S. H. Knight Collection, American Heritage Center, University of Wyoming.

angry decision to quit the Carnegie museum: "In the spring of the year 1900 he impulsively resigned his curatorship because of a minor difficulty with a member of his force, whose dismissal he demanded, but whom the director refused to discharge . . . It is to be regretted that his impulsive temperament led him to abandon his paleontological studies . . . It was a curious act of renunciation, the psychology of which is hard to explain."

When Carnegie sold his steel interests in 1901, he came into possession of a liquid fortune worth more than $350 million. By the time he died in 1919, he'd given away all but about $30 million. So he still died rich, if not nearly as rich or as disgraced, by his own lights, as he might have. But with him to the grave he took his annual add-ons to the Carnegie Museum's budget for paleontological expeditions—the $10,000 per year that for so many years supported the field and laboratory work of men like Reed, Wortman, the Coggeshalls, Hatcher, Gilmore, Douglass, and the rest. Their contributions to vertebrate paleontology, and especially dinosaur paleontology, were incalculable. Big-bone hunting slowed at the Carnegie Museum after that, as it did in the nation's other great museums as well. The shelves were filling up; eventually the museum even quit operations at its magnificent Utah quarry.

Carnegie's *Diplodocus* casts were a different sort of philanthropy from his strictly scientific endowments, the most important of which was the Carnegie Institution in Washington, D.C. The gifts of casts were personal in a way that his support of institutions was not. They arose out of his vanity. They connected him to kings and emperors—right where, in his own mind, he belonged. But they also introduced millions to their first sight of a dinosaur, and in that way—the connection with individual imaginations—the cumulative effect of the gifts is impossible to measure.

As for Holland, one more anecdote seems appropriate. He painted not just landscapes but miniatures—probably a skill he'd taught himself in order to depict his butterflies. On returning to Pittsburgh from a *Diplodocus carnegii* trip, he would take his portrait from the wall where it hung at the University of Pittsburgh, and carefully paint on its chest the new medal he had just won from the kingdom that most recently had honored him. The portrait now hanging in the director's room of the museum shows four medals, three on his chest and one on a ribbon around his neck, each of them painted in exquisite detail, yet not quite looking like they are actually lying there, on him.

Hatcher's grave in Homewood Cemetery went unmarked for ninety-one years. In November 1995 the Society of Vertebrate Paleontology held its annual meeting in Pittsburgh, at the Carnegie Museum. On a bright Sunday morning some of the society members gathered at the spot where Hatcher lies buried next to his daughter, Ruth. They'd bought him a stone. On it are Hatcher's name, Ruth's name, and the outline of a *Triceratops*.

MILESTONES

July, 1899: *Diplodocus* specimen discovered near Sheep Creek, Albany County, Wyo.

May–July 1904: *Diplodocus carnegii* cast erected temporarily at Western Pennsylvania Exposition Society, Pittsburgh, Pennsylvania.

May, 1905: *Diplodocus carnegii* cast unveiled at the British Museum (Natural History) in South Kensington, London.

April, 1907: *Diplodocus carnegii* skeleton erected in new Dinosaur Hall, Carnegie Museum of Natural History, Pittsburgh.

Spring, 1908: *Diplodocus carnegii* casts erected at national museums in Berlin and Paris.

Fall, 1909: *Diplodocus carnegii* casts erected at national museums in Vienna and Bologna.

June, 1910: *Diplodocus carnegii* cast erected at Imperial Academy of Sciences, St. Petersburg. Cast now in Moscow.

October, 1912: *Diplodocus carnegii* cast erected at National Museum, La Plata, Argentina.

November, 1914: *Diplodocus carnegii* cast erected at National Museum, Madrid.

May, 1930: Cast of *Diplodocus carnegii* erected at the National Museum of Natural History, Mexico City.

1934: Cast of *Diplodocus carnegii* shipped to Munich, Germany; never erected.

1957: Cement cast of *Diplodocus carnegii* erected outdoors at Utah Field House of Natural History in Vernal, Utah.

1989: New, fiberglass-and-polyester cast of *Diplodocus carnegii* erected indoors at Utah Field House of Natural History; with new molds made from old cement cast.

1999: New fiberglass-and-gelcoat, life-sized, fleshed-out model of *Diplodocus* erected outdoors at Carnegie Museum of Natural History, Pittsburgh.

NOTES

AHC   American Heritage Center, University of Wyoming

AMNH oc   American Museum of Natural History archives, Osborn Collection

CLPgh   Carnegie Library of Pittsburgh archives

CMNH annex   Carnegie Museum of Natural History annex archives

CMNH br   Carnegie Museum of Natural History big bone room archives

CMNH lib   Carnegie Museum of Natural History library archives

CMNH online   *Diplodocus carnegii* correspondence online at http:// heinz1.library.cmu.edu/imls/

HSWP   Holland papers, Historical Society of Western Pennsylvania archives

LOC   Library of Congress

WSA   Wyoming State Archives

Yale lib   Reed-Marsh correspondence included in the O. C. Marsh Papers, General Correspondence, microfilm reels 13 and 14, Manuscripts and Archives, Yale University Library

1. *DIPLODOCUS CARNEGII*

p. 1   "At one o'clock in the afternoon on Friday, May 12, 1905 ..." The text of the speeches is in Holland's unsigned article, "Presentation of a Reproduction of Diplodocus Carnegiei [sic]."

p. 3   " ... we have recently discovered in the Oxford clays a specimen of a dinosaur not quite as large as Diplodocus ..." Lankester was referring to *Cetiosaurus leedsi,* a Jurassic sauropod discovered earlier that year by the British Museum Paleontologist Dr. Arthur Smith Woodward near Peterborough. The genus had been named in 1841 by the British paleontologist Richard Owen, who thought it was whale-like, or cetacean. On April 18, 1905, Woodward delivered a paper to a meeting of the Zoological Society of London describing the specimen's limbs and tail, and bolstering O. C. Marsh's earlier conclusion that *Cetiosaurus* actually was a sauropod. Also at the April meeting, Holland gave a talk with stereopticon slides on *Diplodocus carnegii*. Both talks were reported in *Science* 21, no. 546 (June 16, 1905):935.

p. 5   "... his dream of a reunion between the two nations, plus Canada, was an open secret." Wall, *Andrew Carnegie*, 673–77. Probably the applauding guests did not know that his scheme went so far as to include a capital of the English-speaking people of the North Atlantic at Washington, D.C., to which the United States, Canada, England, Scotland, Ireland, and Wales would all send their legislators.

p. 8   "... vertebrate paleontology remained a museum-based science ..." For more on the turn-of-the-century rift between university and museum attitudes toward the life sciences, see Rainger, *Agenda for Antiquity*, 18–23.

2. THE FREEHEARTED FRONTIER HUNTER

p. 12   "He'd been born in Connecticut in 1848 ..." Breithaupt, "Biography of William Harlow Reed," 6–7. See also Statement of George Patterson and Dorothy Reed Patterson, Sept. 28, 1961; and letter from the Pattersons to Dr. Carl C. Dunbar, director, Peabody Museum of Natural History at Yale, March 18, 1955. Copies of these documents are in the possession of Michael Kohl, co-editor of *Discovering Dinosaurs in the Old West: The Field Journals of Arthur Lakes*, who kindly shared them with me. Kohl and McIntosh's edition of Lakes' journals (see below) lists the American Heritage Center at the University of Wyoming as the source of the documents, but they are now missing from that archive.

p. 13   "... a mill where worn railroad rails were melted down and rolled into new ones." Kohl and McIntosh, *Discovering Dinosaurs in the Old West* (hereafter referred to as "Lakes"), March 19, 1880, 150.

p. 14   "... four government surveys, supplied from Army posts, whose members explored ..." Lanham, *Bonehunters*, 215–18.

p. 14   "it was Marsh who came out on top ..." Lanham, *Bonehunters*, 233.

p. 14   "... 1,600 species of previously unknown extinct vertebrates."
Lanham, *Bonehunters,* 162.

p. 15   "Marsh received their letter from Laramie in July 1877 ..."
"Harlow and Edwards" (Reed and Carlin) to Marsh, July 19, 1877,
Yale lib.

p. 15   "... one of the greatest troves of dinosaur bones ever found ..."
Ostrom and McIntosh, *Marsh's Dinosaurs,* 10–11.

p. 15   "Flesh decays, but bones may last." See Lageson and Spearing,
Roadside Geology of Wyoming, 30–31; Bakker, *Dinosaur Heresies,* 32–
40; McIntosh, "Second Jurassic Dinosaur Rush," 22–27; and
conversations with Prof. Gerald Nelson, Casper College, Casper,
Wyoming.

p. 18   "By the spring of 1879, Carlin had defected ..." Ostrom and
McIntosh, 19–22, 32.

p. 18   "They were stacked in a wheelbarrow..." Schuchert and LeVene,
O. C. Marsh, 197.

p. 20   "Amongst them was a tall swarthy complexioned man ..." Lakes,
May 14, 1879, 84.

p. 20   "a splendid shot, a keen sportsman, a lover of nature ..." Lakes,
May 23, 1879, 98–99.

p. 21   "... 'with twelve dozen eggs they had collected from the grebes
nests ...' " Lakes, 3 July 1879, 120.

p. 21   " 'R feels particular delight in slaughtering these ...' " Lakes,
June 12, 1879, 109.

p. 21   " 'Mrs. C presented Como with a Fourth of July baby daughter.' "
Lakes, July 4, 1879, 120–22.

p. 22   "... Marsh and Cope paid separate visits ..." Lakes, June 4–6,
1879, 104–07; August 1–2, 1879, 130–31.

p. 22   "... they found a new dinosaur." The dinosaur they found with
Marsh was *Laosaurus consors,* now understood to be the same as
Dryosaurus altus, a beaked two-legged ornithropod of the late
Jurassic. The dinosaur was one of a larger group, the *Hypsilo-
phodons,* that was generally very successful, living through the rest
of the Jurassic and all of the Cretaceous to the dinosaurs' final
extinction 65 million years ago. See Kohl and McIntosh's note in
Lakes, 185.

p. 22   "Relations thawed somewhat on New Year's Day ..." Lakes,
January 1, 1880.

p. 23   "... when Reed froze a foot ..." Lakes, February 12, 1880, 147.

p. 23 "... Lakes could not keep from recording the tales." Lakes, February 5, February 14, March 4, 1879, 146–49.

p. 23 "His brother ... was killed in the summer of 1881 ..." Reed to Marsh, July 19 and July 31, 1881, Yale lib.

p. 23 "... losing 1,100 head ..." Breithaupt, "Biography of William Harlow Reed," 9.

p. 23 "... to ask Marsh if there might be a job collecting fossils in Alaska ..." Reed to Marsh, August 3, 1890, September 12, 1890, Yale lib.

p. 24 " 'Birds with teeth' became a rallying cry ..." Lanham, Bone-hunters, 194, 260–61.

p. 24 "The collection ... rivaled Marsh's ... in size." Breithaupt, "Biography of William Harlow Reed," 8.

p. 24 "... Reed kept his old customer." Reed to Marsh, November 19, 1896, December 4, 1896, December 28, 1896, April 17, 1897, Yale lib.

p. 24 " 'By the way that makes me think of another matter ...' " Reed to Marsh, June 15, 1898, Yale lib.

p. 27 " '... as moss agate Bill I cant do it ...' " Reed to Marsh, June 15, 1898, Yale lib.

p. 27 "The great naturalist was at risk of losing ..." Marsh to Reed, June 21, 1898, Yale lib.

p. 28 "...'I believe you intend to do about right' ..." Reed to Marsh, July 8, 1898, Yale lib.

p. 28 " 'Ower university is so poor that I am thinking of leaving it ...' " Reed to Marsh, September 30, 1898, Yale lib.

3. THE MOST COLOSSAL ANIMAL

p. 29 "... Louise Carnegie was forty-two, and Margaret already two and a half ..." Carnegie was closely attached to his mother, and it was impossible for him to marry until after her death. In 1887 he married Louise Whitfield. She was thirty, and he fifty-one. Their only child, Margaret, named for Carnegie's mother, was born in March 1897 (Wall, Andrew Carnegie, 401, 420, 688).

p. 29 "... reports in the New York papers ..." See unsigned article "The Dinosaur of Wyoming," New York Post, Dec. 1, 1898, CMNH br; unsigned article "Most Colossal Animal On Earth Just Found Out West," New York Journal and Advertiser, Dec. 11, 1898, LOC. The Post and Journal and Advertiser used mostly the same "facts" and even similar turns of phrase as had an article by Grant Jones in the *St. Louis Globe-Democrat*, Nov. 28, 1898. The *Post* and *Globe-Democrat* got Reed's name right, though both inflated his position by calling him an assistant professor of geology at Wyoming State University. On December 3, 1898, the *Laramie Boomerang* noted: "The article by Grant Smith that recently appeared in the Denver papers, describing the animal that once owned the immense femur, now the pride of the Paleontological department of this institution, has been extensively copied by other newspapers and magazines ..." Most likely a reporter from a Denver paper— Grant Smith or Grant Jones—visited Reed in Laramie and wrote the story sometime in November, and it then was picked up by other papers.

p. 33   "Carnegie made his first fortune ..." Wall, *Andrew Carnegie*, 267– 306.

p. 33   "Enact those measures ... and nothing would stand in the way ..." Wall, *Andrew Carnegie*, 47.

p. 34   " ... more time for public affairs on both sides of the Atlantic." Wall, *Andrew Carnegie Reader*, x.

p. 34   " 'Frequently rising to his toes ...' " Wall, *Andrew Carnegie*, 448.

p. 35   " 'All is well, because all grows better' ..." Carnegie uses the motto frequently, almost routinely, throughout his correspondence and other writings. Wall also notes that the motto was among several running around the wall of Carnegie's library-study in his mansion at 2 East 91st St. in New York City. Others included "The Aids To A Noble Life Are All Within," and "The Gods Send Thread For The Web Begun" (Wall, *Andrew Carnegie*, 857).

p. 35   "In a widely read essay in 1886 ..." Wall, *Andrew Carnegie*, 525.

p. 35   "At the Homestead mill, on the Monongahela River near Pittsburgh ..." Wall, *Andrew Carnegie*, 537–82; Lorant, *Pittsburgh*, 214.

p. 37   " 'Say what you will of Frick ...' " Wall, *Andrew Carnegie*, 573.

p. 38   "... his first salvo against the new American imperialism." Carnegie, Andrew, "Distant Possessions: The Parting of the Ways," *North American Review*, August 1898, reprinted in Wall, *Andrew Carnegie Reader*, 294–304.

p. 38   " ... but four thousand American soldiers and forty thousand Filipinos would die over the next four years..." "Crucible of Empire," PBS documentary on the Spanish-American War, online transcript, http://www.pbs.org/crucible/frames/_film.html

p. 38   "Carnegie proposed to pay $20 million of his own funds ..." Wall, *Andrew Carnegie*, 695.

p. 39   "These profits were now increasing geometrically." Wall, *Andrew Carnegie*, 717–18.

p. 39   " 'The man who dies thus rich, dies disgraced' ..." Carnegie, "Wealth," *North American Review*, June 1889, quoted in Wall, *Andrew Carnegie*, 796.

p. 39   "... they owned only small slices, while Carnegie owned 58 percent." Wall, *Andrew Carnegie*, 534–36, 719.

p. 40   "Soon he would direct Frick ... to draw up some cashout options." Wall, *Andrew Carnegie*, 719–20.

p. 40   "Carnegie announced his hope that Yale ... might be able to spare a few dinosaurs ..." Holland, "Story of the Diplodocus," 683. It would have been consistent with Carnegie's methods not to talk this over with Marsh before announcing it publicly. Carnegie finessed Henry Clay Frick into joining the steel business the same way in 1881. See Wall, *Andrew Carnegie*, 484.

p. 41   " 'My Lord—cant you <u>buy</u> this for Pittsburgh—' " Clipping from the *New York Post*, Dec. 1, 1898, CMNH br. The same archives contain a copy of the December 11, 1898, *New York Journal and Advertiser* page, the one with the "Most Colossal Animal" headline and the picture of the dinosaur looking into the skyscraper. Across the top, in Holland's handwriting, is a note—probably written many years later—misidentifying the paper as the *New York Journal,* misdating it back to November 1898, and somewhat inaccurately recalling Carnegie's instructions as "Dear Mr. Chancellor, Buy this for Pittsburgh." Holland's inaccurate date and source for the news story were repeated in many subsequent accounts.

4. CULTURE IN THE IRON CITY

p. 42   "On December 4, 1898, he sent Reed a telegram ..." Holland to Reed, misdated Nov. 4, 1898, CMNH br. Holland in fact appears to have misdated two notes that day—this one to Reed and a second to Carnegie (see below). Holland's reply to Carnegie starts out, "I noted your comments and orders on the newspaper clipping just received." If the November 4 dates are correct, that means Carnegie scrawled find-the-dinosaur instructions on two different newspaper clippings—first on an unknown newspaper around November 4, and then again on the December 1 story in the *New York Post*, as noted in the previous chapter. This seems highly unlikely. If Holland in fact wrote the letters on December 4, not November 4, and telegraphed Reed the same day, then it would make sense that Reed, wanting to sell the dinosaur, would answer promptly with a December 5 telegram and letter back to Holland, as he did.

Elizabeth Hill, collections manager of vertebrate paleontology at CMNH, who has long been familiar with this correspondence, disagrees with me on this. She believes that the letters are dated correctly and that Carnegie's note on the December 1, 1898, *New York Post* article must have been preceded, probably in early November, by an earlier note and news story sent to Holland.

p. 42   "He next wrote to Carnegie for advice." Holland to Carnegie, misdated Nov. 4, 1898, CMNH br.

p. 43   " 'See what you can do. I should like to do the Colossal ...' " Note added on Holland to Carnegie, misdated Nov. 4, 1898, CMNH br. Carnegie also shows here his love-hate relationship toward aristocracy and inherited power. "Lord Chancellor" is one of Britain's highest offices; Carnegie, who loved power and acclaim, makes fun of the title by folding it into phrases that echo the Gettysburg Address, democracy's great hymn.

p. 43   "He had been born in 1848 ..." Unsigned article, "William Jacob Holland, D.D., LL.D," in Fleming, *History of Pittsburgh and Environs*, 813–18; Avinoff, "Holland, William Jacob"; Leighton, "Memorial of William Jacob Holland."

p. 43   "... temporarily posted as missionaries in the Moravian Church." The Moravian sect traces its roots to the fifteenth-century Bohemian reformer Jan Hus; later it arose as a reformist group in the Lutheran tradition in Germany in the early eighteenth century.

p. 43   "... 40 percent of the city's congregations were still Presbyterian." Pritchard, "Religion in Pittsburgh," 333.

p. 43   "... the Moorheads had been prosperous enough to buy an Oakland mansion ..." Lorant, *Pittsburgh*, 153; Alberts, *Pitt*, 39.

p. 44   "... the Hollands found themselves dining ... at a table adjoining Carnegie's." Hendrick, *Life of Andrew Carnegie*, 227.

p. 45   "Worse still was the wreckage of human lives." Kleinberg, *Shadow of the Mills*.

p. 45   "... a third of all deaths in Pittsburgh were of children under five." Lorant, *Pittsburgh*, 287

p. 45   "The city prided itself ... on being a place where work got done ..." Lorant, *Pittsburgh*, 202.

p. 46   "... the elegant Phipps Conservatory ... a zoo in Highland Park ..." Lorant, *Pittsburgh*, 204.

p. 46   "... settlement houses with the goal of 'improving' the poor." Lorant, *Pittsburgh*, 204, and Kleinberg, *Shadow of the Mills*. At the settlement houses, poor families could find solace, order, classroom instruction, and sometimes even direct relief—so long as they weren't in need because the men were out on strike. If the poor were actually trying to change the conditions that brought about their difficulties, they were likely to find charity unavailable.

p. 46   "Pittsburgh proper still had no public libraries ..." Van Trump, *American Palace of Culture*, 2–3.

p. 47   "... against accepting any gift from the man who owned the Homestead mill." Wall, *Andrew Carnegie*, 573.

p. 47   "... a panoramic photo of Oakland from 1900 ..." Lorant, *Pittsburgh*, 292.

p. 47   "... considerable skill and local reputation as an orator." Holland's correspondence in 1899 and 1900 shows that he was in frequent demand to speak at graduations and other public events, for which his fee was $25, about a third the monthly wage of a skilled mill or railroad worker.

p. 47   "He learned Latin and Greek as an adolescent ..." Unsigned article, "William Jacob Holland, D.D., LL.D.," in Fleming, *History of Pittsburgh and Environs*, 814.

p. 48   "... his work in paleontology was just adequate ..." Rainger, "Collectors and Entrepreneurs," 15.

p. 49   "... and the number of students increased eightfold." Alberts, *Pitt*, 41, 50.

p. 49   "... politicians were no longer able to ignore the skyrocketing number of typhoid fever cases ..." Tarr, "Infrastructure and City-Building," 236–38; Tierno, "Search for Pure Water in Pittsburgh"; Klein and Hoogenboom, *History of Pennsylvania*, 368.

p. 49   "Bitter battles ensued over who would get the construction contracts ..." Tarr, "Infrastructure and City-Building," 236, 241; Klein and Hoogenboom, *History of Pennsylvania*, 368.

p. 49   "… as proud of … bringing clean water to Pittsburgh as of anything he'd done." Unsigned article, "William Jacob Holland, D.D, LL.D.," in Fleming, *History of Pittsburgh and Environs*, 817.

p. 49   " '… unless the institution be kept in touch with the masses …' " Carnegie to Frew, in Kinard, *Celebrating the First 100 Years*, 36.

p. 50   "… a dramatic, life-sized diorama of two lions attacking a desert Arab on a camel." Kinard, *Celebrating the First 100 Years*, 162; Van Trump, *American Palace of Culture*, 51. The diorama stands in a glass case in the hall of mammals on the museum's second floor, and shows a lion in the desert sand, clawing up at the Arab, who is mounted on a camel and is wielding a curved knife. The lioness lies dead beneath them, the Arab's single-shot gun, discarded, has fallen across her body. French taxidermist Jules Verreaux won a gold medal for this display at the Paris Exposition of 1867. The American Museum of Natural History in New York bought it, supposedly for several thousand dollars, but museum officials later decided it was too sensational, and the AMNH curator contacted Carnegie preparator Frederic Webster to arrange a sale. Pittsburghers' tastes, apparently, were more lurid than New Yorkers'. The Carnegie Museum bought the mount for $50 plus shipping charges in 1898. The work was restored in 1994. The lions are a North African subspecies, now extinct.

p. 50   "… the most … productive of which was the Bone Cabin Quarry …" The AMNH shipped sixty-five tons of dinosaur bones out of the Bone Cabin Quarry during the next four years (Preston, *Dinosaurs in the Attic*, 67).

p. 50   "Reed answered Holland's query the next day…" Telegram quoted in Holland to Carnegie, Dec. 9, 1898, CMNH br.

p. 50   "The letter Reed sent restored Holland's hopes …" Reed to Holland, Dec. 5, 1898, CMNH br.

p. 50   "Holland wrote Carnegie first." Holland to Carnegie, Dec. 9, 1898, CLPgh.

p. 50   "Next day, writing Reed …" Holland to Reed, Dec. 10, 1898, CMNH br.

p. 51   "Three different times between December and March …" Holland to Reed, Dec. 10, 1898; Feb. 7, 1899; March 16, 1899; all CMNH br.

p. 51   "He doled out information slowly …" Reed to Holland, Dec. 5 and Dec. 22, 1898, CMNH br; and March 2, 1899, HSWP.

5. A LIZARD IN WYOMING POLITICS

p. 52 "Reed met him at the train, and they spent the afternoon together ..." Holland to Carnegie, March 27, 1899, CMNH annex.

p. 52 "... huge fossil collection, then crammed into offices, closets, and classrooms ..." Breithaupt, "Dinosaurs to Gold Ores," 19–20, 23.

p. 53 "... the snowiest winter he'd known in twenty-nine years in the Rockies ..." Reed to Holland, March 2, 1899, HSWP.

p. 53 " 'It occurred to me on mature reflection ...' " Holland to Carnegie, March 27, 1899, CMNH annex.

p. 53 "... for the chief executive of one university to call on the president of another." Then, as now, the universities were quite different from each other. The Western University of Pennsylvania had boomed since Holland became chancellor in 1891; Wyoming University was still struggling to survive in a depressed economy, with little true demand for its services.

p. 54 "The president of the board, Otto Gramm ..." Gramm had served a single four-year term as state treasurer beginning in 1890, the year Wyoming Territory became a state. He served on the university board of trustees from 1895 to 1911, as board president for all but the first two of those years. In 1907 he became manager and lessee of the state penitentiary in Rawlins, during which time he also held contracts to feed the prisoners and kept for himself the proceeds from the sale of all the brooms made in the prison broom factory. Wyoming State Directory, 1991; Hardy, *Wyoming University*, 45–46; Larson, *History of Wyoming*, 321.

p. 54 "... to sit in the village drug-store and wait ..." Holland, "Story of the Diplodocus," 684–85.

p. 55 " '... worth a hundred thousand dollars to us.' " Holland to Carnegie, March 27, 1899, CMNH annex.

p. 55 " 'The lizard ... has gotten into Wyoming politics' " Holland to Carnegie (cable), March 27, 1899, CLPgh.

p. 55 "... Holland wrote Gramm a letter recapitulating their discussion." Holland to Gramm, March 23, 1899, CMNH br.

p. 55 "... article had run in one of the Cheyenne papers about Carnegie's recent purchase ..." *Cheyenne Daily Sun Leader*, Feb. 14, 1899, WSA.

p. 56 "... the idea ... came to him from 'an old entomological acquaintance ...' " Holland, "Story of the Diplodocus," 685.

p. 56   "... Downey was intimately connected with state and university politics." Larson, *History of Wyoming*, 137, 141, 145, 147, 161, 245, 256–57, 300.

p. 57   "There were two ways, Downey replied." The land-scrip option Holland and Downey discussed was just one piece of the crazy quilt of federal land law at the time. There were perhaps half a dozen different ways to take up federal land, often complicatedly conflicting with each other, and the law was poorly enforced or not enforced at all. Fraud and shady deals were routine, among high government officials as among much of the rest of the population, leading to a culture of distrust and contempt for the federal government which continues today in the West.

p. 58   "He sent Carnegie a long cable, and a much longer letter." Holland to Carnegie, cable and letter, March 27, 1899, CLPgh.

6. UNCLE SAM'S LAND

p. 59   "... Carnegie quickly wired back ..." Telegram, Carnegie to Holland, March 27, 1899. CMNH lib.

p. 60   "... 'that minute information' ..." Holland to Reed, Holland to Downey, March 27, 1899, CMNH annex. Starting with the Northwest Ordinance in 1787, U.S. public land in the West was divided into townships six miles square. Each township was further divided into thirty-six square-mile sections. Any land could thus be located by describing the fraction of the section of the township in which it lay.

p. 60   "Reed ... was off by an entire township ..." Holland to Downey, April 1, 1899, CMNH annex.

p. 60   "... Reed confessed to Holland ..." Reed to Holland, April 5, 1899, CMNH br.

p. 60   " 'You do not tell me how in the world you came to make the error ...' " Holland to Reed, April 11, 1899, CMNH annex.

p. 60   " 'Let there be no error in locating [the claim] this time'..." Holland to Downey, April 11, 1899, CMNH annex.

p. 61   "... 'there is no claim to contend with except the notice at the quarry ...' " Reed to Holland, April 15, 1899, CMNH br.

p. 61   "Federal and state law made acquiring clear title to a mining claim complicated but cheap ..." U.S. Department of the Interior, "Mining claims and sites on Federal Lands," BLM brochure no. BLM-WO-GI-91-002-4130, April 1996.

p. 62   " 'I wil help you in this business so far as I can ...' " Reed to Holland, April 15, 1899, CMNH br.

p. 63   " '...make sure by the seeing of the eye and the touch of the hand ...' " Holland to Carnegie, April 17, 1899, CLPgh.

p. 63   "... [Owen] had little flexibility in his schedule ..." Owen had held various private and public surveying jobs for 20 years, and in 1894 was elected state auditor. He'd recently been appointed examiner of federal surveys, a job that soon would take him to South Dakota.

p. 63   "... there was no guarantee he could keep Carnegie's name out of it ..." Downey to Holland, April 20, 1899, CMNH annex.

p. 63   "You know that I do not believe in antagonizing ..." Carnegie to Holland, April 19, 1899, CMNH lib.

p. 63   " 'I was nearly insane with a gathering in my head ...' " Reed to Holland, April 23, 1899 (first letter that day), CMNH br.

p. 64   "Reed was stunned to hear that the survey had *not* been completed ..." Reed to Holland, April 23, 1899 (second letter that day), CMNH br.

p. 65   " 'Town, as they called it, pleased me the less ...' " Wister, *Virginian*, 25.

p. 66   "... about twenty houses, and stockyards big enough to hold thousands of sheep or cattle ..." Holland, "Bone Hunters Starting Well Their Work."

p. 66   " 'We have no law here ...' " Holland, "Bone Hunters Starting Well Their Work."

p. 66   "... a little construction job of their own." Holland, "Story of the Diplodocus," 686–87.

p. 67   "... Owen billed Holland for six days' surveying ..." Owen-Holland, May 2, 1899, CMNH br.

7. HEWN INTO FRAGMENTS

p. 68   " 'The offer is altogether and unconditionally withdrawn.' " Holland to Gramm, March 29, 1899, CMNH br.

p. 68   "Don't make enemies, but get the dinosaur." See telegram, Carnegie to Holland, March 27, 1899 ("... do not think it judicious to antagonize the state of Wyoming ..."), and Holland to Downey, May 10, 1899 ("He [Carnegie] has set his heart on obtaining this particular specimen."), CMNH br.

p. 69   "Sternberg ... left the younger man to work the fossil quarry alone ..." Sternberg, *Life of a Fossil Hunter*, 170–200. Then, as now, the John Day beds were rich in plant and mammal fossils of the Tertiary period, a post-dinosaur time. Sternberg remembered those months clearly a generation later, when he came to write his book, because he and Wortman at one point had to cache fossils in a hurry and get out of the country in advance of angry Snake Indians.

p. 69   "working first as a curator at the Army and Navy Medical Museum." This and subsequent biographical details are found in Holland, "Obituary of Dr. Jacob L. Wortman."

p. 69   " 'It was indeed a rare bit of one's education ...' " Osborn, "J. L. Wortman," 652.

p. 71   " '... the younger men ... derived great benefit ...' " Holland, "Obituary of Dr. Jacob L. Wortman, 200.

p. 71   "... paleontologists would remember the early years ..." See, e.g., Matthew, "Early Days of Fossil Hunting on the High Plains."

p. 71   "... [Osborn] wanted mountable specimens ..." Rainger, *Agenda for Antiquity*, 88.

p. 72   "... Osborn hired a recent University of Kansas graduate ..." Rainger, *Agenda for Antiquity*, 94–95. Brown went on to a colorful career digging dinosaurs for the American Museum all over the North American West, as well as in Mexico, Greece, and India. (Rainger, *Agenda for Antiquity*, 79).

p. 72   "... even richer diggings ... at the Bone Cabin Quarry ..." The quarry was named by Wortman for a cabin foundation of dinosaur bones nearby—all that remained of some earlier shack. See Wortman to Osborn, June 18, 1898, AMNH oc. There was never an entire cabin made of bones there, as has often mistakenly been asserted. About thirty-five years later, an entrepreneur named Thomas Boylan opened a gas station and roadside attraction on U.S. Route 30 east of Medicine Bow on the south slope of Como Bluff. It included a "65 million year old cabin" built entirely of dinosaur bones Boylan had picked up over the years.

p. 72   "He almost certainly felt passed over ..." Rainger, *Agenda for Antiquity*, 280 n.88, and Rainger, "Collectors and Entrepreneurs," 17.

p. 72   "He had believed that he was the logical successor ..." Holland to Carnegie, April 1, 1899, CMNH annex.

p. 72 "Wortman may have inferred ..." Rainger, "Collectors and Entrepreneurs,"17; Osborn to Granger, May 18, 1899, AMNH oc; Holland to Downey, May 10, 1899, CMNH br.

p. 73 " 'I was led to feel that if I could obtain the services ...' " Holland to Carnegie, April 1, 1899, CMNH br.

p. 73 "Wortman ... stayed at Holland's house ..." Holland to Wortman, April 12, 1899, CMNH archives. The building, at Fifth Avenue and Bellefield Street in Oakland, now houses the University of Pittsburgh's music department. See Alberts, *Pitt*, 39.

p. 73 "... directing [Wortman's] attention to recent news reports ..." Holland to Wortman, April 20, 1899, CMNH br.

p. 73 "... friends threw a farewell dinner ..." Osborn to Granger, May 18 and May 28, 1899, AMNH oc.

p. 74 "Downey and Carnegie had already advised him ..." Downey to Holland, April 20, 1899, and Carnegie to Holland, March 27, 1899, CMNH br.

p. 74 " 'the ground is open to location by anyone' " Holland to Gramm, May 2, 1899, CMNH archives.

p. 74 "... Warren, already for more than a decade the most powerful politician ..." Francis Warren first served as territorial governor in the mid-1880s, was elected first state governor in 1890, then, within months, was elected to the U.S. Senate. He remained in the Senate until he died in 1929, and he gathered considerable power there, thanks to a long and vindictive memory, a quiet charm, and an understanding that Wyoming's economic survival depended on a steady, orderly flow of federal subsidies. See L. Gould, *Wyoming*.

p. 75 " 'After we had swapped stories for a while ...' " Holland to Carnegie, May 5, 1899, Carnegie correspondence, CLPgh.

p. 76 "Gramm ... chose to read the offer ..." Gramm to Holland, May 4, 1899, CMNH br.

p. 76 "On May 10 Holland urged Downey to continue ... to pull strings ..." Holland to Downey, May 10, 1899, CMNH br.

p. 77 ".... Carnegie was cashing in all his steel interests." Newspapers began on May 5 to report that Carnegie's companies were about to be sold and shares to be placed on the stock market. This deal would eventually fall through. Wall, *Andrew Carnegie*, 723–30.

p. 77 " ... completely ignoring Gramm's specific thanks ..." Holland to Gramm, May 10, 1899, CMNH br.

p. 77   "… enlist Owen, too, in his efforts to pull Wyoming strings."
Holland to Owen, May 13, 1899, HSWP.

p. 77   " '… another proof that genius, always imperious …' " Carnegie
to Holland, May 20, 1899, "Diplodocus" file, big bone room,
CMNH br.

p. 77   "Reed left Laramie for the Freezeouts May 6 … " Downey to
Holland, May 7, 1899, CMNH br.

p. 77   "… 'to mouse around your "Happy Valley' …" Holland to Reed,
May 12, 1899, CMNH annex.

p. 78   "… stopped in Chicago for an extra tent …" Wortman to Holland,
May 30, 1899, CMNH br.

p. 78   "Knight was already back in the Freezeouts by mid-May" Wortman to Holland, May 17, 1899, CMNH br.

p. 78   "… the Bone Cabin Quarry, which would prove so productive …"
Between 1898 and 1903, American Museum crews shipped a total
of 483 different fossil specimens, about 160,000 pounds of bones
in 275 boxes. They provided a huge boost to the understanding of
Jurassic fauna, though very few of the specimens proved useful in
the race to mount big skeletons. See Colbert, *Great Dinosaur
Hunters,* 153.

p. 78   "The Union Pacific Railroad … had sent out a circular in April …"
Wall Street Journal, April 4, 1899.

p. 79   "Coggeshall got to carry the 100-pound sacks of dry plaster."
Coggeshall, "How Dippy Came to Pittsburgh," 239. Contrary to
Coggeshall's recollection, the plaster was actually carried over the
bridge at a later date. See Wortman to Holland, June 6, 1899,
CMNH br.: "I have ordered 1000 # of plaster."

p. 80   " 'All of Reed's prospects proved disappointing …' " Wortman to
Holland, June 6, 1899, CMNH br.

p. 80   " '… Reed had to admit, as we suspected …' " Coggeshall, "How
Dippy Came to Pittsburgh," 240.

p. 80   "… a long swing southwest to the head of Troublesome and
Difficulty creeks …" Wortman to Holland, June 18, 1899, CMNH
br.

p. 82   "… Holland had been making openly contemptuous remarks …"
Holland to Owen, May 13, 1899, HSWP; Holland to Wortman,
May 20, 1899, CMNH br.

p. 82   "The university trustees at their meeting June 22 …" Downey to
Holland, June 8; Holland to Downey, June 16; Downey to

Holland, June 27; CMNH br. The full board of trustees of the University of Wyoming met only two, or at most three, times a year; the June meeting would have been one of the full meetings. Month-to-month matters were handled by an executive commit-tee. Presidents' annual reports survive from those years, but no meeting minutes. See Hardy, *Wyoming University*, 27.

p. 82   "Knight, meanwhile, had been making various trips to the Freezeouts ..." Wortman to Holland, May 17, 1899, CMNH annex; Granger to Osborn, May 22, 1899, AMNH oc.

p. 83   " 'I found the same bones last summer ...' " Reed to Holland, May 26, 1899, CMNH br.

p. 83   " 'We want you eastern chaps to understand ...' " Jack Bowie to Holland, June 5, 1899, Holland papers, HSWP.

p. 84   " 'Everything has turned out badly ...' " Holland to Wortman, July 3, 1899, CMNH br.

p. 84   " 'I am in receipt of a letter informing me that Prof Knight ...' " Holland to Downey, July 3, 1899, CMNH annex.

p. 85   "... a mid- or late-June visit while Wortman and Reed were off prospecting other sites seems much more likely." The only problem with this scenario is that it reduces to mere coincidence Holland's ominous remarks about bone smashing in the letters he wrote in May.

Another, more sinister scenario also suggests itself, but has been rejected here as more complicated and therefore less likely. Holland may have realized after he got back to Pittsburgh, and perhaps received some criticism from his staff about the lack of care with which the half femur had been extracted, that he and Owen had made a bad mess of the quarry—so bad that it seemed unlikely the dinosaur could be extracted in mountable condition. Embarrassed, Holland may have started spreading the rumor that Knight was responsible as early as in his May 13 "bone butcher" letter to Owen and, more particularly, in his May 20 ("I only hope that Knight will not have torn the whole thing to pieces") letter to Wortman, quoted and cited above. When Wortman finally got to the field, Holland directed him specifically to check out the site ("My informant in regard to these matters is Dr. Wortman, who, at my request, visited the locality to report ..."). Whatever Wortmann found there, Holland could loudly blame on Knight.

p. 86   "He buried them to guard against discovery by rival parties ..." Reed to Holland, May 26, 1899, CMNH br.

8. SOME GOOD LUCK AT LAST

p. 87   "... probably guided to the spot by cairns Reed had left there ..."
Reed to Holland, May 26, 1899, CMNH br. The best-known
account of the discovery of the *Diplodocus* is Coggeshall's "How
Dippy Came to Pittsburgh," which has been cited in a number of
other publications since. Writing fifty-two years after the event,
Coggeshall recalled nothing of any markers Reed might have set
up. He remembered only that the party arrived the evening of
July 3, 1899, at a spot along Sheep Creek where there were good
grass and water and promising outcrops of Jurassic rock. The
next morning, Reed and Wortman went off on horseback to
check out a likely escarpment two miles away. Coggeshall was left
behind to prospect on foot. At that point his account retreats
politely into the passive voice:

> The first indication of "Dippy" was a toe bone of a hind foot. After
> very close scanning of the ground, a few pieces of weathered bone
> were found. It was then that the heartbeats of the writer really
> became loud, for it was the best prospect any of us had discovered
> in over two months of hard and disappointing work, and we did so
> want to make good with a dinosaur for Mr. Carnegie.

The *Diplodocus* should perhaps have been named "The Star-
Spangled Dinosaur" on account of the date of its discovery,
Coggeshall noted. Reed and Wortman returned at noon, empty-
handed. By then "there was enough of the pelvis cleared away for
us to feel sure we had at last found something that, while it might
not be the "Most Colossal Dinosaur" ever discovered, indicated a
splendid find." Six years after the discovery, Holland, in "The
Story of the Diplodocus," similarly placed the discovery on July 4.
But thirty-one years later, in "The Diplodocus Goes to Mexico,"
he wrote that he received a telegram from Wortman on July 1,
1899, announcing the discovery "of an apparently complete
skeleton of a Diplodocus imbedded in block-clay near Sheep
Creek, Wyoming." Such a telegram, if it ever was written, has not
survived. Wortman's July 4 letter to Holland has, however, and its
detailed descriptions of the two good prospects appear to show
the crew had been digging for at least a day or two. That fits well
with Holland's article sent back to the *Pittsburg Dispatch* on July
28, 1899, and published on August 10 (see below), indicating that
the outcrop was spotted the evening of July 2 and the bones

found July 3. For those reasons I've chosen Holland's newspaper account of the discovery as the most reliable, even though Holland wasn't there.

p. 87 "… Wortman spotted a line of huge vertebrae …" Holland, "Diplodocus Is a Great Find." The article is datelined "Camp Carnegie, Sheep Creek Basin, Wyoming, July 28."

p. 87 "… 'very happy to report some good luck at last.' " Wortman to Holland, July 4, 1899, CMNH br.

p. 88 "… while Holland sat in the depot and wrote …" Holland, "Bone Hunters Starting Well At Their Work."

p. 88 "… Osborn, in particular, was eager to avoid the bigger crowd …" Osborn to Granger, July 13, 1899, AMNH oc.

p. 89 "… no museum in Europe possesses, and of which only fragments exist in American collections." Holland, "Bone Hunters Starting Well At Their Work." "Fragments" is the interesting word here. So far, very few complete dinosaur skeletons were on permanent display anywhere. There apparently were none in North America, though the idea of erecting fossil skeletons for the public dates back to 1789, when a *Megatherium* skeleton from Lujan, sixty miles west of Buenos Aires, was erected at the royal museum of natural history in Madrid (see Simpson, *Discoverers of the Lost World*, 3–9). By 1899 the major museums were hunting for dinosaur specimens that would make good, permanent mounts. Osborn was eager to get a look at a "Brontosaur," that is, an *Apatosaurus*, that American Museum paleontologists Walter Granger and William Diller Matthew had found earlier in the summer near the Nine Mile Crossing of the Little Medicine Bow River, just a few miles from the Bone Cabin Quarry. Wortman, disappointed in his prospects in the Freezeouts, had visited Nine Mile late in June, when he had not yet found the Sheep Creek prospect. Matthew speculated Wortman may have gone to the spot, as he'd noticed it the previous summer while still in the American Museum's employ. See Matthew to Osborn, July 2, 1899, in Colbert, *William Diller Matthew*, 68–69.

p. 91 "Osborn at that time was Dean of Pure Science at Columbia University …" Rainger, *Agenda for Antiquity*, 83–87.

p. 91 "Matthew … into conflict with Osborn …" Rainger, *Agenda for Antiquity*, 182–215.

p. 92 "Lull had been one of Osborn's first Ph.D. students …" Rainger, *Agenda for Antiquity*, 53, 85, 163.

p. 93   " 'Our success in fact has been simply phenomenal ...' " Wortman to Holland, Aug. 19, 1899, HSWP.

p. 93   "... an idyllic week of camping and feasting ..." Holland, "Fossil Hunters on the Plains." The article is datelined Aug. 12.

p. 93   "... a behavior ...[Holland] found 'simply brutal.' " Holland to Wortman, Aug. 15, 1899, CMNH annex.

p. 94   "A week later, he was still in bed ..." Holland to Wortman, Aug. 22, 1899, CMNH annex.

p. 94   "Coggeshall and Willie Reed worked on the *Apatosaurus* ..." Wortman to Holland, Aug. 19, 1899, HSWP.

p. 95   "... 'hovering between life and death' ..." J. A. Shafer to Carnegie, Aug. 26, 1899, CMNH annex.

p. 95   "... out of danger ..." C. C. Mellor to Reed, Sept. 1, 1899, CMNH annex.

p. 95   "... kept the appendix as a souvenir ..." Holland to A. Darlow, Oct. 10, 1899, CMNH annex.

p. 95   "Standard procedure was ..." Bell, "Fossil Hunting in Wyoming," 268.

p. 96   "Z. H. Fales, of Medicine Bow, charged $7.50 per ton ..." Wortman to Holland, Sept. 11, 1899, CMNH br.

p. 97   "Fales's final bill of $92.60 ..." Holland to Mellor, Oct. 4, 1899, CMNH lib.

p. 97   "... 'to collect a Baptanodon or so' ..." Wortman to Holland, Sept. 27, 1899, CMNH br.

p. 98   "... the bones shipped free the whole way." That is, on the Union Pacific from Medicine Bow to Omaha, on the Chicago and Northwestern to Chicago, and finally on the Pittsburgh, Fort Wayne and Chicago Railroad, a Pennsylvania Railroad subsidiary, the rest of the way to Pittsburgh. Despite all Holland's efforts, the C&NW mistakenly billed him for the $148.80 for transporting the bones over the middle third of their journey.

p. 98   "The freight car arrived in Pittsburgh in mid-October." Holland to Hughitt, Oct. 14, 1899, CMNH annex.

p. 98   "Wortman and Reed arrived about the same time." E. B. Williamson, the museum staffer who had traveled with Holland and the other two young men to Wyoming, left the museum to teach high school in Salem, Ohio, but before leaving wrote letters to help Coggeshall and Reed find places to live for the winter. Williamson directed Reed to the boarding house where he'd been

staying, on Fillmore Street, just two blocks from the museum.
Williamson to Coggeshall, and Williamson to Reed, both Sept. 9,
1899; CMNH annex.

9. THE AMPLE FOSSIL FIELDS

p. 99   "… three bandits held up a Union Pacific train …" For stories
about the Wilcox train robbery, see *Laramie Boomerang*, June 2, 3,
5, 6, 7, 8, 9, 10, 12, 13, 15, 16, 19, 20, 21, and July 12 and 14, 1899.

p. 101   " 'The Union Pacific officials and others of the officers …' "
Laramie Boomerang, June 12, 1899.

p. 101   "The railroad paid up promptly, at five dollars a day." *Laramie
Boomerang*, June 12, 1899.

p. 101   "Under the leadership of Edward H. Harriman …" The passage
that follows, about Harriman's investment and construction plans,
relies largely on Klein, *Union Pacific*, 11–55.

p. 102   "… a trip to Alaska would be both relaxing and invigorating."
Klein, *Life and Legend of E. H. Harriman*, 183–98.

p. 102   "Fifty passengers boarded the steamer there …" Goetzman and
Sloan, *Looking Far North*, 207–12.

p. 103   "… including totem poles, grave monuments, and other ceremo-
nial artwork …" Harriman gave artifacts from the village to the
California Academy of Science, the Field Museum in Chicago, the
University of Michigan, the University of Washington, and the
Peabody Museum at Harvard. Most accounts of the expedition
list the village as "abandoned," but the families that had made the
artifacts almost certainly still felt attached to them. See Victoria
Wyatt's introduction, "The Harriman Expedition in Historical
Perspective," to Grinnell, *Alaska 1899*, xliv–xlv.

p. 103   "The *Boomerang* did notice the special train this time …" *Laramie
Boomerang*, Aug. 8, 1899. The Laramie newspaper's account
reflected Harriman's rapidly growing public presence, calling him
"probably the greatest railroad man in the country today." Klein,
in *The Life and Legend of E. H. Harriman*, notes that newspapers
across the nation "heaped praise on the expedition" after its
return (198).

p. 103   "The same month Harriman began planning …" The brochure, in
a footnote, mentions the death of O. C. Marsh "as we go to
press." Marsh died March 18, 1899. No correspondence between
Knight and Lomax has surfaced.

p. 103 "Knight's close work with Lomax ..." The booklet is unsigned, though it quotes Knight at great length. It was written before Reed defected to the Carnegie Museum and reveals high hopes for a university building in which to display the huge dinosaur, as well as for the dinosaur itself.

p. 105 " '... no equal area in the world, has done so much for the theory of evolution ...' " Union Pacific Railroad, "Some of Wyoming's Vertebrate Fossils," 3.

p. 105 "... museums to match the ones at Yale, Harvard, and Princeton—or even the ones at the universities of Kansas, Nebraska, Wyoming, and California ..." Rainger, *Agenda for Antiquity*, 21–22.

p. 105 "... and that camp life itself produces unpredictable events ..." The same idea turns up in correspondence among members of the Harriman expedition, and in Holland's correspondence and newspaper articles: outdoor work and recreation are to be anticipated with pleasure because they will produce good stories to be told and retold. These men lived in a culture of raconteurs in love with the strenuous life.

p. 105 "... an invitation to pay the railroad fare for any scientists ..." "Union Pacific Progresses," *Wall Street Journal*, April 4, 1899, 1.

p. 106 "The population of Laramie at the time was only about eight thousand ..." Wyoming Economic Analysis Division figures, available online at eadiv.state.wy.us/pop/citypop.htm

p. 107 "The *Boomerang* that summer carried stories ..." See "Death by the Bottle" and "The Grader's Inquest," July 24 and 26, 1899; "Waylaid by Footpads," Aug. 18, 1899; "Tarrant Runs A-muck" [sic], July 28, 1899; "Winchester and Colt," July 28, 1899; "Shotting [sic] at Rawlins," Aug. 19, 1899; "Cleveland Riots," July 22, 1899; and "His Leg Amputated," June 6, 1899.

p. 108 "Violence even touched the university ..." *Laramie Boomerang*, June 19 and 20, 1899.

p. 108 "[Downey] ... tried to persuade the Albany County commissioners ..." "A Possible Emergency," *Laramie Boomerang*, Aug. 1, 1899.

p. 109 "In October the onset of snow and cold weather ..." "Italian Line Wavered," *Laramie Boomerang*, Oct. 17, 1899.

p. 109 "Knight and ... Slosson wrote papers for scientific publications and industry bulletins ..." *Laramie Boomerang*, June 3, 1899.

p. 109 "... prospectors and their financial backers appear to have complained ..." *Laramie Boomerang*, March 27, 1899.

p. 109 "By the third week in June he was ill with the measles ..."
Colbert, *William Diller Matthew*, 69.

p. 110 "... they looked just like anyone else ..." Holland, "Bone Hunters
Starting Well At Their Work."

p. 110 "... they met to establish a mini-government ..." Holland, "Bone
Hunters Starting Well At Their Work."

p. 110 "Osborn ... appears to have stopped in Laramie only briefly."
Osborn to Granger, July 13, 1899, AMNH oc.

p. 111 "... a public reception in the university auditorium drew two
hundred people ..." *Laramie Boomerang*, July 20, 1899.

p. 111 "During the night some students shot off a cannon...." *Laramie
Boomerang*, July 22, 1899.

p. 111 "By lunchtime of the second day ..." Knight, "Wyoming Fossil
Fields," 453.

p. 113 "... fossil deciduous leaves and coral ..." *Laramie Boomerang*, July
26, 1899.

p. 113 "Como Bluff, it reported, 'is on a huge anticlinal fold ...' " *Laramie
Boomerang*, July 31, 1899.

p. 113 "... stopping to visit with the American Museum paleontologists
..." *Laramie Boomerang*, July 31, 1899.

p. 113 "... 'that great crowd of curiosity and bone hunters' with its
'miscellaneous scrambling for Dinosaurs'..." Osborn to Granger,
June 8, 1899, and July 13, 1899, AMNH oc.

p. 114 " 'Men could be seen everywhere ...' " *Laramie Boomerang*, Aug. 3,
1899.

p. 115 "The men took five hundred photographs." Knight, "Wyoming
Fossil Fields," 457, and Knight's account in the *Laramie Boomerang*,
Aug. 22, 1899. He said that "500 plates and films" were exposed,
implying that some men had large-format, tripodded cameras
while others carried more portable Kodaks.

p. 115 " 'determined in the near future to be one of the famous resorts
of the Rocky Mountains.' " Knight, "Wyoming Fossil Fields," 461.
But irrigation for downstream farmers and ranchers took prece-
dence over tourism; Pathfinder Dam was built in 1904 of huge
granite blocks in a narrow spot below the Platte-Sweetwater
confluence. Alcova Dam was built in the 1930s near a hot springs
a few miles below the opening of the canyon, flooding the springs
and most of the canyon floor. The main stream of the Platte now
funnels through tunnels to run turbines for hydropower. Fremont

Canyon's floor is watered only by occasional local runoff from the cliffs above it, and by water backed up from Alcova Dam below.

p. 115 "… about half the party started back for Medicine Bow." *Laramie Boomerang,* Aug. 10, 1899.

p. 115 "… two dozen cooks and drivers, and seventy-five or eighty scientists …" These numbers bring the expedition close to the size of the posses that pursued the Wilcox train robbers the previous June. The posses appear never to have maintained their size for more than a few days at a time, however, and probably traveled without wagons.

p. 116 " 'The hard rocks have not been reduced to the general levels of the country …' " George L. Collie, "Topography of Central Wyoming," in Fossil Fields Expedition, 50–51.

p. 116 " 'The most sublime sight I ever beheld …' " Yates, "Observations on the Expedition," in Fossil Fields Expedition, 11.

p. 117 "… establish a permanent summer school …" *Laramie Boomerang,* July 26, 1899.

10. NOBLE CHAMPIONS OF TRUTH

p. 118 "… Frick and another partner had brought to Carnegie a pair of speculators …" Wall, *Andrew Carnegie,* 728–44.

p. 119 " 'You know I am a creature which feeds upon encourage-ment …' " Holland to Carnegie, Jan. 1, 1900, CMNH lib.

p. 119 "… Carnegie appeared in Pittsburgh just a week later …" Holland to James M. Swank, Jan. 8, 1900, CMNH annex.

p. 119 "Their famous last meeting …" Wall, *Andrew Carnegie,* 753.

p. 120 "… Holland was steadily frustrated …" Alberts, *Pitt,* 50–52. Late in the decade, Holland realized it would make sense for the university to move from the city of Allegheny, on Pittsburgh's north side, to the university's present site in Oakland. But that meant persuading Mrs. Schenley, the rich widow who still owned so much land in the East End, to part with more of her property, a tricky proposition. Holland and Carnegie met with her in London in 1897; a year later she came back with a price. The Pennsylvania legislature refused to come up with the money, however. Carnegie likewise refused. Holland was discouraged by, even resentful of, Carnegie's refusal. In a speech he gave when he finally resigned his chancellorship, Holland said, "You cannot kill this institution. It will grow. It is rooted deep in the affections of the men it has served and the community it has honored. I trust the day is coming when the rich men of Western Pennsylvania, and the poor men, too ... will realize that to live and die without in some way having helped their University is to die disgraced." Quoted in Alberts, *Pitt*, 52. The last sentence echoes Carnegie's famous line from "The Gospel of Wealth": "The man who dies thus rich, dies disgraced."

p. 120 "... a joke Holland often told about a Scotsman ..." Wortman to Osborn, Nov. 4, 1899, AMNH oc.

p. 121 " '...one or two expressions which I thought were likely to offend ...' " Holland to Mellor, Jan. 31, 1900, CMNH annex.

p. 121 "Wortman's article in *Science* was published February 2." Wortman, "New Department of Vertebrate Paleontology."

p. 122 " 'Onward Ye Braves ...' " Holland to Carnegie, CMNH br. The letter is undated, but the attached newspaper clipping, otherwise unidentified, bears a dateline of Feb. 6, 1900, under a small headline, "Dr. J. L. Wortman resigns."

11. PATAGONIA

p. 123 "Hatcher was born in Illinois and grew up in Iowa ..." Schuchert, "John Bell Hatcher," 131–41. This article also contains a bibliography of Hatcher's publications, prepared by his brother-in-law, O. A. Peterson.

p. 123 "He took the novel approach of locating the bones on a grid map ..." Lanham, *Bone Hunters*, 199–200.

p. 123 "... carload after carload of the bones and big skulls of *Brontotherium*..." Schuchert, "John Bell Hatcher," 132.

p. 124 "... parts of several huge, horned dinosaur skulls ..." Hatcher, "Some Localities for Laramie Mammals," 112–20.

p. 125 " 'The small mammals are pretty generally distributed ...' " Hatcher, "Some Localities for Laramie Mammals," 119. Most Cretaceous mammal teeth are so tiny they are best viewed under a low-power microscope.

p. 126 " 'If we accept literally Marsh's statement ...' " Hatcher, "Some Localities for Laramie Mammals," 115–16. All italics are Hatcher's.

p. 127 "... [Hatcher] 'hated pretense of any sort.' " Schuchert, "John Bell Hatcher," 138.

p. 128   " 'Regions affording such contradictory evidences ...' " Hatcher, "Ceratops Beds of Converse County," 144.

p. 128   "... Florentino wrote articles on the fossils Carlos shipped home ..." Simpson, *Discoverers of the Lost World*. I've drawn heavily in this section on Simpson's chapters 4 and 5, pp. 59–93, on the Ameghino brothers. Chapter 7 on Hatcher's trips to Patagonia and chapter 8 on Scott's work with the South American fossils, pp. 105–12, are also useful. The thoughts on Florentino Ameghino's chauvinism and on similar qualities in Hatcher are my own, however.

p. 129   " 'The discoveries announced by the Ameghinos were of such an interesting nature ...' " Hatcher, "Explorations in Patagonia," 328.

p. 129   " 'Since no one else seemed ready to undertake this work ...' " Hatcher, "Explorations in Patagonia," 328.

p. 130   "... Hatcher rode overland to see to the shipments at Punta Arenas ..." Hatcher, *Bone Hunters in Patagonia*, 88–90. This book, a reprint of the original narrative of the Patagonia expedition, is one of the great pieces of the literature of travel and exploration of its era and deserves a wider readership. My account here is based largely on the narrative and also on the more scientific articles Hatcher published at the time.

p. 132   "... 'a persistence that in retrospect seems more maniacal than brave.' " Simpson, *Discoverers of the Lost World*, 118.

p. 132   "By now he was out of money ..." In his introduction to Hatcher's *Narrative*, reprinted in the Ox Bow Press edition, Princeton professor William Berryman Scott thanks a number of wealthy Princeton alumni and friends who helped pay for Hatcher's trips, among them John W. and Horatio Garret of Baltimore, Cleveland H. Dodge, Morris Jesup, Henry Fairfield Osborn, William C. Osborn, Rudolf Schirmer and Charles Scribner of New York, and Cyrus and Stanley McCormick of Chicago. Hatcher himself, in his own introduction in the same volume, lists the Garretts, Dodge, and Jesup among a smaller group of "chief contributors." Hatcher also notes that he paid for most of the third expedition himself and, at several points in the narrative, remarks how poorly equipped the expeditions were.

    Simpson (*Discoverers of the Lost World*, 110) records that Hatcher wangled reduced steamship fares and won free passage on various ships traveling among Patagonian ports, but he is skeptical about Hatcher's claim to have covered many of the expenses himself, questioning how a man with no financial resources beyond his salary—and with a wife and five children to support—could have come up with the extra money.

Through the middle of the twentieth century at least, Princeton-based geologists' lore held that Hatcher had financed his trips with poker winnings. An article in the *Atlantic Monthly* in September 1937 by James Terry Duce, an oil geologist, paints a vivid picture of Hatcher backing out through a saloon door, pistol drawn and pockets full of just-won pesos, as his steamboat blows its whistle down at the harbor (Duce, "Patter-gonia"). Simpson has the sense to call the poker story "obviously garbled" but goes on to say, reasonably, that some card-playing expertise on Hatcher's part seems not out of character (*Discoverers of the Lost World*, 110).

p. 133 "... young Barnum Brown, Osborn's rising star ..." Osborn's decision to send Brown on this expedition, rather than Wortman, contributed to the discontent Wortman was feeling when Holland came to New York in April 1899 to recruit him for the Carnegie Museum curatorship.

p. 133 "In the southern winter of 1898, he met Carlos [Ameghino] in the port of Santa Cruz ..." Hatcher to William Dall, Oct. 14, 1903, CMNH br.

p. 133 "They were thorough and clear—but ... incorrect." Simpson, *Discoverers of the Lost World*, 85–87, 128. Ortmann later followed Hatcher to the Carnegie Museum, where he became curator of invertebrate paleontology.

p. 134 "... Scott's close work with the big vertebrates ..." Simpson, *Discoverers of the Lost World*, 128–33.

12. NO MORE REEDS, NO MORE WORTMANS

p. 135 "... Hatcher angrily had refused." Simpson, *Discoverers of the Lost World*, 118. Simpson also quotes Scott's resignation letter. "The understanding between Prof. Henry F. Osborn and Mr. Barnum Brown," handwritten document, Dec. 6, 1898, AMNH oc.

p. 136 "... Peterson left Princeton to take a job at the Carnegie Museum ..." Wortman to Osborn, Jan. 6, 1900 (misdated 1899), AMNH oc.

p. 136 "Osborn had also had his eye on Peterson ..." Osborn to Scott, Sept. 14, 1899, AMNH oc; Wortman to Osborn, Jan. 6, 1900 (misdated 1899), AMNH oc.

p. 136 "... Holland was in Princeton, having a long conversation ..."
Holland to C. C. Mellor, chairman of the museum committee,
Carnegie Institute, Feb. 8, 1900, CMNH annex.

p. 136 "Hatcher wrote Holland on February 12 ..." Hatcher to Holland,
Feb. 12, 1900, CMNH br.

p. 137 " 'We have the three ablest bone sharks ...' " Holland to
Carnegie, March 19, 1900, CMNH annex.

p. 137 "Reed... 'will probably leave in the spring ...' " Wortman to
Osborn, Feb. 1, 1900, AMNH oc.

p. 137 "Hatcher ... now requested the funds from Holland to do
everything right." Hatcher to Holland, March 31, 1900, CMNH
br.

p. 138 "... Reed remembered five skulls ..." Hatcher to Holland, April 7,
17, and 21, 1900, CMNH br.

p. 138 "Hatcher expected Reed and Peterson back with the skulls ..."
Hatcher to Holland, April 28, 1900, CMNH br.

p. 138 "The older man confessed ..." Reed to Hatcher, May 3, 1900,
CMNH br. The letter in the archive is clipped to a large manila
Carnegie Museum envelope from the Holland era, on which is
written in large, blue crayon: "Famous letter of Reed to Hatcher
Excusing himself for not finding the bones which he cashed [sic]
in 1885 He had never found them O.A.P." The note apparently
was written by Olaf August Peterson. Peterson's judgment on
Reed permeates the thinking of generations of Carnegie Mu-
seum professionals, turning up, for instance in such places as
Coggeshall's September 1951 article about the discovery of the
Diplodocus, with its belittling tone about Reed's contribution.

p. 138 " 'the field north of the ratle snake hills' ..." Reed to Hatcher,
May 3, 1900, CMNH br. Reed may be referring here to Eocene
fossil fields near Lysite, Wyoming, worked by Wortman and
others from the American Museum in the 1890s and worked
again in the 1980s by paleontologists from the Carnegie Museum.

p. 138 "... Reed's claim ... that he had 'picked up half a bushel of small
skulls in half an hour.' " Hatcher to Holland, May 9, 1900, CMNH
br.

p. 139 "Hatcher would stay where he was, looking for horned dinosaurs." And not finding any, it is worth noting here. He did find
something he assured Holland was of far greater scientific
interest—the skeleton of a *Claosaurus,* a duckbilled Cretaceous
dinosaur, with some of the skin still on it (see Hatcher to Hol-

land, May 31, 1900, CMNH br). But Hatcher must have known Holland was promising Carnegie big *Triceratops* skeletons for display, and the failure to find any most likely contributed to his anxiety.

p. 139 " 'I trust you will not take this in an offended spirit ...' " Hatcher to Reed, May 18, 1900, CMNH br.

p. 140 " 'You will remember that you told me that you were my friend ...' " Reed to Holland, May 27, 1900, CMNH br.

p. 141 " 'I am very familiar with the work he did for Marsh ...' " Hatcher to Holland, June 4, 1900, CMNH br.

p. 141 "Hatcher professed ... 'the kindliest feelings' ..." Hatcher to Holland, June 7, 1900, CMNH br.

p. 141 "... he could consider Reed's 'withdrawal' as dating from ..." Hatcher to Reed, June 6, 1900, CMNH br.

p. 141 " '... & if we are careful we can get men who are truthful also.' " Hatcher to Holland, June 7, 1900, CMNH br.

p. 142 " 'Reed is afflicted ...' " Holland to Hatcher, June 12, 1900, CMNH br.

p. 142 "... Holland went on to recap ..." Holland to Carnegie, March 26, 1900, CMNH lib.

p. 142 " 'Such men are far less apt to be conceited and troublesome ...' " Holland to Hatcher, June 12, 1900, CMNH br.

13. SOUTHERN DREAMS

p. 144 "... a scattering of publications ..." For a sampling, see Hatcher's articles "On the Geology of Southern Patagonia," "Patagonia," " 'The Mysterious Mammal of Patagonia, Gryptotherium Domesticum,' by Rudolph Hauthal, Santiago Roth, and Robert Lehman Nitsche" (review), "Explorations in Patagonia," and "Some Geographic Features of Southern Patagonia."

p. 144 " 'While there is a striking and universal dissimilarity ...' " Hatcher, "Explorations in Patagonia," 329.

p. 145 "... Libbey ... was ... well connected ..." Libbey had attempted the ascent of Mt. St. Elias in Alaska in 1888, and by 1899 had traveled twice to Greenland on expeditions led by or relieving Robert Peary. See Princeton University, Department of Geosciences website.

p. 145 "... Bruce had grown tired of waiting ..." Baughman, *Pilgrims on the Ice*, 3, 28–29. Bruce cooled his heels for eleven months before he gave up waiting for an answer from Sir Clements Markham of the Royal Geographic Society, fundraiser and organizer for the British expedition. Markham may have feared that, if Bruce were appointed director of the scientific staff, he would be too strong a rival to Robert Falcon Scott, the young navy officer Markham had picked to lead the effort. Scott's first expedition spent the period 1901–04 on the Pacific side of Antarctica. They were based on Ross Island in McMurdo Sound and explored the Ross Ice Shelf and Victoria Land.

p. 145   " 'Now my plan is just this …' " Hatcher to Holland, May 1, 1900, CMNH br.

p. 147   "… he hoped to have two summers …" Hatcher to Holland, May 1, 1900, CMNH br.

p. 148   " '… I cannot believe that you are physically up to such an undertaking …' " John Garrett to Hatcher, June 29, 1900, CMNH br. Garrett graduated from Princeton in 1895. He spent many years in the diplomatic corps and eventually was named U.S. ambassador to Italy during the Hoover administration.

p. 148   "… the brand-new and only marginally seaworthy vessel …" The *Discovery* cost £51,000 to build, an amount which could have bought and outfitted two whalers for scientific research. Persuading Parliament to bear this expense represented a cultural triumph of adventure, the true goal of Scott's expeditions, over science. It also represented the triumph of the Royal Geographical Society's faction of the scientific community, led by Sir Clements Markham, over the Royal Society faction, led by the geologist Sir Archibald Geike (see Baughman, *Pilgrims on the Ice*, 51–52). It was Geike who, in chapter 1 of this account, spoke eloquently for the true value of *Diplodocus carnegii*, as a fossil to which other fossils could usefully be compared.

p. 148   "… appointments have already been made …" Scott to Libbey, March 4, 1901, CMNH br.

p. 148   " 'Do I understand correctly your offer …" Bruce to Libbey, March 5, 1901, CMNH br.

p. 148   "It was not uncommon in the early British polar explorations …" Baughman, *Pilgrims on the Ice*, 30–32.

p. 149   " 'Since my conversation with you last evening …' " Hatcher to Holland, March 21, 1901.

p. 149   "The earth sciences around 1900 were tangled …" Oreskes, *Rejection of Continental Drift*, 3–80.

p. 151 "… no one could yet conceive the mechanics of drift—how it actually worked …" Oreskes, in *The Rejection of Continental Drift*, notes that other important phenomena—gravity and electricity, for example—were widely accepted as real long before it was understood how they work. This leads her to argue persuasively that Wegener's ideas were rejected more for social reasons than for scientific ones.

p. 151 "… ships began to use echo-sounding devices …" Sullivan, *Continents in Motion*, 52–54.

p. 152 "… measurements of heat rising … showed it was coming up much than would be predicted …" Sullivan, *Continents in Motion*, 64.

p. 152 "… Hess began articulating a theory …" Sullivan, *Continents in Motion*, 68–70.

p. 153 "… sound fossil evidence that Antarctica had been part of Gondwanaland …" Sullivan, *Continents in Motion*, 178–87.

p. 154 "In recent years, scraps of Late Cretaceous dinosaurs have turned up there, as well as rare remains of Eocene mammals and birds." Michael Woodburne, paleontologist at the University of California at Riverside, personal communication, Nov. 2, 2000. Vertebrate fossils on the Antarctic Peninsula are still very rare, invertebrates relatively common. Dinosaurs include hypsilophodonts and, possibly, hadrosaurs. Mammals include marsupials and some placental South American ungulates (hoofed animals); birds include phororhachoids, a flightless type, and various penguins.

p. 154 " '… no amount of kindness … is capable of satisfying you …' " Holland to Hatcher, March 21, 1901, CMNH br.

p. 155 " '… I shall take my defeat philosophically.' " Hatcher to Holland, March 23, 1901. CMNH br.

p. 155 "… Hatcher attended scientific meetings …" Hatcher to Holland, monthly report, April 30, 1902, CMNH br.

p. 155 "… request for $65,000 to support a Hatcher-led expedition to Antarctica." Hatcher, Holland and Mellor, "To The Executive Committee of the Carnegie Institution, Washington D.C.," April 21, 1902, CMNH br.

p. 156 "… parts of the Andes … were pulled eastward when Gondwanaland broke up." Sullivan, *Continents in Motion*, 189–90.

p. 156 "The Carnegie Institution … was brand new in the spring of 1902." Wall, *Andrew Carnegie*, 860–63.

p. 157 "but an executive committee ... found it 'inexpedient to recommend' the proposal ..." Holland to Frew and Holland to Walcott, both Dec. 4, 1903, CMNH lib.

14. WHEN THE FLAG DROPS

p. 158 "... parts of two *Diplodocus* skeletons ..." Hatcher, *"Diplodocus* Marsh."

p. 161 " 'It is a bigger beast ... Now the biggest thing on earth of its kind bears your name.' " Holland to Carnegie, May 15, 1901, and May 28, 1901, CLPgh. In the second letter, Holland reminds his patron that he'd once named a new genus of African moth for him also— "small, but beautiful" (see *Entomological News* [May 1896]: 33 et. seq. and plate 6). Holland had promised Carnegie a similar immortality when he first wrote him about the moth genus in 1896: "No[w] then there is a genus named after you, and when you think of Livingstone, and Stanley, and our Mutual friend [the French-born American explorer of Africa Paul] DuChaillu, and the continent, which they with others have opened to the eyes of men, it will perhaps be with the pleasure of the passing thought that one of the fairy forms which rise at dusk toward the light of the moon, and hover over the giant tree-tops flooded with the splendor of equatorial night, bears your name, and will continue to bear it as long as science has a language. I would have liked to have named some great thing in your honor, but the great things of the animal kingdom have all been sought out and named already, unless it be the dead brutes of the past ages, which Marsh and Cope and others are unearthing. My province is the delicate, the softly beautiful, the curious in form and color" (Holland to Carnegie, May 2, 1896, CMNH br).

p. 161 "... by far the more compelling of the two." Gilmore, "On a Newly Mounted Skeleton of Diplodocus," 7–8 and plate 6.

p. 161 "Louis Dollo, in his way, contributed as much to the era's understanding of dinosaurs ..." See Kenneth Carpenter, "Dinosaurs as Museum Exhibits," in Farlow and Brett-Surman, *Complete Dinosaur*, chap. 12, 150–64; Wilford, *Riddle of the Dinosaur*, 152–55; Gardom and Milner, *Natural History Museum Book of Dinosaurs*, 96–97.

p. 162 " 'Have you ever thought about casting the bones ...' " Dollo to Hatcher, Dec. 11, 1901, author's translation, CMNH br.

p. 163 "[Marsh] published a sheet of illustrations ..." Hoagland, "They Gave Life to Bones," 114–33; Schuchert and LeVene, *O. C. Marsh,* 385.

p. 163 "Beecher ... had decided to set up Marsh's *Apatosaurus* ..." Holland to Carnegie, Jan. 10, 1902, CLPgh.

p. 163 "... a young University of Wyoming graduate named Charles Gilmore." In the spring of 1900, after Reed was fired, Peterson hired Charles W. Gilmore, a recent University of Wyoming graduate and student of Wilbur Knight, to work the Sheep Creek quarry. By the summer of 1901 Hatcher was willing to leave Gilmore in charge there, and he found and excavated an *Apatosaurus.* He was rewarded the following fall by being hired for the permanent museum staff in Pittsburgh. Not long afterward, he went to the U.S. National Museum, where he had a long and distinguished career, rising to curator of vertebrate paleontology. In 1909, however, Carnegie collectors in Utah found a site that eventually yielded an even better *Apatosaurus.* As a result, Gilmore's *Apatosaurus* spent about fifty years in pieces, sitting on shelves at the Carnegie Museum. Finally, in the mid-1950s it made its way back to Wyoming, and, under the supervision of geology professor Sam Knight, Wilbur Knight's son, the *Apatosaurus* was mounted in the University of Wyoming's geology museum, where it remains today.

p. 164 " 'The hugest quadruped that ever walked the earth, a namesake of mine.' " Holland, "Diplodocus Goes to Mexico," 84.

p. 164 " 'The King was attracted to the Diplodocus when here' ..." Carnegie to Holland, Oct. 2, 1902, CMNH br.

p. 164 "... made a formal offer ... to the trustees of the British Museum ..." Correspondents of the time use the term "British Museum" somewhat loosely. They are not referring to the museum in Bloomsbury which contains the Elgin Marbles and the Rosetta Stone. In the early 1880s the natural history collection was moved from that building to the one in South Kensington now called the Natural History Museum, where the collection still can be found. More formal references at the turn of the last century used the term "British Museum (Natural History)." At the time both institutions were under the same governing board. For more information go to the Natural History Museum website's history page at http://www.nhm.ac.uk/info/history/index.html.

p. 164 "… 'ought to bring a royal return, more than a thank you.' "
Holland to Carnegie, Jan. 31, 1903, CMNH lib.

p. 164 "… two skilled Italian modelers …" Holland to R. A. Franks, May
1, 1903; Holland to Carnegie, May 9, 1903; CMNH lib. In the first
letter, Holland mentions "two modelers"; in the second, he
mentions hiring "a young Italian, who apparently is very capable
and has extensive knowledge of manipulative methods, and will
undoubtedly succeed far better than many who have already
wider reputations for this kind of work."

p. 165 "A huge European fossil collection …" Holland to Carnegie, May
9 and June 8, 1903, CMNH lib; Holland to Hatcher, June 6, 7, and
10, 1903, CMNH br.

p. 166 "Holland sailed for Europe July 8." Holland to Carnegie, July 3
and Sept. 28, 1903, CMNH lib; Holland to Hatcher, July 27, 1903.

p. 167 "… filled more than 250 boxes." Holland to Carnegie, Dec. 7,
1903, CMNH lib. Carnegie collectors working in Wyoming,
Montana, and Kansas that summer, by comparison, shipped home
180 boxes of fossils.

p. 167 "Carnegie, the experienced manufacturer, agreed …" Carnegie to
Holland, Aug. 4, 1903, CMNH br.

p. 167 "In his annual fall thank-you note … Holland told Horace Burt
…" Holland to Horace Burt, Oct. 7, 1903, CMNH lib.

p. 167 "Hatcher wrote to Boule, proposing a swap." Hatcher to
Marcellin Boule, Oct. 8, 1903, CMNH br.

p. 168 "… and Holland had to scramble." Holland to Boule and Holland
to Carnegie, Jan. 13, 1904, CMNH lib.

p. 168 " 'My breath was taken away …' " Holland to Carnegie, Jan. 13,
1904, CMNH lib.

p. 168 "… work on the reproductions had doubled." Holland to
Carnegie, Dec. 7, 1903, and March 4, 1904, CMNH lib.

p. 168 "… the reproduction would be finished … by August …" Holland-
Carnegie, March 4, 1904, CMNH lib.

p. 169 "On May 13 … Hatcher reported to Holland …" Hatcher to
Holland, May 13, 1904, CMNH br.

p. 170 "For the next two years … he would work an average of seven
hours a day on the project." Osborn, "Explorations of John Bell
Hatcher," in Hatcher, Ceratopsia, xx.

p. 171 " 'Hatcher has indeed told us that … he saw no Pierre deposits
beneath the Judith River beds …' " Hay, "On Some Recent Literature," 117–18.

p. 171 "… one observed fact is worth any amount of expert opinion."
Hatcher, *Ceratopsia*, 8.

p. 171 "… Hatcher's letters try but fail to conceal his bitterness."
Hatcher to Hay, Sept. 7 and Sept. 11, 1903; Hay to Hatcher, Sept.
15, 1903, CMNH br.

p. 171 "… 'we were able to assure ourselves …' " F. Ameghino to
Hatcher, April 20, 1903 (author's translation), CMNH br.

p. 171 "He had proposed just such a solution to Carlos Ameghino in
1898." Hatcher to William H. Dall, Oct. 14, 1903, CMNH br.

p. 171 "In 1904 he again proposed a joint field trip with the Ameghinos …"
Hatcher to Florentino Ameghino, Feb. 23, 1904, CMNH br.

p. 171 "… a memoir on a sauropod entirely new to science …" Hatcher,
"Osteology of Haplocanthosaurus."

p. 172 "By June 4, 1904, the crews had mounted the long neck …"
Hatcher to A. Hermann, June 4, 1904, CMNH lib.

p. 172 "… we will avoid the unsightly and cumbrous mass of scaffolding …" Holland to Carnegie, June 10, 1904, CMNH lib. Carpenter, in "Dinosaurs as Museum Exhibits" (Farlow and Brett-
Surman, *Complete Dinosaur*), notes that when the English sculptor
Waterhouse Hawkins mounted *Hadrosaurus foulkii* at the Academy of Natural Sciences in Philadelphia in 1868, he drilled holes
in the vertebrae and strung them along an iron rod. He attached
limb bones to a supporting armature with steel bands. Similarly,
when Dollo mounted the *Iguanodon* skeletons in Brussels in the
late 1870s and early 1880s, he used metal bands to attach the
bones to a steel armature. Photos show that Dollo assembled the
structure in front of a life-sized drawing of the skeleton. The
bones hung from a wooden scaffolding, ready to be attached to
the armature. Dollo also kept ostrich and kangaroo skeletons
nearby for reference.

p. 172 "The dinosaur's front feet had been cast from an American
Museum specimen …" For a detailed description of the parts that
made up *Diplodocus carnegii*, I thank John S. McIntosh, a paleontologist and professor of physics at Wesleyan University, now
retired (conversation Oct. 8, 2000).

p. 174 "The skull … proved to be the greatest problem." Holland,
"Osteology of *Diplodocus* Marsh," 227–30.

p. 175 "… because he was ever a Pittsburgh booster, Holland would later
believe …" Holland to Osborn, July 29, 1904, CMNH lib. Details
of the events leading up to Hatcher's death are also in this letter.

p. 175 " 'Wire from Douglas [Stewart, Holland's assistant] tells me of our great loss, Professor Hatcher.' " Carnegie to Holland, July 11, 1904, CMNH lib.

p. 175 "[Utterback] ... found two *Triceratops* skulls." Holland to Utterback, Aug. 17, 1904, CMNH lib.

p. 178 "Carnegie appears to have provided Anna Hatcher with financial assistance after Hatcher's death." Carnegie to Church, July 19, 1904, CMNH br.

p. 178 "... Hatcher's policy with the Union Mutual Life Insurance Company paid $3,000." W. H. Lushear to Douglas Stewart, Oct. 25, 1904, CMNH br.

p. 178 "She and the four surviving children ... moved back to Lamont, Iowa ..." Anna Hatcher-Stewart, April 5, 1905, CMNH br; Hatcher's children are named in Simpson, *Discoverers of the Lost World*, 107.

15. HEADS AND TAILS

p. 180 " '... beauty ought not to be secured at the expense of truth' " Hay, "On the Restoration of Skeletons," 94.

p. 180 "... [Hay's] irritation with Hatcher and Holland ..." Hay, "On the Habits and Pose of the Sauropodous Dinosaurs," 672–81.

p. 180 "Richard Owen ... in 1841 ... invented the concept of dinosaurs." John S. McIntosh, M. K. Brett-Surman, and James O. Farlow, "Sauropods," chapter 20 in Farlow and Brett-Surman, *Complete Dinosaur*, 264–90. In the same book, see Hugh Torrens, "Politics and Paleontology: Richard Owen and the Invention of Dinosaurs," 175–90. See also Hugh Torrens, "Dinosaurs and Dinomania Over 150 Years." In both publications Torrens clears up a longstanding confusion over the date of Owen's famous report.

p. 181 "... [Osborn] was tempted, he wrote, to discard modern theories of evolution and 'to revive the old teleological explanation'..." Osborn, "A Skeleton of Diplodocus," Osborn was, in fact, tempted by teleological explanations all his life. See Rainger, *Agenda for Antiquity*.

p. 182 "Osborn went so far as to believe the animal could raise its forequarters *while swimming* ..." Osborn, "Additional Characters of Diplodocus," 315–16.

p. 182 "Osborn concluded ... that it ate nutritious water plants ..."
Osborn, "A Skeleton of Diplodocus," 874.

p. 182 " 'In contrast with Brontosaurus it was essentially long and light-
limbed and agile.' " Osborn, "A Skeleton of Diplodocus," 874.

p. 182 "His conclusions follow Osborn's ..." Hatcher, "*Diplodocus*
Marsh," and "Additional Remarks on *Diplodocus.*"

p. 183 "Admitting the decision was 'largely conjectural' ..." Osborn,
"Skull and Skeleton," 374–76.

p. 183 "By analogy to the modern animals, they came up with two
important features..." Osborn, " Skeleton of *Brontosaurus* and
Skull of *Morosaurus.*"

p. 184 "There is still room for wide differences of opinion ..." Osborn,
"Skull and Skeleton," 376.

p. 184 "... Holland published a large monograph in 1906." Holland,
"Osteology of *Diplodocus* Marsh."

p. 184 "Osborn had found similar fusing in the tail bones ..." Osborn,
"Skeleton of *Brontosaurus* and Skull of *Morosaurus*," 283.

p. 185 "Hay entered the dispute ... on the gait-and-posture question."
Hay, "On the Habits and Pose," 672–81.

p. 185 "In a second paper the same month ..." Hay, "Dr. Holland on
Diplodocus."

p. 186 "Holland was stung." Holland, "Dr. Hay on *Diplodocus.*"

p. 186 " 'The plain indication of the restored parts ... is ... a matter of
common honesty.' " Hay, "On Restoration of Skeletons," 94–95.

p. 187 "... pursuing his claim for *Diplodocus*' crocodile-like gait ..." Hay,
"On Locomotion of Dinosaurs."

p. 187 " 'It was a bold step ... to proceed with the help of a pencil ...' "
Holland, "Review of Criticisms of Sauropod Dinosaurs," 262.
Holland delivered the substance of the paper, in a talk illustrated
with stereopticon slides, to the paleontological section of the
Geological Society of America on December 30, 1909. The paper
was published in the following spring.

p. 188 " 'The *Diplodocus* must have moved in a groove or a rut.' "
Holland, "Review of Criticisms of Sauropod Dinosaurs," 268.

p. 189 "Sauropod footprints discovered in Texas ..." Bakker, *Dinosaur
Heresies*, 206.

p. 189 "He was unconvinced about another ... matter as well ..." Hay,
"Further Observations on Pose."

p. 189 "... Carnegie collector Earl Douglass found three sauropod skeletons ..." Holland, "Review of Criticisms of Sauropod Dinosaurs," 283.

p. 189 "In 1915 he politely raised the flag of uncertainty." Holland, "Heads and Tails." 273–78. The paper was first read in Philadelphia before a meeting of the Paleontological Society of America on December 31, 1914.

p. 191 "... Holland's doubts about Marsh's head choice were as strong as ever ..." Holland, "Skull of *Diplodocus*."

p. 192 "... Bakker was describing dinosaurs as generally agile and warm blooded." Bakker, *Dinosaur Heresies*.

p. 193 "The Jurassic conifers and cycads grew slowly ..." Bakker, *Dinosaur Heresies*, 190–93.

p. 193 "... sauropods didn't like swamps." Bakker, *Dinosaur Heresies*, 120–24.

p. 193 "... two other paleontologists were ... ready to challenge Marsh's authority ..." See Berman and McIntosh, "Skull and Relationships"; McIntosh and Berman, "Description of the Palate and Lower Jaw"; McIntosh et al., "Sauropods," 268; and West, "Dinosaur Head Hunt."

p. 194 "But not until 1997 did a pair of dinosaur scientists distinguish between two kinds of whips." Myhrvold and Currie, "Suspersonic Sauropods?"

p. 195 "Some scientists now say the engineering of the diplodocids' skeletons ..." R. McNeill Alexander, "Engineering a Dinosaur," chapter 30 in Farlow, *Complete Dinosaur*, 414–24.

p. 196 "To better understand the physical capabilities inherent in the diplodocids' neck ..." Stevens and Parrish, "Neck Posture and Feeding Habits."

16. CELEBRITY

p. 198 "Holland visited a church in the city of Tucuman ..." Holland, *To the River Plate and Back*, 277.

p. 199 "The number of plasterers swelled to a small army." Van Trump, *American Palace of Culture*, 27.

p. 199 "His most cherished hope ..." Wall, *Andrew Carnegie*, 924–26.

p. 200 "With these gifts in hand ..." According to Holland, Carnegie telephoned on the second morning of the opening celebrations to say, "Did you not once tell me that when you were making the replica of the Diplodocus for the British Museum you had made a couple of additional castings?"(Holland, *To the River Plate and Back*, 12). But it seems unlikely that Carnegie would have forgotten the multiple casts he had earlier approved in his eagerness to have gifts ready to bestow on monarchs and presidents.

p. 200 "He instructed Holland to ask the Germans and the French ..." The Germans present were Minister of State Theodor von Moeller and a General von Loewenfeld; the French were Baron d'Estournelles and M. Paul Doumer (Holland, *To the River Plate and Back*, 12).

p. 200 " 'an attitude ... far more graceful and lifelike'..." Holland to Marcellin Boule, Nov. 12, 1907, CMNH online. See photo on p. 2.

p. 200 "The crates ... were shipped in mid-March 1908." Holland estimated the expedition would cost just under $5,000, including freight for the dinosaur bones, his and Coggeshall's steamer fares, three months' wages for Coggeshall, two months' stay for the two of them in Paris and Berlin, some hired laborers on the European side, and, the most expensive item, $2,200 to build the platforms and buy the ironwork with which to mount the dinosaur (Holland to R. A. Franks, March 23, 1908, CMNH online).

p. 200 "Parisians of all ranks crowded the Jardin des Plantes outside the Museum d'Histoire Naturelle ..." Taquet, *Dinosaur Impressions*, 116–17.

p. 201 "[Grand Duke Wladimir] asked Holland to tell Carnegie to remember Russia, too." Holland, *The River Plate and Back*, 248–52.

p. 201 "Crowned heads of Europe/ All make a royal fuss ..." Holland, *To the River Plate and Back*, 248.

p. 202 "... a moment of truth came when the backbone was suspended high in the air ..." Holland, *To the River Plate and Back*, 248–52.

p. 203 "I wish I were an ichthyosaurus / And could swim the Lias ocean ..." Holland, *To the River Plate and Back*, 1.

p. 203 "A final banquet on October 15, 1912 ..." Holland, *To the River Plate and Back*, 255–56.

p. 204 "... Holland and Coggeshall traveled to neutral Spain ..." Holland, "Editorials," 3–4.

p. 204 "... Holland visited him in those last months ..." Hendrick, *Life of Andrew Carnegie*, vol. 2, 383.

p. 204 "... [Holland] took on the duties of president of the Carnegie Hero Fund ..." The fund was the only one of Carnegie's philanthropies that was entirely his own idea. It rewarded civil heroes—often, the protagonists in dramatic rescues—with medals, publicity, and financial help according to their needs (Wall, *Andrew Carnegie*, 894–97).

p. 204 "... Mexican-American relations at that moment were at a low ebb." James, *Mexico and the Americans*, 238–40, and Krauze, *Mexico*, 417–19.

p. 205 "Holland was game ..." Holland to Louise Carnegie, Nov. 3, 1927, and Feb. 15, 1928; Holland to F. P. Keppel, Feb. 23, 1928; Holland to Franks, May 22, 1928; CMNH br.

p. 206 "Holland had to correct his misapprehension that the dinosaur skeleton would be made of bronze ..." Holland to Herrera, Oct. 1, 1928, CMNH br.

p. 206 "... Herrera sent out fundraising letters almost immediately." Herrara to "Estimado Señor," undated to-whom-it-may-concern fundraising letter, probably October 1928, CMNH br.

p. 206 "... 'a mighty stimulus toward the erection of new buildings ...' " Holland to Keppel, Oct. 9, 1928, CMNH br.

p. 206 " 'Your dear husband once said to me ...' " Holland to Louise Carnegie, Oct. 23, 1928, CMNH br.

p. 207 " 'Owing to the disturbed condition of affairs in Mexico ...' " Holland to Herrera, May 7, 1929; Herrera to Holland, May 13, 1929 CMNH br. The Cristiada, the fierce War for Christ, was nearing its end. For three years mounted guerrillas fought a newly mechanized federal army that had a hard time following them through territory where roads were bad or absent. President Calles hated the church and had insisted on absolute enforcement of articles of the 1917 Constitution requiring the closing of church schools and government registration of priests. The poor, who had little at all other than their religion, refused to submit (see Krauze, *Mexico*, 419–24). Morrow, the U.S. ambassador, finally got representatives of both sides to agree to a compromise in the spring of 1928, but the war dragged on until June 1929.

p. 207 "Holland finally shipped the crates ..." Holland to Herrera, Sept. 11 and Oct. 21, 1929, CMNH br.

p. 207 "... Herrera quit his job." Herrera to Holland, Nov. 14, 1929, CMNH br.

p. 207 "... shifting political waters ..." In a presidential election that month, Calles's protegé and chosen successor, Pascual Ortiz Rubio, defeated opposition candidate José Vasconcelos, who, with the wide support of university students and intellectuals, had hoped to return Mexico to the more democratic roots of its revolution. Ortiz Rubio was "declared the victor in elections that he most probably would have lost had they been honest" (Krauze, *Mexico,* 429–30).

p. 207   " 'I am wholly at sea …' " Holland to Herrera, Nov. 26, 1929, CMNH br.

p. 208   "Yes, Ochoterena telegraphed back …" Ochoterena to Holland, Nov. 28 and Dec. 17, 1929, and early March, no date, 1930; Holland to Ochoterena, Dec. 10, 1929, CMNH br.

p. 208   "Holland stopped vacillating and decided to go." Holland to Ochoterena, March 28, 1930, CMNH br.

p. 208   "… he saved the letters… his wife wrote him while he was away." Carrie Moorhead Holland to William Holland, April 4, 6, 8, 12, 14, 16, and 21, 1930, CMNH br.

p. 208   "[Holland] socialized with … Johnston … and … d'Harnoncourt." d'Harnoncourt to Holland, April 7, 1930; Julia Johnston to Holland, and Gordon Johnston to Holland, (no date, both before April 10, 1930); Gordon Johnston to Holland, April 23, 1930; Holland to Gordon Johnston, May 14, 1930; CMNH br.

p. 208   " 'The beautiful roses you brought to the train …' " Holland to Hoffman, May 14, 1930, CMNH br.

p. 209   "… the polished top of the base was finally laid under the dinosaur's feet… . Ochoterena had a sign put up nearby …" Ochoterena to Holland, May 21, 1930, CMNH br.

p. 209   " 'Here are nothing new. I am sad as ever.' " Herrera to Holland, July 29, 1930, CMNH br.

p. 209   "… Herrera wrote to Holland … to complain." Herrera to Holland, July 11, 1931, and Holland to Herrera, Aug. 18, 1931, CMNH br.

p. 210   " 'When will you come back to Mexico?' " Anita Hoffman to Holland, April 30, 1932, CMNH br.

p. 210   "One cast was traded … to the natural history museum in Munich …" McGinnis, *Carnegie's Dinosaurs,* 17.

p. 210   "In the spring of 1952 …" J. Leroy Kay to Ernest Untermann, Utah Field House of Natural History, May 13, 1952; Untermann to Kay, May 20, 1952; M. Graham Netting to Kay, May 23, 1952; Untermann to Kay, (telegram), June 4, 1952; Kay to Untermann, June 6, 1952, CMNH br; and labels at the Utah Field House of Natural History.

p. 210 "From Vernal the old molds kept traveling ..." McIntosh, conversation, Oct. 12, 2000.

p. 211 "Finally ... the Carnegie Museum unveiled a full-sized, outdoor ... cast ..." Gangewere, "This is Huge."

EPILOGUE

p. 212 "Photos show free-standing dinosaur femurs ..." Photos in the Knight Collection of the American Heritage Center, University of Wyoming, show various displays in the university geology museum when Reed was in charge. See also Reckling and Reckling, *Samuel Howell "Doc" Knight*, 15–24.

p. 214 "Jacob Wortman worked for about two years at the Peabody Museum ..." For information on Wortman in this section, see Wortman to Osborn, Feb. 24 and April 18, 1902, AMNH oc; Holland to Barnum Brown, Dec. 7, 1926, AMNH oc; and Holland, "Obituary: Dr. Jacob L. Wortman."

p. 215 "... he'd given away all but about $30 million." Wall, *Andrew Carnegie*, 1042.

p. 216 "As for Holland, one more anecdote seems appropriate." Conversation with Don Baird, retired curator of Princeton University's natural history museum, October 8, 2000. Baird grew up in Pittsburgh and heard this story from his father, George Baird, who knew Holland.

p. 216 "Hatcher's grave ... went unmarked for ninety-one years. Unsigned article, "Vertebrate Paleontologists Honor John Bell Hatcher," from *The Homewood*, a newsletter published by the Homewood Cemetery Historical Fund, vol. 5, no. 1, Spring/Summer 1996.

BIBLIOGRAPHY

Alberts, Robert C. *Pitt: The Story of the University of Pittsburgh, 1787–1987.* Pittsburgh: University of Pittsburgh Press, 1986.

Alexander, R. McNeill. "Engineering a Dinosaur." In Farlow and Brett-Surman, *Complete Dinosaur.* Bloomington and Indianapolis: Indiana University Press, 1997, chap. 30, 414–24.

Anderson, William T., ed. *Mermaids, Mummies, and Mastodons: The Emergence of the American Museum.* Washington, D.C.: American Association of Museums, 1993.

Avinoff, Andrey. "Holland, William Jacob." *Dictionary of American Biography,* Supplement 1, Harris E. Starr, editor. New York: Scribner's Sons, 1944.

Bakker, Robert T. *The Dinosaur Heresies.* New York: Zebra Books, 1986.

Baughman, T. H. *Pilgrims on the Ice: Robert Falcon Scott's First Antarctic Expedition.* Lincoln: University of Nebraska Press, 1999.

Bell, Howard W. "Fossil Hunting in Wyoming," *Cosmopolitan* (January 1900): 268.

Berman, D. S., and J. S. McIntosh. "Skull and Relationships of the Upper Jurassic Sauropod *Apatosaurus.*" *Bulletin of the Carnegie Museum* 8 (1978): 1–35.

Breithaupt, Brent H. "The Geological Museum at the University of Wyoming." *Fossils Quarterly* 5 (1986): 8–19.

———. "Biography of William Harlow Reed: The Story of a Frontier Fossil Collector." *Earth Sciences History* 9, no. 1 (1990): 6–13.

———. "Dinosaurs to Gold Ores: The 100 Year History of the University of Wyoming Geological Museum." *Fiftieth Anniversary Field Conference, Wyoming Geological Association Guidebook.* Casper, Wyoming: Wyoming Geological Association, 1993.

Bridge, James Howard. *The Inside History of the Carnegie Steel Company, A Romance of Millions.* New York: Aldine, 1903.

Carpenter, Kenneth. "Dinosaurs as Museum Exhibits." In Farlow and Brett-Surman, *Complete Dinosaur,* chap. 12, 150–164.

Clawson, Marion, and Burnell Held. *The Federal Lands: Their Use and Management* Baltimore: Johns Hopkins University Press, 1957.

Clough, Wilson O. *A History of the University of Wyoming, 1887–1964.* Laramie: University of Wyoming, 1965.

Coggeshall, Arthur S. "How 'Dippy' Came to Pittsburgh." *Carnegie Magazine* 25 (September 1951): 238–41.

———. "'Dippy Crashes Royalty.'" *Carnegie Magazine* 25 (October 1951): 276–78.

———. "More about 'Dippy' and Royalty." *Carnegie Magazine* 25 (November 1951): 312–15.

Colbert, Edwin H. *The Great Dinosaur Hunters and Their Discoveries.* New York: Dover, 1984.

———. "W. D. Matthew's Early Western Field Trips." *Earth Sciences History* 9, no. 1 (1990): 41–44.

———. *William Diller Matthew, Paleontologist: The Splendid Drama Observed.* New York: Columbia University Press, 1992.

Couvares, Francis G. *The Remaking of Pittsburgh: Class and Culture in an Industrializing City, 1877–1919.* Albany: State University of New York Press, 1984.

Duce, James Terry. "Patter-gonia." *Atlantic Monthly* 160, no. 3 (September 1937): 367–72.

Faires, Nora. "Immigrants and Industry: Peopling the Iron City." In Hays, *City at the Point,* 10–12.

Farlow, James O., and M. K. Brett-Surman, eds. *The Complete Dinosaur.* Bloomington: Indiana University Press, 1997.

Fleming, George Thomton, et. al., eds. *History of Pittsburgh and Environs.* New York and Chicago: The American Historical Society, Inc., 1922.

Fossil Fields Expedition. Reports by Members. *Fossil Discoveries in Wyoming.* Omaha: Union Pacific Railroad Company Passenger Department, 1909. AHC, Hebard Collection, Box 8, Folder 5.

Gangewere, R. Jay. "A Century of Influence: The Carnegie Library and Institute." *Carnegie Magazine* 62 (September/October 1995): 18–32.

———. "This is Huge, Really Huge." *Carnegie Magazine* (July/August, 1999): 12–18.

Gardom, Tim, with Angela Milner. *The Natural History Museum Book of Dinosaurs.* London: Carlton, 1998.

Gilmore, Charles W. "On a Newly Mounted Skeleton of Diplodocus in the United States National Museum." *Proceedings of the United States National Museum,* vol. 81, art. 18, pp. 7–8, and plate 6.

Glasco, Laurence, "Double Burden: The Black Experience in Pittsburgh." In Hays, *City at the Point,* 69–109.

Goetzman, William H., and Kay Sloan. *Looking Far North: The Harriman Expedition to Alaska, 1899.* New York: Viking, 1982.

Gould, Lewis L. *Wyoming: From Territory to Statehood.* Worland, Wyoming: High Plains, 1989. First published as *Wyoming: A Political History, 1868–96.* New Haven: Yale University Press, 1968.

Gould, Stephen Jay. *Wonderful Life: The Burgess Shale and the Nature of History.* New York, London: W. W. Norton, 1988.

Gratacap, L. P. "The Great Jurassic Dinosaur." *Scientific American* 86 (Jan. 4, 1902): 5.

Grinnell, George, with Introductions by Polly Burroughs and Victoria Wyatt. *Alaska 1899.* Seattle: University of Washington Press, 1995. A reprint of Grinnell's essays from volumes one and two of the original reports of the 1899 Harriman expedition to Alaska.

Hardy, Deborah. *Wyoming University: The First 100 Years, 1886–1986.* Laramie: University of Wyoming, 1986.

Hatcher, John Bell. "The Ceratops Beds of Converse County, Wyoming." *American Journal of Science,* 3d ser, vol. 45, no. 266 (February 1893): 135–44.

———. "Some Localities for Laramie Mammals and Horned Dinosaurs." *American Naturalist* 30 (February 1896): 112–20.

———. "Patagonia." *National Geographic* 8 (November 1897): 305–19, 2 figs. and map, plates 35–37.

———. "On the Geology of Southern Patagonia." *American Journal of Science* 4, no. 23 (November 1897): 327–54, figs. 1–11 and sketch map.

———. "Explorations in Patagonia." *Scientific American* 81 (Nov. 18, 1899): 328–29, 9 figs.

———. "The Mysterious Mammal of Patagonia, *Gryptotherium domesticum,*" by Rudolph Hauthal, Santiago Roth, and Robert Lehmann Nitsche. (Revista del Museo de La Plata 9: 409–74). Review in *Science,* n.s., 10, no. 257, (Dec. 1, 1899): 814–15.

———. "Some Geographic Features of Southern Patagonia; with a Discussion of Their Origin." *National Geographic* 40 (February 1900): 41–55, 3 figs., plate 2.

———. "*Diplodocus* Marsh: Its Osteology, Taxonomy, and Probable Habits, with a Restoration of the Skeleton." *Memoirs of the Carnegie Museum* 1, no. 1 (July 1901): 1–63, figs. 1–24, plates i–xiii.

———. *Bone Hunters in Patagonia.* Woodbridge, Conn.: Ox Bow, 1985. Reprint of "Narrative and Geography." *Reports of the Princeton University Expeditions to Patagonia,* 1896–1899, vol. 1, 1903, xvi–314, plates and map.

———. "Osteology of *Haplocanthosaurus,* with Description of a New Species and Remarks on the Probable Habits of the Sauropoda and the Age and Origin of the Atlantosaurus Beds." *Memoirs of the Carnegie Museum* 2 (November 1903): 1–72, figs. 1–28, plates i–v.

———. "Additional Remarks on *Diplodocus*." *Memoirs of the Carnegie Museum* 2 (November 1903): 72–75, figs 1–2, plate vi.

Hatcher, John Bell, based on preliminary studies by Othniel C. Marsh, edited and completed by Richard S. Lull. "The Ceratopsia." *Monographs of the United States Geological Survey*, vol. 49. Washington: GPO, 1907. Contains a complete bibliography of Hatcher's fifty-two scientific publications. Pp. xxv–xvi.

Hay, Oliver P. "On Some Recent Literature Bearing on the Laramie Formation." *American Geologist* (August 1903): 115–20.

———. "On the Habits and Pose of the Sauropodous Dinosaurs, Especially Diplodocus." *American Naturalist* 42, no. 502 (October 1908): 672–81.

———. "Dr. W. J. Holland on the Skull of Diplodocus." *Science*, n.s, 28, no. 720. (Oct. 16, 1908): 517–19.

———. "On the Restoration of Skeletons of Fossil Vertebrates." *Science*, n.s., 30, no. 759 (July 16, 1909): 93–95.

———. "On the Manner of the Locomotion of the Dinosaurs, Especially Diplodocus." *Proceedings of the Washington Academy of Sciences* 12, no. 1 (Feb. 15, 1910): 1–26.

———. "Further Observations on the Pose of the Sauropodous Dinosaurs." *American Naturalist* 45, no. 535 (1911): 398–412.

Hays, Samuel, ed. *City at the Point: Essays on the Social History of Pittsburgh*. Pittsburgh: University of Pittsburgh Press, 1989.

Hendrick, Burton J. *The Life of Andrew Carnegie*. New York: Doubleday, Doran, 1932.

Hoagland, Clayton. "They Gave Life to Bones." *Scientific Monthly* (February 1943): 114–33.

Holland, William J. "A New African Saturnid." *Entomological News* (May 1896): 133–35.

———. "Bone Hunters Starting Well At Their Work." *Pittsburg Dispatch*, July 25, 1899, CLPgh. Reprinted in the *Laramie Boomerang*, Aug. 2, 1899, under the headline "Good Words for Laramie."

———. "The Diplodocus Is a Great Find, Says Dr. Holland." *Pittsburg Dispatch*, Aug. 10, 1899.

———. "Fossil Hunters on the Plains of Wyoming." *Pittsburg Dispatch*, Aug. 19, 1899.

———. "Geology and Paleontology." Unsigned article. *The Carnegie Museum, Annual Report to the Director for the Year Ending March 31, 1900*. Publications of the Carnegie Museum: no. 7, 16–19.

———. "Geology and Paleontology." Unsigned article. *The Carnegie Museum, Annual Report to the Director for the Year Ending March 31, 1901*. Publications of the Carnegie Museum: no. 10, 19–21.

———. "The Story of the Diplodocus." *Westminster Review* 163 (June 1905): 683–92.

———. "The Presentation of a Reproduction of Diplodocus Carnegiei [sic] to the Trustees of the British Museum." Unsigned article. *Annals of the Carnegie Museum* 3 (1905): 443–52.

——— "The Osteology of *Diplodocus Marsh*, with Special Reference to the Restoration of the Skeleton of Diplodocus Carnegiei [sic] Hatcher, Presented by Mr. Andrew Carnegie to the British Museum, May 12, 1905." *Memoirs of the Carnegie Museum* 2, no. 6 (1906): 225–64, 30 figs., 29 plates.

———. "Dr. O. P. Hay on the Skull of Diplodocus." *Science*, n.s., 28, no. 723. (Nov. 6, 1908): 644–45.

———. "A Review of Some Recent Criticisms of Sauropod Dinosaurs Existing in the Museums of the United States, with Special Reference to That of *Diplodocus carnegiei* [sic] in the Carnegie Museum." *American Naturalist* 44, no. 521 (May 1910): 259–83.

———. "Museums of Science." Initialed article, with first-floor plan of Carnegie Museum. *Encyclopedia Britannica*, 1911, 64–69.

———. *To the River Plate and Back*. New York: G. P. Putnam's Sons, 1913.

———. "Editorials." Unsigned note on Holland's and Coggeshall's trip to Madrid. *Annals of the Carnegie Museum* 9 (1915): 3.

———. "Heads and Tails: A Few Notes Relating to the Structure of Sauropod Dinosaurs." *Annals of the Carnegie Museum* 9, (1915): 273–78.

———. "The Skull of *Diplodocus*." *Memoirs of the Carnegie Museum* 9, no. 3 (1924): 379–403, illustrated.

———. "Obituary: Dr. Jacob L. Wortman." *Annals of the Carnegie Museum* 17 (1926): 199–201.

———. *Twenty-Five Years of the Carnegie Hero Fund*. Pittsburgh: Carnegie Hero Fund Commission, 1929.

———. "A Diplodocus Goes to Mexico." *Carnegie Magazine* 4, no. 3 (1930): 83–86.

Howard, Robert West. *The Dawnseekers: The First History of American Paleontology*. New York: Harcourt Brace Jovanovich, 1975.

Ingham, John H. "Steel City Aristocrats." In Hays, *City at the Point*, 69–109.

James, Daniel. *Mexico and the Americans*. New York: Frederick A. Praeger, 1963.

Johnson, Kirk. Personal interviews, Jan. 8, 1999, and Jan. 11, 1999.
Johnson, a paleobotanist, is curator of paleontology at the Denver
Museum of Natural History.

Jones, Grant, "An Animal 130 Feet in Length." *St. Louis Globe-Democrat.*
Nov. 27, 1898.

Kinard, Agnes Dodd. *Celebrating the First 100 Years of the Carnegie in
Pittsburgh, 1895–1995.* Pittsburgh: Carnegie Museum of Art, 1995.

Klein, Maury. *Union Pacific: The Rebirth, 1894–1969.* New York:
Doubleday, 1990.

———. *The Life and Legend of E. H. Harriman.* Chapel Hill: University of
North Carolina Press, 2000.

Klein, Philip S., and Ari Hoogenboom. *A History of Pennsylvania.*
University Park: Pennsylvania State University Press, 1980.

Kleinberg, S. J. *The Shadow of the Mills: Working-Class Families in Pittsburgh, 1870–1907.* Pittsburgh: University of Pittsburgh Press, 1989.

Kleppner, Paul. "Government Parties and Voters." In Hays, *City at the
Point, 151–80.*

Knight, Wilbur C. "The Wyoming Fossil Fields Expedition of July 1899."
National Geographic 11, no. 12 (December 1900): 449–65.

Kohl, Michael F., and John S. McIntosh, eds. *Discovering Dinosaurs in the
Old West: The Field Journals of Arthur Lakes.* Washington: Smithsonian
Institution Press, 1997.

Kohlstedt, Sally Gregory, ed. *The Origins of Natural Science in America:
The Essays of George Brown Goode.* Washington: Smithsonian Institution Press, 1991.

Krauze, Enrique. *Mexico: A Biography of Power.* New York: HarperCollins,
1997.

Krishtalka, Leonard. *Dinosaur Plots and Other Intrigues in Natural History.*
New York: William Morrow, 1989.

Lageson, David R., and Darwin R. *Roadside Geology of Wyoming.*
Missoula: Mountain Press, 1988.

Lakes. See Kohl, Michael F., and John S. McIntosh, *Discovering Dinosaurs
in the Old West: The Field Journals of Arthur Lakes.*

Lanham, Url. *The Bone Hunters: The Heroic Age of Paleontology in the
American West.* Reprint ed. New York: Dover, 1991. Originally
published by Columbia University Press, 1973.

Laporte, Leo F. "George G. Simpson (1902–1984): Getting Started in the
Summer of 1924." *Earth Sciences History* 9, no. 1 (1990): 62–71.

Laramie Boomerang. Unsigned articles, 1899.

Larson, T. A. *History of Wyoming,* second ed., revised. Lincoln: University
of Nebraska Press, 1978.

Leighton, Henry. "Memorial of William Jacob Holland." *Bulletin of the Geological Society of America* 44 (1933): 347–52. Includes a bibliography of Holland's publications.

Lindsay, William, with illustrations by Giuliano Fornari. *The Great Dinosaur Atlas*. Englewood Cliffs, N.J.: Julian Messner, a division of Silver Burdett Press, Inc., Simon and Schuster, Inc., 1991. First published, London: Dorling Kindersley, 1991.

Lorant, Stefan. With contributions by Henry Steele Commager, Oscar Handlin, J. Cutler Andrews, Sylvester K. Stevens, John Morton Blum, Henry David, Gerald W. Johnson, David Lawrence. *Pittsburgh: The Story of an American City*. Garden City, N.Y.: Doubleday, 1964.

[London] *Daily Telegraph*. Unsigned article. "The Biggest Quadruped: An 84 Ft. Backbone. Interview with the Discoverer." May 12, 1905. CMNH online.

Lucas, Frederic A. "Constructing an Extinct Monster from Fossil Remains." *Scientific American* 86 (Jan. 18, 1902): 43.

McGinnis, Helen J. *Carnegie's Dinosaurs*. Pittsburgh: The Board of Trustees, Carnegie Institute, 1982.

McIntosh, John S. Personal interview, Ocober 8, 2000.

———. "The Second Jurassic Dinosaur Rush." *Earth Sciences History* 9, no. 1 (1990): 22–27.

McIntosh, John S., and D. S. Berman. "Description of the Palate and Lower Jaw of Diplodocus with Remarks on the Nature of the Skull of Apatosaurus." *Journal of Paleontology* 49 (1975): 187–99.

McIntosh, John S., M. K. Brett-Surman, and James O. Farlow. "Sauropods." In Farlow and Brett-Surman, eds. *The Complete Dinosaur*. Bloomington: Indiana University Press, 1997, chap. 20, 264–90.

Matthew, William Diller. "Early Days of Fossil Hunting on the High Plains." *National History* (September/October 1928): 449–54.

Monasterky, Richard. "Psst ... Wanna Buy a T-Rex? Paleontologists Fret about Dinosaur Sales." *Science News* 152, no. 24 (Dec. 13, 1997): 382–83.

Myhrvold, Nathan P., and Philip J. Currie. "Suspersonic Sauropods? Tail Dynamics in the Diplodocids." *Paleobiology* 23, no. 4. (1997): 393–409.

New York Journal and Advertiser. Unsigned article. "Most Colossal Animal Ever on Earth Just Found Out West." Dec. 11, 1898. LOC.

New York Post. Unsigned article. "The Dinosaur of Wyoming." Dec. 1, 1898. CMNH br.

Oles, James, *South of the Border: Mexico in the American Imagination, 1914–1947*. Washington: Smithsonian Institution Press, 1993.

Oreskes, Naomi. *The Rejection of Continental Drift: Theory and Method in American Earth Science.* New York: Oxford University Press, 1999.

Osborn, Henry Fairfield. "Models of Extinct Vertebrates." *Science.* n.s., 7, no. 182, (June 24, 1898): 841–45.

———. "Additional Characters of Diplodocus." *Science.* n.s., 9, no. 218, (March 3, 1899): 315–16.

———. "Fore and Hind Limbs of Carnivorous and Herbivorous Dinosaurs from the Jurassic of Wyoming." *Bulletin of the American Museum of Natural History* 12, dinosaur contributions No. 3, (October, 1899): 161–72.

———. "A Skeleton of Diplodocus." *Memoirs of the American Museum of Natural History,* vol. 1, part 5 (October 25, 1899): 191–214, plates 24–27.

———. "A Skeleton of Diplodocus, Recently Mounted in the American Museum." *Science.* n.s., 10, no. 259 (Dec. 15, 1899): 870–74.

———. "On the Position of the Bones of the Forearm in the Opisthocoelia or Sauropoda." *Science,* n.s., vol. 19, no. 476 (Feb. 12, 1904): 255–56.

———. "Fossil Wonders of the West: The Dinosaurs of Bone Cabin Quarry." *Century* 48, no. 4 (August 1904): 680–94.

———. "Manus, Sacrum and Caudals of Sauropoda." *Bulletin of the American Museum of Natural History* 20 (1904): 181–90.

———. "Skull and Skeleton of the Sauropodous Dinosaurs, Morosaurus and Brontosaurus." *Science,* n.s., 22, no. 560. (Sept. 22, 1905): 374–76.

———. "The Skeleton of Brontosaurus and the Skull of Morosaurus." *Nature* 73, no. 1890 (Jan. 18, 1906): 282–84.

———. "Explorations of John Bell Hatcher for the Paleontological Monographs of His Contributions to American Geology and Paleontology," A biographical sketch of Hatcher and a bibliography of his work. In Hatcher, "Ceratopsia," 8.

———. " J. L. Wortman—A Biographical Sketch." *Natural History* 26, (1926): 652–53.

Ostereicher, Richard. "Working-Class Formation, Development and Consciousness in Pittsburgh, 1790–1860." In Hays, *City at the Point,* 127.

Ostrom, John H., and John S. McIntosh. *Marsh's Dinosaurs: The Collections from Como Bluff.* New Haven: Yale University Press, 1966.

Pittsburg Dispatch. Unsigned articles. 1899. CLPgh.

Preston, Douglas J. *Dinosaurs in the Attic: An Excursion into the American Museum of Natural History.* New York: St. Martin's Press, 1986.

Princeton University, Department of Geosciences website, departmental history section, online at http://geoweb.princeton.edu/deptinfo/history/home.html.

Pritchard, Linda. "Religion in Pittsburgh." In Hays, *City at the Point,* 327–53.

Public Broadcasting System. *The Richest Man in the World: Andrew Carnegie.* Website for PBS documentary, including script: www.pbs.org/wgbh/pages/annex/carnegie/index/html

——."Crucible of Empire: The Spanish-American War." Website for PBS documentary, including script: www.pbs.org/crucible

Pyne, Stephen J. *Grove Karl Gilbert: A Great Engine of Research.* Austin: University of Texas Press, 1980.

——. *The Ice: A Journey to Antarctica.* Iowa City: University of Iowa Press, 1986.

Rainger, Ronald. "Collectors and Entrepreneurs: Hatcher, Wortman, and the Structure of American Vertebrate Paleontology Circa 1900." *Earth Sciences History* 9, no. 1 (1990): 14–21.

——. *An Agenda for Antiquity: Henry Fairfield Osborn and Vertebrate Paleontology at the American Museum of Natural History, 1890–1935.* Tuscaloosa: University of Alabama Press, 1991.

Rexer, Lyle, and Rachel Klein. *The American Museum of Natural History: 125 years of Exploration and Discovery.* New York: Harry N. Abrams, in Association with the American Museum of Natural History, 1995.

Roberts, David, with photos by Ted Wood. "Digging for Dinosaur Gold." *Smithsonian,* 28, no. 12 (March, 1998): 40–53.

Schuchert, Charles. "John Bell Hatcher." *American Geologist* 35, no. 3. (March 1905): 130–41. Contains a forty-eight-item bibliography of Hatcher's publications.

Schuchert, Charles, and Clara Mae LeVene. *O. C. Marsh, Pioneer in Paleontology.* New Haven: Yale University Press, 1940.

Simpson, George Gaylord. *Discoverers of the Lost World: An Account of Some of Those Who Brought Back to Life South American Mammals Long Buried in the Abyss of Time.* New Haven: Yale University Press, 1984.

Stegner, Wallace. *Mormon Country.* New York: Duell, Sloan and Pearce, 1942.

Sternberg, Charles H. *The Life of a Fossil Hunter.* Bloomington: Indiana University Press, 1990. Originally published, New York: Henry Holt and Company, 1909.

Stevens, John D. *Sensationalism and the New York Press.* New York: Columbia University Press, 1991.

Stevens, Kent A., and J. Michael Parrish. "Neck Posture and Feeding Habits of Two Jurassic Sauropod Dinosaurs." *Science* 284 (April 30, 1999): 798–800.

Sullivan, Walter. *Continents in Motion: The New Earth Debate.* New York: McGraw-Hill, 1974.

Swetnam, George, and Helene Smith. *The Carnegie Nobody Knows.* Revised edition. Greensburg, Pa.: McDonald/Sward Publishing Company, 1989.

Taquet, Phillippe, *Dinosaur Impressions: Postcards from a Paleontologist.* Translated by Kevin Padian. Cambridge: Cambridge University Press, 1998.

Tarr, Joel A. "Infrastructure and City Building." In Hays, *City at the Point,* 223–41.

Tierno, Mark J. "The Search for Pure Water in Pittsburgh: The Urban Response to Water Pollution, 1893–1914." *Western Pennsylvania Historical Magazine* (January 1977): 23–36.

Torrens, Hugh. "Politics and Paleontology: Richard Owen and the Invention of Dinosaurs." In Farlow and Brett-Surman, *Complete Dinosaur,* chap. 14, 175–90.

———."Dinosaurs and Dinomania Over 150 Years." *Modern Geology* 18, (1993): 257–86.

Union Pacific Railroad. *Some of Wyoming's Vertebrate Fossils.* Omaha: Union Pacific Railroad, 1899. WSA, Paleontology folder.

Van Trump, James D. *An American Palace of Culture: The Carnegie Institute and Carnegie Library of Pittsburgh.* Pittsburgh: Carnegie Institute and Pittsburgh History and Landmarks Foundation, 1970.

Wall, Joseph Frazier. *Andrew Carnegie.* New York: Oxford University Press, 1970.

Wall, Joseph Frazier, ed. *The Andrew Carnegie Reader.* Pittsburgh: University of Pittsburgh Press, 1992.

Wall Street Journal, April 4, 1899. Unsigned article. "Union Pacific Progresses."

Wallace, David Rains. *The Bone Hunters' Revenge: Dinosaurs, Greed and the Greatest Scientific Feud of the Gilded Age.* Boston: Houghton Mifflin, 1999.

West, Susan. "Dinosaur Head Hunt." *Science News* 116, no. 18. (Nov. 3, 1979): 314–15.

Wilford, John Noble. *The Riddle of the Dinosaur.* New York: Vintage, 1987.

"William Jacob Holland, D.D., LL.D." Unsigned biographical article. In Fleming, *History of Pittsburgh and Environs,* vol. 3, 813–18.

Williams, Roger L. *Aven Nelson of Wyoming*. Boulder: Colorado Associated University Press, 1984.

Wister, Fanny Kemble, ed. *Owen Wister Out West: His Letters and Journals*. Chicago: University of Chicago Press, 1958.

Wister, Owen. *The Virginian*. Pleasantville, N.Y.: Reader's Digest, 1988. With an Afterword by John L. Cobbs. First published 1902.

Woodburne, Michael. Paleontologist, University of California at Riverside. Personal communication, November 2, 2000.

Wortman, Jacob. "The New Department of Vertebrate Paleontology of the Carnegie Museum." *Science*, n.s., 11, no.266 (Feb. 2, 1900): 163–66.

Yochelson, Ellis L. *The National Museum of Natural History: 75 Years in the Natural History Building*. Edited by Mary Jarrett. Washington, D.C.: Smithsonian Institution Press, 1985.

INDEX